SO-BFE-019

DATE DUE

TEN YEARS AFTER

Ten Years After

THE HUNGARIAN REVOLUTION IN THE
PERSPECTIVE OF HISTORY

Edited by Tamas Aczel

HOLT, RINEHART AND WINSTON

New York   Chicago   San Francisco

Copyright © 1966 by MacGibbon & Kee, Ltd.
First published in the United States, May 1967.
All rights reserved, including the right to reproduce
this book or portions thereof in any form.

"The Message of the Hungarian Revolution" by
Michael Polanyi was first published in Vol. XXVI,
No. 18, the October 31, 1966 issue of *Christianity
and Crisis: A Christian Journal of Opinion.*

Library of Congress Catalog Card Number: 66-21626.

First Edition

8599607
Printed in the United States of America

CONTENTS

DB
957
A56
1967

TEN YEARS AFTER

MICHAEL POLANYI

The Message of the Hungarian Revolution

IT IS ten years, almost to the day, since the 20th Party Congress at which Khrushchev denounced the insane regime of Stalin. After another four months, in June 1956, the repercussions of this act led to an open rebellion of the Hungarian writers at the meetings of the Petőfi Circle in Budapest. This was the actual beginning of the Hungarian revolution which broke out violently in October.

It has often been mentioned, but I believe it has never been realized in its full importance, that this was a rebellion of Communist Party members. There were many among them who had won high honours and great financial benefits from the government and had—until fairly recently—been its genuine passionate supporters.

The Petőfi Circle, where this first rebellion broke out, was an official organ of the party and the meetings were presided over by trusted representatives of the ruling clique. But other party members, forming the bulk of the audience, overcame the platform. They demanded a reversal of the position assigned to human thought in the Marxist-Leninist scheme. Marxism-Leninism taught that public consciousness is a superstructure of the underlying relations of production. Public thought under socialism, therefore, must be an instrument of the party controlling socialist production.

The meeting rejected this doctrine. It affirmed that truth must be recognized as an independent power in public life. The press must be liberated to tell the truth. The murderous trials based on faked charges must be publicly condemned and their perpetrators punished; the rule of law must be restored. And, above all, the arts corrupted by sub-servience to the party must be set free to speak to the imagination and to tell the truth. It was this outbreak that created the centre of opposition which later overthrew the communist government.

Has the response of the West to these events been adequate? I am not asking whether we ought to have aided the Hungarian revolution by

9

money or the force of arms. I am asking about our intellectual and moral responses.

What did we think, what do we think today, of this change of mind among many of the most devoted Hungarian Stalinists ? Do we realize that this was a wholesale return to the ideals of nineteenth-century liberalism ? In the Hungarian revolution of 1956 its fighters were clearly going back to the ideals of 1848, to Liberty, Equality, Fraternity. After the French revolution these ideas had filtered from Paris to Eastern Europe and they inspired the Hungarian patriots rebelling against the Habsburgs in 1848. The Hungarian revolutionaries of 1956 revived these ideas; they believed that the ideals of truth, justice and liberty, were valid and were resolved to fight for them and to conquer in their name.

What do we say to this ? It has been a long time since history was last written in the English language as the inevitable progress of truth, justice and liberty. I think J. B. Bury was the last to do so fifty years ago. Our current interpretations of social change and of the rise of new ideas are nearer to the theories of Marx than to the views of Bury, or of J. S. Mill, or Jefferson, or Gibbon. Interpretations today are couched in terms of a value-free sociology, of a historicist historiography, or of depth psychology. They can hardly be expected to acknowledge the motives which the Hungarian rebels professed to be fighting for. The most popular explanation of such movements was sociological. It said that the methods of Stalin had fulfilled their purpose of carrying out the rapid industrialization of the Soviet Union, but that these methods were no longer suited to a more complex society and hence the need had arisen for new ideals appropriate to the new situation. This was said to be the origin of the renewal of thinking in the Soviet countries since Stalin's death.

This liberation of the mind, which might be a decisive force for the future of mankind has been interpreted as a response to technical changes. Such theories, explaining away man's basic need for truth, were put forward without supporting evidence and nobody has asked for evidence. The fact that two of the most highly industrialized regions of Europe—Eastern Germany and Czechoslovakia—have produced the hardest Stalinist government and resisted reform longest, was disregarded. In our days any mechanical explanation of human affairs, however absurd, is accepted unquestioningly.

This reluctance of modern scholarship to envisage ideal needs as a motive power of historical change is illustrated by a story told two years ago in *Encounter*[1] by a distinguished expert on Soviet nationalities, Professor Richard Pipes, Associate Director of Harvard's Russian Research Centre. Professor Pipes wrote:

> Four years ago, when writing an essay on the Russian intelligentsia for the journal *Daedalus*, I wanted to conclude it with a brief statement to the effect that the modern Russian intellectual had a very special mission to fulfil: 'to fight for truth'. On the advice of friends I omitted this passage since it sounded naive and unscientific. Now I regret having done so, because the literature that has appeared in the intervening period has demonstrated repeatedly how important the concept, and even the word, 'truth', is for the Soviet intellectuals.

At the most influential academic centre studying Soviet affairs, it took three years after the rebellion of writers at the Petőfi Circle to be mooted for the first time that this kind of unrest was due to a craving for truth. Even then this suggestion was suppressed in deference to expert opinion because to speak of intellectuals fighting for truth was held to be naive and unscientific.

Professor Pipes continues this passage by explaining why he thinks now (four years later) that in the case of Russian intellectuals it is not unscientific to attribute to them a passionate desire for truth. Since these reasons apply also to the conditions under which Hungarian intellectuals rebelled, the argument applies to them too. Professor Pipes writes:

> The reason the word 'truth' is in disrepute among us is because we attach to it generally moral connotations; that is, we understand it as a concept which implies the existence of a single criterion of right and wrong—something we are not willing to concede. We react thus because in the environment in which we live our right to perceive is not usually questioned; what can be questioned is our interpretation of the perceived reality. But in an environment where the very right to perception of reality is inhibited by claims of the State, the word 'truth' acquires a very different meaning. It signifies not true value but true experience: the right to surrender to one's impressions without being compelled for some extraneous reason to interpret and distort them.

We are told that it is unscientific to speak among us of 'truth' and the word merits its current discredit here because we attach moral values to

[1] *Encounter*, Vol. XXII, Jan. 1964, p. 83.

it. It is legitimate to recognize that the Soviet intellectuals fight for truth, because they are demanding merely the right to 'the perception of reality' and not to convey any interpretation of it in terms of values believed to be true. However, the writers who rebelled in the Petőfi Circle ten years ago were not demanding the right to have certain perceptions of reality. They demanded that the execution of Rajk based on faked charges be publicly admitted and that they be free to denounce the tyranny forcing its false values on the people; and they demanded freedom to write the truth in novels, in poetry and in the newspapers.

Was Pasternak's *Doctor Zhivago* or Ahmatova's poetry suppressed in Soviet Russia because of the factual information that it conveyed? Was this the issue about them?

I will not contest here the current views about the criteria of scientific knowledge. The question whether something is to be described as scientific or not is generally unimportant and here quite pointless. The purpose of any observation is to acquire knowledge that is both illuminating and trustworthy. An ideal of strict impersonality would blind us to all that is essential in human affairs; though some may call this ideal scientific, it would still be nonsensical.

Such academic pursuit of scientific darkness can perhaps be excused if, owing to its absurdity, its implications are disregarded. It is not unusual for our minds to lead a double life, our practice being wiser than the teachings of our theory. David Hume observed this for the teachings of his own scepticism. He wrote that while the errors of theology may be disastrous, the follies of philosophy were merely ridiculous. Bentham's utilitarianism is another case in point. England was guided during many fruitful decades by the influence of Bentham's absurd calculus of pleasure and pain which claimed to account scientifically for morality as well as all other noble values. 'Utility is the supreme object,' Bentham wrote, 'which comprehends in itself law, virtue, truth, and justice.' English reformers used this theory for attacking narrow dogmatism and unreasonable practice. But never spelled out the implications of a utilitarian calculus as for example Hitler was to do, when sanctioning that human beings be used for lethal experiments, that might benefit a vastly greater number of other people.

Bentham's inhuman implications remained suspended in England. But Hitler's case indicates that we are no longer as safe in practice from the immoral implications of sceptical philosophies as men were in the days of Hume and Bentham. When Freud wrote in his famous essay on

Civilization and its Discontents: 'This alone I know with certainty, namely that men's value judgements are . . . merely an attempt to bolster up their illusions by argument', such teachings spread confusion among modern men's moral principles.

And there exists today a sceptical interpretation of man's ideals which claims to comprehend—to use Bentham's words—all 'law, virtue, truth, and justice', and which has swept by its convincing power through the minds of many millions, setting them up against the other half of mankind which resisted this persuasion. I mean Marxism. Marxism embodies all the ideals of man in a struggle for power alleged to bring about automatically all the boundless moral aspirations of man. Marxist theory protects these ideals from modern scepticism by denying the reality of moral motives in public life, and it lends them, at the same time, incomparable driving power by feeding them covertly into the engines of communist action. Such is the famous transformation of socialism from an utopia into a science.

It is clear that we cannot turn away from the sceptical conclusions of our philosophies today as comfortably as Hume turned to a game of backgammon from the conclusions of his own scepticism. For modern man the follies of philosophy can be disastrous. And conversely, when the young Stalinists who had been fanatically convinced that all real truth and justice was embodied in the power of the party, rebelled against the party by declaring that truth must be recognized as an independent power in public life, this was a matter of life and death for them.

I think it is also a matter of life and death for us that we recognize the power which made them rebel as they did.

I cannot trace here the rise of this power in detail. But I can indicate three lines of its progress which should be seen jointly. First we have the defection of leading intellectuals of the West, abandoning 'the god that failed'. Some turned away during the trials of 1937–38, others after the Stalin–Hitler pact of 1939, others still later. By the end of the Second World War there was an ardent band of former communists who desperately warned against trusting the Soviets to establish free governments in the spheres of influence conceded to them.

The next decisive change occurred in Soviet Russia itself on the day Stalin died. The first act of his successors was to release the thirteen doctors of the Kremlin, who had recently been sentenced to death on their own false confession of murderous attempts against Stalin and other members of the government. This action had a shattering effect on the party. If party-truth was now to be refuted by mere bourgeois objectivism, then Stalin's whole fictitious universe would presently dissolve.[2]

The alarm was justified. Since the further revelations of the 20th Party Congress it should be clear, that the new masters of the Kremlin acted as they did, because they believed their position would be safer if they had more truth on their side and less against them. They sacrificed for this sake the most dreaded weapon of terror, the weapon of faked trials; no such trial was ever held in the Soviet empire after this date.

The third event in the growth of the power vindicating truth, and the values depending on the right to tell the truth was the rebellion of Hungarian writers. It should be seen now as a stage in the historical process which started the numerous defections from communism among Western intellectuals about fifteen years before. Since there are many highly articulate men and women who changed their minds at that time, it should be possible to get a fuller account of their motives than we have today. When these will be compared with the recollections of the Hungarian dissenters, we shall have before us the dynamics of the force which underlies the whole intellectual and moral transformation accompanying the decline of Marxism.

We shall then stop offering to those who have achieved this transformation our theories of the technological or psychological mechanism of their action. We shall realize that this is to confess that we ourselves do not believe in the truth and power of the ideals for which we stand and that by our false theories we are actually propagating that very determinism from which those who achieved this transformation have liberated themselves. We shall realize that this is to spurn those who have come to us after having fought for our ideas and to insult them by denying the genuine motives of their action.

And there is still more to this. The rebellion of Hungarian writers was a change of mind of dedicated communists. Their action, undertaken at great peril against the overwhelming background of ruling Stalinism, was the action of an intellectual avant-garde. It spread rapidly under the very eyes of the still powerful secret police until one day it brought the workers out into the streets and enlisted the army in

---

[2] I have recorded an instance of this unsettling effect on one particular fervent Stalinist in my Eddington Lecture, *Beyond Nihilism*, Cambridge University Press, 1960.

its support. The government was overthrown and a few days later the Russians moved in with new tanks, but not to restore the Stalinists to power. Since 23 October ideas have never ceased to circulate freely in Hungary. Though you cannot fully print them, you can yet effectively spread them by word of mouth.

Hungarian newspapers have recently published complaints by party members that scant respect is paid to them today. They say that the government itself prefers non-party members. We can understand what is happening here. Those who still hotly profess the Marxist interpretation of history, who proclaim the surpassing achievements of revolutionary socialism and predict the proximate coming of communism—these people are increasingly looked upon as ignorant fools. The young are immune against their teachings; the Old Believers' authority is drained away by the superior intelligence surrounding them.

The Hungarian revolution was not a unique event. It was unique only in exemplifying most clearly the change of mind going on throughout the Soviet countries, except perhaps in China. Everywhere outside China this change is clearly in progress.

It is bound to be accelerated by the gradual acceptance, since 1963, of Liberman's critique of detailed planning as inferior to market operations controlled by profit. It is becoming clear that there is in fact no viable socialist alternative to the market. Thus the Russian revolution that conquered power in order to achieve a radically distinct form of economic organization that would be far more productive and also morally superior to commercial management, has now revealed that there is no such possibility. By the time its fiftieth anniversary is celebrated, the revolution may be widely recognized by its very successors as having been virtually pointless. It may live on thenceforth in its emblems, as for example the Mexican revolution has lived on without making much difference in substance.

Judging by the Hungarian revolution and other movements akin to it elsewhere in the Soviet countries, this great tide of thought is flowing back to the original ideals of modern society. This process is just as important for statesmanship, as is the spreading of nuclear weapons or the menace of world-wide famine by over-population. It is a movement akin to our ideals, to which we must respond by trusting its power.

It was dangerous and foolish to expect that we could evoke a friendly response from totalitarian rulers, so long as these rulers were convinced that we were about to collapse and leave them to take over our heritage.

But just as it was imperative to know that such an opponent would respond to every voluntary concession by making more inordinate demands on us, so it is imperative today that we recognize in the Soviet countries a growth of thought which alone can save us, and indeed the world, from disaster.

We can recognize this historical process and its power only by casting out our mechanistic theories of human affairs. We must re-establish instead the grounds of our true ideals, in which we can join those who are liberating themselves from the party for the service of these ideals.

This is the message of the Hungarian revolution.

PART I

Hungary and the World

The Meaning of Destiny

NO EVENT has moved the conscience of the free world as deeply as the Hungarian revolution of 1956. No other event has assumed such equivocal political significance in the space of ten years. This historic moment can best be characterized by the psychoanalytical formula of *over-determination*, the plurality of meanings inherent in a single act, a single thought.

In order to decipher the obscure language of forgotten facts and past experiences let us evoke our own feelings that, in spite of the years, are still close and vivid.

★　★　★

When the Hungarian revolution erupted and, for a few days, appeared triumphant, it seemed nothing short of a miracle. It refuted our scepticism: a totalitarian regime, we had said, has nothing to fear from those it oppresses; propaganda accustoms people to servitude, the police discourages all attempt at rebellion. Mussolini was overthrown by the defeat of the Italian army, not by a conspiracy, nor by the king. Hitler continued to exert his reign of terror to the very end. Even after 20 July 1944, the majority of military leaders, the functionaries and the people itself followed their Führer to the brink of the abyss and almost to collective suicide. The Hungarian revolution reminded us of simple truths that we had almost forgotten.

A totalitarian regime is also vulnerable. In Hungary it crumbled in the end because it was abandoned by the intellectuals, the men in the street, the party members and even the army.

In 1848 it was Marx's dream that the revolution should have philosophy as its head and the proletariat as its heart. In 1956 this dream became reality. The intellectuals claimed their right to truth and the proletariat its right to freedom—the real freedom of the nation and of the working class. Together they defeated despotism supported by a foreign power. And despotism could not resist the attack because those who were supposedly its beneficiaries aligned themselves *en masse* with the insurgents.

Historians or sociologists usually explain the fall of a regime by the weakness of its governing elite or by its lack of confidence in itself. Cynics, in the manner of Pareto, would add that one does not govern innocently. A minority that has lost its capacity for remaining in power, even through the use of force, is, from a short or long-term point of view, doomed. The Hungarian intellectuals of the Petőfi Circle who, like Imre Nagy and his friends, were party members, proved the inaccuracy of this belief in an unexpected fashion. Charles X or Louis Philippe, indeed, hastened to go into exile because they had lost faith in the monarchy; the militant wing of the Hungarian Communist Party, however, abandoned its cause (or that cause that appeared to be its own) for other and more profound reasons: its members were ashamed of themselves. In the material sense of the word, intellectuals and party members were privileged; from a moral point of view, however, they were victims of the regime just like the rest of the population.

Could the events that occurred in Hungary have taken place in the Soviet Union? We were not certain. In Hungary, nationalism and liberalism were linked together in 1956 as they had been in 1848, and, though the two could not be crushed simultaneously, Soviet pseudo-socialism was well able to crush at least one, and was not the suppression of nationalism one of the principal causes of the explosion? Socialism, that is, the state control of economy, must be national, for it requires the adhesion of the masses to the state. Why should the masses adhere to a state that is not theirs? Ideological faith is no substitute for patriotism.

No less significant was the emergence of several parties during the days of revolutionary fervour; it surprised even those who should have expected it as normal and inevitable. After all, the majority of anti-communists in the West had denounced the single-party system as the principal cause, the symbol and essence of pseudo-socialist despotism. The tragedy of Marxism, we said, sprang from the monopoly enjoyed by one party of all political activity, the subordination of that party itself to the near-discretionary authority of one or a few persons (even where the leaders are not privileged slaves of a foreign general staff). These were the roots, we said, of the corruption of bolshevism which was originally inspired by aspiration of liberty and then resulted in totalitarianism. In spite of the fact that the revolution corresponded with our convictions, or perhaps because of it, we were staggered: we had been right, even more right than we realized. The nations of Eastern Europe had not been converted to Marxism–Leninism, nor had they been taken in by the propaganda or the ideologies which so many Western intellectuals, great or otherwise, absorbed so avidly. They demanded freedom in the political sense of the term. And there can be no political freedom without a plurality of parties. In Europe, at least, the alternative which we had begun to doubt, was still valid: despotism by a monopolistic party, or freedom through the competition of several parties.

The crushing of the revolt, the victory of the Khrushchevist—if not Stalinist—counter-revolution at the time when the French and British were engaged in the insane Suez adventure, brought us rapidly down to earth. The romantic illusion was destroyed. It was clear that the regimes imposed by the Soviet Union were foreign to the traditions and sentiments of the peoples. But the Soviet Union has claimed for itself the same right exercised a century ago by the sovereigns of the Holy Alliance: to repress the rebellions (now called counter-revolutions) against the established order, here alleged to be socialist. The sovereigns of the Holy Alliance defended the order of the past. The communist Holy Alliance claimed to defend the order of the future, of which the Marxist–Leninist parties of all countries consider themselves the builders.

At the same time, we did not know whether the passivity of the West, especially the United States, should be praised or condemned. Were we to reproach the *Voice of America* or *Radio Free Europe* for encouraging the Hungarian freedom fighters? Were we to reproach the United States for watching the suppression of the insurgents without doing anything about it but talk? How far had American propaganda led the revolutionaries to believe that the West would come to their aid? Would the Americans have acted differently had the French and British not landed in Egypt? But beyond these uncertainties we all had the feeling that from then on there existed a hidden *Russo-American pact against war*, an agreement probably more binding than any other alliance, and of which we did not even know whether it should be acclaimed as a guarantee of peace (or at least of non-total war) or bitterly condemned as a sanctioning of injustice: the sacrificing of Moscow's victims—and Washington's allies—to the predominating interest of the two great powers not to fight, that is, not to destroy each other mutually.

In the United Nations when the Suez problem was discussed, the

Russians and Americans acted together against France and Great Britain, while in the Hungarian question they found themselves in opposite camps. But while the Americans supported motions of protest they recognized, *de facto*, the Soviet hegemony within the Eastern European zone. Would the European nations that reproached them for it have lightly assumed a risk of war ? One might be tempted to reply that the risk was slight, numerous intermediate possibilities were conceivable between total war and inaction, but Washington showed neither imagination nor a capacity for initiative. I, personally, agree with this and believe that the President of the United States was not restricted to an immediate choice between the danger of total war and complete inactivity camouflaged by solemn protestations. The fact remains, however, that the President of the United States believed himself to be confronted with this alternative and no one can honestly state that an *effective* intervention would not have constituted a risk of war.

It will be argued that six years later, in 1962, the United States took a risk just as great or even greater when they felt themselves directly threatened. This is true, but the circumstances were different. The setting up of medium-range rockets facing the coast of Florida constituted an attempt to modify the military *status quo*. Since the end of the war the unwritten rule governing Soviet–American relations was the old rule of zones of influence with one important innovation. The principle of mutual respect for these zones of influence is valid only in the strictly military domain, or, to be more precise, in the case of regular armies. American propaganda tried to cross the line of demarcation and the Russians did much more by means of propaganda, money, instructions to Western communist parties and, in some parts of the world, subversive agents, without encountering the same obstacles. In October–November 1956, an effective intervention by the United States would have had to envisage at least the possibility of regular armies crossing the demarcation line between the two Europes.

One could argue that in October–November 1962, when Soviet rockets crossed the Atlantic, there was no clear violation of an implicit rule. In the *Tiers-Monde*, where the two Great Powers, or two camps, are engaged in a permanent competition, the US have profited from alliances with the different countries in order to establish military bases encircling the Soviet Union. The Kremlin tolerated these bases because it lacked the means not to tolerate them. The United States, however, did not permit the Soviet Union to pay them back in kind and to use Cuba's conversion to Marxism–Leninism in order to set up a rocket base.

In spite of this reasoning, the American refusal is in keeping with Soviet–American relations in the post-war period. The American Air Force had bases in Scotland, Turkey, Saudi Arabia, Japan, Okinawa, the Philippines and Formosa, but the USSR maintained twenty-five Russian divisions in East Germany and created an East German army before the Western powers decided to rearm Bonn. The USSR saw to it that North Korea's military strength was superior to that of South Korea. A sort of balance was achieved, for the superiority of the Soviet armed forces was evened out, on the one hand, by the nuclear monopoly of the United States, on the other by the great number of transport vehicles and bases (aerodromes and launching sites) at the disposal of the Americans. American acceptance of the Soviet rocket bases in Cuba would have had a military, and beyond that, psychological and political importance that none of the American bases throughout the world has achieved. It would have weakened the strategy of deterrents which forms the foundation of world peace.

A weapon alone cannot deter a determined adversary if the latter regards the possessor of the weapon as morally incapable of using it. The meeting of the two K's in 1962 bolstered the American strategy of deterrents for several years. However, had America remained passive in the Cuba affair, Soviet impunity would have opened a period of extreme instability in Berlin and elsewhere. In this sense there is an obvious difference in nature between the 1956 Hungarian crisis and the Cuban crisis of 1962: the lack of action in one case, and action in the other served probably the same purpose, at least in relation to the Soviet–American duel, the confirmation of the *status quo*, territorial and military, and the reduction to a minimum of the risk of armed conflict.

Ten years ago, while Mr Kádár's so-called peasant and worker government dissolved the workers' councils and 200,000 Hungarians fled their country, I was inclined to draw various lessons from what took place: moral victory for freedom, material victory for the Marxist–Leninist counter-revolution, Western passivity, the priority of peace over justice, and Soviet–American agreement on a certain form of spheres of influence adapted to the circumstances. Once again, as in 1846, a small nation wedged in between Slavs and Germans, had tragedy as its lot. Once again this small nation lived a great moment of its history in pride and suffering. It would retain the memory of an achievement that was also a defeat.

★   ★   ★

Ten years have gone by. We have forgotten none of our emotional re-actions, none of the interpretations that came to mind. The Hungarian revolution has remained a revolution, it has *not become a counter-revolution*. In Moscow's language, any revolt against a state that claims to be based on Marxism–Leninism is a counter-revolution. Within the internal terminology of this system, the Budapest revolt was therefore counter-revolutionary but in our view the counter-revolution continues to be embodied by those who need Russian tanks to oppress their own people. It is counter-revolution first in the literal sense of the word, because the revolution was fought by the intellectuals and the workers to free themselves of foreign tyranny. But counter-revolution also in the strictly political sense of the word, since the order established by the Russian troops was the rule of a single party, a state ideology, a police-maintained discipline.

I am fully aware that the controversy as to who was counter-revolutionary in Hungary in 1956 is purely terminological or philosophical in character. János Kádár 'restored' a regime that had been overthrown by a revolution supported by the people. By definition, therefore, he was a counter-revolutionary, like Louis XVIII. To this the Marxist–Leninists will reply that Imre Nagy and his followers were in the process of 'restoring' a system that had historically preceded 'Soviet socialism', bourgeois democracy or, worse, the rule of the landowners and capital-ists. This question, pertaining to the philosophy of history passes judge-ment on the historical significance of the system that the revolutionaries would have established had they been spared by their enemies.

For once, it is not impossible to give an answer to the question: what would have happened if . . .? Imre Nagy was a Marxist–Leninist even at the time when events placed him at the helm of the revolution. He could have played the role Gomulka played in Poland: he could have given a revolution of national-liberal inspiration an appearance accep-table to the Soviet Union and found a compromise between the aspira-tions of the Hungarian people and the international situation. The main reason for his failure where Gomulka succeeded and his inability to prevent Russian intervention, was the weakness, the falling apart of the Hungarian Communist Party. It was Rákosi and Gerő themselves who provoked the uprising of which they then lost control. Imre Nagy, in turn, presided over a government which was incapable of either directing or curbing the revolution. The proclamation of neutrality, following upon the recognition of several parties, only hastened, but was not the cause of Russian intervention.

Let us suppose that Imre Nagy had been the Gomulka of Hungary. Would even a Marxist–Leninist of the strictest Muscovite discipline call him a counter-revolutionary? The Chinese would call him a revisionist or a Khrushchevist, but in their eyes all the men in power in Eastern Europe are revisionists, all betray the heritage of Marx and Lenin. But let us forget about Chinese polemics for the moment. In Europe, an Imre Nagy government which, in Gomulka's manner, would have halted the revolution on the brink of the irreparable, would not have been called counter-revolutionary. It would merely have accomplished more rapidly and more completely the task of de-Stalinization which Kádár's so-called worker-peasant government had also partially accomplished as an outcome of, or in spite of, the revolution smothered in blood.

There is no contradiction between our 1956 and 1966 interpretation of the tragedy, but we are more aware of an aspect which we did not ignore at the time, but did not sufficiently appreciate; namely, that the Hungarian uprising took place during the process of de-Stalinization, it neither initiated it nor interrupted it for any length of time. In the perspective of ten years it now appears like a tragic vicissitude; neither as a beginning, nor as an end. It reveals much more what Stalinism has been than what the Eastern European regimes are today. An accident along the way, a cynic would describe it.

This interpretation coincides with a theory of revolution, classic since Alexis de Tocqueville. When despotism relaxes vigilance, it is in peril. The governed, whose lot is improving, become aware, simultaneously, of the wrongs they are suffering and the future perspectives. It is hope rather than misery that inspires revolutionaries. During Stalin's lifetime the lack of freedom of speech stifled both scruples and questions in the long run. The moment the intellectuals were no longer forced to tell *total lies* they felt an irresistible need for the *total truth*. Partial freedom restores the appetite for absolute freedom. Ten years after their rebellion Hungarians and Poles are still on parole and enjoy only partial freedom, but the former are not worse off than the latter. The revolution crushed by military force and the revolution directed by the Communist Party have produced more or less the same results.

A detailed comparative study would be beyond the scope of this short essay, but as far as can be judged from the outside, the differences—and they do exist—are not all in Poland's favour. Poland, it seems to me, has made more concessions to her peasants than Hungary. There, collectivization has not been carried to the extreme limit, while János Kádár has returned, after a lapse of a few years, to orthodox collectivization, although with less sacrifice to the peasants than the Stalinist methods cost them. As far as the workers' committees are concerned, Gomulka and Kádár have acted in precisely the same way: they have gradually liquidated the institutions created by the proletariat but incompatible with Marxism–Leninism. Kádár intends to retain the direction of the proletarian movement in the hands of the party; spontaneity, expressed by the workers' committees, is in contradiction to the revolutionary doctrine which has been in effect since 1917 and the mode of control typical of the Soviet regimes.

Apart from this difference and this similarity the same tendencies can be observed in the two countries, more accentuated perhaps in Hungary than in Poland. For several years Hungarian economists have not hesitated to question centralized authoritarian planning and they discussed necessary reforms, whether it is a question of replacing the traditional quantitative indicators by the profitability of the enterprise, or of restoring a more important function to the mechanism of the market. As regards the living standard, the way of life, travel abroad and the position of intellectuals, Hungary is on the same level with Poland, perhaps even a little more advanced. It cannot be proven but it is probable that had Imre Nagy succeeded in moderating the revolution, as Gomulka did, he would have put into effect a policy not radically different from that followed by Kádár, the man who betrayed him.

While Moscow's accusation of counter-revolution collapses, another question comes to mind. The revolutionaries have not attained their objectives either in Poland or in Hungary. The former missed the experience of triumph, glory and martyrdom, while a great number of the latter are in exile, thousands were deported immediately after the suppression of the revolt, many died, and hundreds who are still alive have, it is said, not yet returned to their country. Does this mean that the Hungarian people fought for nothing, or that they would have obtained the same results without paying the same price had they been wise enough or lucky enough not to cross the limits set so ruthlessly by international circumstances? The question is heartbreaking for the Hungarians and for their friends throughout the world, but in spite of this, we must find the courage to ask it.

Let us now return to the theme of the counter-revolution. We have put forward a hypothesis: a party directed by Imre Nagy, like Gomulka's party in Poland, would have attempted a compromise between communism and popular feeling, between a desire for freedom and the interests of Moscow. Thanks to the Hungarian revolution we know that this solution—de-Stalinization and revisionism—would have been a compromise. What the Hungarians and Poles wanted in 1956, and what they still want today, are the liberties scornfully described by Marxists for a whole century as 'formal'. Should these 'formal' liberties include a multi-party system and free elections? I feel that this is still decisive for anyone wishing to interpret the Hungarian revolution and differentiate honestly between its objectives and those of Khrushchevist and post-Khrushchev revisionism. Adapting the famous phrase from the Communist Manifesto a political writer stated recently: 'A spectre haunts the Soviet world, the spectre of the multi-party system.' Were the Hungarians right when they carried the logic of revisionism to its bitter end? Is not a multi-party system, implying the freedom of propaganda and free elections, the *sine qua non* of formal liberties in the twentieth century? The institutions which the Soviets regard as part and parcel of bourgeois democracy and consequently counter-revolutionary as compared to a 'people's democracy' or socialism, have they not retained their freshness, in spite of Western scepticism, precisely where they have been eliminated in the name of a so-called socialism?

Two remarks will serve as introduction. In theory the Soviet regimes have not suppressed representational institutions. In the USSR they hold elections and the Supreme Soviet, composed of members elected by the people, meets regularly. In reality, however, even at best, these elections allow but a meagre freedom of choice. The Assembly is in session for a few days only, it hears previously prepared speeches and approves unanimously or by acclamation, the budget and the proposed laws laid before it. Whether these ceremonies represent the homage paid by vice to virtue or a camouflaging of despotism as the traditional Potemkin villages, the essential fact remains: the Soviet regimes do not reject the principle of representational institutions, elections, and an

Assembly. The spokesmen of these regimes like to comment on the number of non-party candidates figuring on their lists, the gap between the number of candidates and the number of those elected, and on the increasing seriousness of parliamentary debates (in Poland, for example). In the same way, indirectly, the dogmatics admit that the choice of candidates is what is essential in elections, and that the function of deputies is to deliberate and debate, not only to approve.

Beyond this they are compelled to justify the rule by a single party which is not the logical outcome of the democratic idea. Justification varies between two extremes: the *formula of the avant-garde*, the active minority called upon to lead the masses in the attack on the capitalist Bastille, and the *formula of social homogeneity* which deprives the multi-party system of all authentic significance. In other words: either this plurality is the expression of a class society, and, pretending to respect diversity, bourgeois democracy favours the maintenance of the power of the capitalists; or the working class has seized the state through the intermediary of the Marxist–Leninist party. In that case, the party was compelled to exercise dictatorship in the name of the proletariat during the initial phase so as to eliminate the classes condemned by history. Once the building of socialism is on its way, or even accomplished, the state is no longer the state of the proletariat alone but that of the peasants and workers, it becomes the state of the entire people. During the first phase a plurality of parties would constitute an obstacle, and during the second phase it no longer serves a purpose. The entire people is one with the state and with the party that supports it.

It is difficult to achieve a social revolution by legal means, respecting private interests and the positions of the various social groups. Thus, it will be admitted that these revolutionaries, determined to substitute collective ownership for private ownership of the means of production, establish for a period of time what they call the dictatorship of the proletariat but which is, in fact, the absolute dictatorship of the party that regards itself the agent of historical necessity, unleasher of the catastrophe that leads to salvation. But when the enemy classes have disappeared, when the state belongs to the entire people, why are the electors not allowed to choose their own representatives? A single party and the state of the people are, in the ultimate analysis, contradictory propositions. Stalin had thought up the perverted theory that during the building of socialism the class struggle becomes intensified. Where will the class enemies be found half a century after the collectivization of all the means of production? But the theory of his successors, though perhaps less harebrained, is hardly more satisfactory. Why should there be but one party? Why should a free competition of candidates be forbidden if the entire population identifies itself with the state? The so-called socialist regime, the reign of a single, monopolistic party, made possible the 'personality cult' and the crimes accompanying it, which were publicly acknowledged by Mr Khrushchev. Is not the only logical conclusion the one adopted by the Hungarians? De-Stalinization is not enough; what is needed is the removal of the conditions in which Stalinism could develop and, most of all, the removal of the pseudo-dictatorship of the proletariat: the single-party despotism.

At this juncture both the Russians and the Chinese, reconciled for a moment against those whom they both describe as reactionaries, shout in unison: counter-revolution! Their reconciliation, however, is precarious, for the Chinese have no difficulty in proving that Khrushchevism leads not to the re-establishment of the private ownership of the means of production but to the restoration of the individual, hence bourgeois, freedoms. As far as the natural sciences are concerned the party no longer considers itself the repository of the ultimate truth, it is trying to find the most effective methods of planning, and it now allows writers and artists to express themselves more freely, the only condition being that they do not question the dogma of Marxism–Leninism. It permits the individual to hope for a progressive rise in the standard of living instead of promising him 'blood, sweat and tears' in the struggle against the hydra-headed monster of capitalism and imperialism. How can the last 'untouchable' dogma be safeguarded in a society which is beginning to prefer comfort to crusade? In the ultimate analysis, the most fragile dogma is that of the one-party monopoly, not to be found in Marx's Marxism, the justification of which disappears in the measure the classes disappear.

The Chinese accusation of revisionism levelled at Stalin's successors is well founded, but so is the Russian counter-accusation of dogmatism. Why should one not apply the most effective methods of planning? Why lay claims to a scientific approach and, at the same time, deprive the intellectuals of freedom? Why produce if not to raise the living standard of the masses? The self-fulfilment of the individual has always been a Marxist ideal. Does anyone who tries to put the Marxist ideal into practice betray Marxism–Leninism?

Both the Chinese and Russians are right, or, rather, right in their attacks on each other. It is difficult to defend revisionism but it is also difficult to justify totalitarianism beyond the initial phase of the revolution and the first stage of industrialization in the name of a philosophy of enlightenment. Post-Stalinism leads logically to the restoration of the liberties that the Leninists have for long called 'formal'. And Mao Tse-tung's Marxism–Leninism must either break with Western rationalism, or it can be valid only for a period of privations, struggle and poverty.

In 1956 the Hungarian revolutionaries revealed, simultaneously, the historical, that is past, truth of Stalinism and the imminent truth of Khrushchevism which was still unrealized. All observers of this revolution confirmed that the intellectuals played a decisive role in it. Now, the revolt of the intellectuals was first and foremost a revolt against the falsehood in which, they now realized, they themselves have lived. In this sense the Hungarian revolution was a 'victory of truth'. The revolutionaries were defeated but the meaning of their action survives because it was '*wirklich*', as Hegel would have said, that is, genuine and efficient.

We know since 1956 that within the existing international situation Eastern Europe must not, and cannot, hope for a sudden and dramatic liberation. Liberation will be the issue of an internal transformation and no one can foretell how long that will take. The opportunity was lost and will not re-occur in the foreseeable future. The Hungarian revolution throws light on a bitter truth: the peoples on whom a Soviet regime has been imposed can rely on themselves alone. Thanks to the sacrifice of the Hungarian people, other peoples of Eastern Europe have learned that the hope of an external liberation was, for reasons I have referred to, in vain and now trying to find other, less dramatic but perhaps nonetheless effective ways and means for their area 'internal' liberation.

★ ★ ★

I have restricted myself to using the language of politics only, and it is a poor language. It impels us to contrapose means and ends, cost and profit. Inevitably, it ignores the essential: moral significance, the value of symbols. The attribute of greatness, greatness of men and greatness of nations, is that it lifts us above the mediocrity of calculation, above the prosaic quality of everyday existence.

No one has the right to incite a people to greatness when it costs so

many sacrifices and ends in martyrdom. But when, in a sort of heroic
madness, a people chooses a destiny of greatness, when it sacrifices
itself to bear witness, it is the duty of the analyst to realize the limits of
the interpretation to which he has restricted himself.

The Hungarian revolution, a historic tragedy, a triumph in defeat,
will for ever remain one of those rare events that restore man's faith in
himself and remind him, beyond his proper lot, of the meaning of his
destiny: truth.

Against the Stream

RESISTANCE TO TOTALITARIANISM WITHIN
THE SOVIET EMPIRE 1917-66

'HISTORY IS the propaganda of the victors,' said Ernst Toller. Up to a point this is true: what we know, for instance, about Carthage, we have learned from her most implacable enemies, and we tend to view Greek history through Athenian eyes. Yet meek acquiescence in this state of affairs would mean the abdication of the historian's responsibility. For the past two hundred years, since the study of history came into its own as an independent and critical discipline, historians have seen as one of their main tasks the redressing of this inequity, and the reconstruction of the past in a shape as many-sided and as true to the facts as their abilities and the data at their disposal allow them. One can be rightly sceptical about Ranke's famous claim to reconstruct the past *wie es eigentlich gewesen*, 'as it actually was', yet this aim, however unattainable, is surely the ideal which the historian should for ever strive to achieve.

In our time the idea of determinism and the search for causality has resulted in the losers often being regarded as tiresome irrelevancies, undeserving of the student's attention. A few years ago an eminent English historian stirred up a lively controversy by his observations on the subject matter of history: 'History is, by and large, a record of what people did, not of what they failed to do: to this extent it is inevitably a success story . . . By and large, the historian is concerned with those who, whether victorious or defeated, achieved something.'[1] In other words, the historian was firmly ranged on the side of the big battalions. But what was to be the criterion for inclusion in this 'success story'? Is not the success of today frequently the defeat of tomorrow, and the loser of yesterday the victor of today? Did this mean that the object of the historian's attention should be whoever and whatever seemed successful at the given moment in time at which he was producing his work?

[1] E. H. Carr, *What is History?*, London, 1961, pp. 120-1.

'It's always best on these occasions to do what the mob do.' 'But suppose there are two mobs ?' suggested Mr Snodgrass. 'Shout with the largest,' replied Mr Pickwick.

At what stage can the historian consider the stigma of defeat to have been rubbed off sufficiently to allow its bearer to enter the annals of history ? In one of his stories Anatole France describes Pontius Pilate in retirement, being approached by an acquaintance with a request for details about a minor Jewish agitator, who had been sentenced to death many years earlier, and being unable to remember anything about the case, even the culprit's name. What failure could have been more absolute ?

History is not a success story, and the historian's task is to look beyond the seemingly straightforward record of successes and failures that is contained in the great bulk of his sources.

If the writing of history from the point of view of the victor—or of 'achievement'—is a deplorable practice at all times, how much more misleading, and even dangerous, has it become in our age, the age of the totalitarian dictatorship, the monolithic ruling party, and the compulsory, uniform and all-embracing ideology. For the communist dictatorships (and their inept 'third world' imitators) the perversion of history, the fabrication of ever newer definitive versions of the past is far more than a matter of vanity or political expediency. It provides not merely the basis for their political legitimacy, but the vital core of their whole system: the justification for their claim to act as the embodiment of the Laws of History, for their messianic faith in the righteousness of their cause. 'A profound understanding of the laws of history' is officially given as the source of the party's omniscience and the reason for its supremacy. Surely it was not by chance that George Orwell, with his uncanny understanding of totalitarianism, chose as the central figure of his *1984* one of the insignificant manipulators of history, a man whose fall from grace into the abyss of 'crime-think' originated in his obsessive search for the truth about the past. And, in the final analysis, Big Brother's total control over the minds and souls of his subjects was based not on the torture-chamber, but on his mastery of the past, on his power to refashion history at will. ('All history was a palimpsest, scraped clean and re-inscribed as often as was necessary.')

Under totalitarianism history no longer means 'knowledge of the past', and the historian himself is transformed from a cloistered chronicler of remote events into an active moulder of the present and the future. One striking illustration instantly springs to mind. During the half-century of its existence the Soviet empire has experienced many dire predicaments: cruel military reverses, economic failures, widespread famine, sharp turnabouts in policy, forced collectivization, mass purges, sudden changes of leadership, executions and deportations, great waves of dissatisfaction. But the gravest and most lasting crisis of the Soviet system, which for a time endangered its very continuance and is still nowhere near solution, was caused by none of these, but by Nikita Khrushchev ascending the rostrum of the 20th Party Congress on 25 February 1956, and relating to the delegates a few of the previously concealed facts about their party's past. No longer is the spectre of communism haunting Europe: from that day it is the spectre of the past that has been haunting communism. No atom bomb can compare with it for destructiveness.

The communist 'success story' is turning sour. With 'losers' being rehabilitated and 'victors' degraded, with ever graver doubts being cast upon 'achievements', and strenuous efforts being made to re-vitalize 'failures', the history of the opposition to what for more than forty years was the dominant totalitarian trend in communist politics, to the party 'general line', acquires a new importance. For all that it is a story of unqualified defeat it may yet turn out to have a greater significance for the present and the future than the history of the Leninist–Stalinist Juggernaut that has for so long monopolized the history books.

The development of the totalitarian system was not fortuitous; neither did it happen unresisted. At every stage of its growth the monolith was defied. It can be said that, in a sense, the whole history of the communist movement, both inside and outside Russia, is in large part the story of a long succession of people, party members and non-communists alike, having finally to face up to the true meaning of what was being built up in their names.

Indeed, the opposition to totalitarianism began well before the revolution of October 1917, and even before the basis of the future system had been first formulated in Lenin's organizational principles for the 'party of the new type'. Throughout the history of the nineteenth-century Russian revolutionary movement the authoritarian Jacobin tendency had always been present, and often occupied a commanding position. It was in fierce conflict with this trend that Marxism first appeared in Russia. In the earliest of his theoretical works Plekhanov poured scorn on the *narodnik* plans of achieving power by means of a minority revolution, and etched a prophetic picture of the kind of system they would be compelled to introduce in the—to him inconceivable—event of the success of their plans: 'It [the revolutionary government] will be forced to seek salvation in the ideals of a "patriarchal and authoritarian communism", modifying these ideals only to the extent that, instead of the Peruvian "sons of the Sun" and their officials, the national production will be managed by a socialist caste.'[2] In his next book, published in the following year (1884), Plekhanov was even more explicit: 'Such a revolution could result in a political monstrosity similar to the ancient Chinese or Peruvian empires—or, in other words, in a resuscitated Tsarist despotism supplied with a communist lining.'[3] By a supreme irony of history, it was the Russian Marxists who were to effect the design their pioneers had so abhorred.

Twenty years later, after the first blueprint of 'democratic centralism' had been revealed to the party in 'What is to be done?', Plekhanov, Axelrod, Martov, Martynov and others bitterly accused Lenin of defiling Marxism and of reviving the dictatorial, elitist *narodnik* ideas of Nechaev, Tkachev and Tikhomirov. In a famous passage Trotsky perceptively summed up the inevitable development of Lenin's system: 'Lenin's methods lead to this: the party organization at first substitutes itself for the party as a whole; then the Central Committee substitutes itself for the organization; and finally a single "dictator" substitutes himself for the Central Committee.'[4]

In the course of the ensuing factional struggle the great guns of European social-democracy were brought to bear on Lenin. Most wounding of all were the remarks of Rosa Luxemburg, the leading spirit of the Marxist Left, for whom the idea of a proletarian revolution divorced from democracy was intolerable: 'We can conceive of no greater danger to the Russian party than Lenin's plan of organization. Nothing will more surely enslave a young labour movement to an intellectual elite hungry for power than this bureaucratic straitjacket, which will immobilize the movement and turn it into an automaton manipulated by a Central Committee.'[5]

For the next fifteen years Lenin patiently and methodically built up

[2] G. V. Plekhanov, *Sochineniya*, Vol. II, Moscow–Leningrad, 1925, p. 81.
[3] Ibid., p. 306.
[4] Quoted in Isaac Deutscher, *The Prophet Armed*, Oxford, 1954, p. 90.
[5] Rosa Luxemburg, *The Russian Revolution and Leninism or Marxism*, Ann Arbor, 1961, p. 102.

his monolithic, disciplined party, based on the principles of 'democratic centralism', and comprising an elite of professional revolutionaries. It was several months after this party had achieved supreme power
in Russia that Rosa Luxemburg—imprisoned by the Kaiser's government and relying on only the scantiest of information—though
exhilarated by the news of the Russian revolution, uttered her sombre
warning about the evils inherent in Lenin's version of socialism. With
amazing foresight she described the consummation of a society then
existing only in embryo, but which was to become different from
anything that had ever been seen before:

> The remedy which Trotsky and Lenin have found, the elimination
> of democracy as such, is worse than the disease it is supposed to cure;
> for it stops up the very living source from which alone can come the
> correction of all the innate shortcomings of social institutions . . .
>
> Freedom only for the supporters of the government, only for the
> members of one party—however numerous they may be—is no free-
> dom at all. Freedom is always and exclusively freedom for the one
> who thinks differently . . .
>
> Without general elections, without unrestricted freedom of press
> and assembly, without a free struggle of opinion, life dies out in every
> public institution, becomes a mere semblance of life, in which only
> the bureaucracy remains as the active element. Public life gradually
> falls asleep, a few dozen party leaders of inexhaustible energy and
> public experience direct and rule. Among them, in reality only a
> dozen outstanding heads do the leading and an elite of the working
> class is invited from time to time to meetings, where they are to
> applaud the speeches of the leaders, and to approve proposed resolu-
> tions unanimously—at bottom, then, a clique affair—a dictatorship,
> to be sure, not the dictatorship of the proletariat, however, but only
> the dictatorship of a handful of politicians . . . Yes, we can go even
> further: such conditions must inevitably cause a brutalization of
> public life: attempted assassinations, shooting of hostages, etc.[6]

Rosa Luxemburg did not live to see the fulfilment of her prophecy. But
there were many others who did, and who tried, desperately but
ineffectually, to stem the tide of totalitarianism. At one time or another
the progress of the communist monolith was resisted, with varying

[6] Rosa Luxemburg, *The Russian Revolution and Leninism or Marxism*, pp. 62,
69, 71–72.

degrees of intensity, by diverse and large segments of the Soviet population: by 'kulaks' and medium peasants, national minorities, industrial workers, intellectuals, even by influential elements within the party and the party leadership itself. Taken together, this heterogeneous list makes impressive reading. The essential point is, of course, that they never were taken together, that each and every disaffected or disillusioned category took up their stand in total isolation from the others, and only when their own turn had come to be trampled underfoot. The atomization of totalitarian society could only breed a long succession of tragic 'losers'.

It is this long story of futile, fragmented resistance that draws into such sharp relief the uniqueness of the Hungarian revolution of 1956, the only occasion when all the divergent foci of political, economic, national and religious discontent suddenly coalesced within a single unified stress of popular opposition to communist one-party dictatorship.

Given the circumstances, the Hungarian revolution could have achieved its striking success only because it was actively supported, and even led, by a section of the ruling party. Conversely, the single most important reason for the inevitable failure of all other anti-totalitarian movements within the Soviet empire has been the isolation of the discontented non-communist masses from the oppositionists within the party, and vice versa. Under a severely regimented system, where the Communist Party is the sole existing political organization, a political initiative can hardly issue from outside its ranks. And it was the mystique of the Leninist party—the demiurge of History, of the revolutionary elite to which all members owed utter and unquestioning loyalty, that in almost every case prevented the communist, however opposed to the general line, from taking the final irrevocable step and making common cause with the non-party malcontent. 'My party, right or wrong', as Trotsky declared on the eve of his own expulsion. Although the members of the various successive opposition groupings gradually came to comprise a virtual majority of the old bolsheviks, their efforts were doomed from the start. The myth of the party was the irresistible weapon by which each and every one of them was driven to submission, capitulation, and death.

Resistance to totalitarianism (as it later came to be called) appeared within the party practically on the aftermath of the seizure of power. Few, if any of the leading bolsheviks had ever given much thought to the practical running of the future proletarian dictatorship, but it had always been vaguely assumed that the basic democratic liberties were to be preserved, even strengthened, and that a minority party dictatorship was out of the question. Therefore when Lenin made known his intention of abolishing the freedom of the press and of maintaining a purely bolshevik government, even his closest colleagues were shocked. Ten days after the October coup five of the twelve original People's Commissars, together with Kamenev and Zinoviev, resigned from their posts in protest against Lenin's refusal to establish a broad coalition government of socialist parties: 'We believe that apart from this only one path remains open: the preservation of a purely bolshevik government by means of political terror. This is the path now taken by the Council of People's Commissars. We cannot and shall not take it. We clearly see that this will lead to the exclusion of the proletarian mass organizations from the direction of political life, to the establishment of an irresponsible regime, and to the defeat of the revolution and of the country.'[7]

Their defiance was short-lived: it collapsed after the first appeal to their party loyalty. As was to become customary, Zinoviev led the retreat. A precedent had been set, and the first step taken upon a long and agonizing journey.

With the outbreak of the Civil War dissensions were cast aside. Discipline, unity and regimentation seemed the only means by which the tiny band of embattled communists could withstand the onslaught of a host of enemies. These qualities became transfigured into the central mystery of the communist creed. Yet it would be wrong to believe, as many historians do, that it was the exigencies of war which led to the withering away of inner-party democracy and to the transformation of the party into an unreasoning instrument of totalitarianism. On the contrary, compared with what came later, the years of Civil War stand out as the period of the greatest freedom of discussion, of a rough-and-ready equality and solidarity between communists. Basic issues were left until later, but great questions of military, economic and foreign policy were heatedly and openly debated. These, it was clearly understood, were privileges extended only to communists, and therefore jealously guarded—and soon revealed as essentially worthless.

As the Civil War drew to a close, leaving the Soviet government in firm control of the country, many communists felt the time had come to

[7] *Protokoly Tsentral 'nogo Komiteta RSDRP(b). Avgust 1917–fevral' 1918*, Moscow, 1958, pp. 136–7.

repeal the state of siege, and to put an end to developments which they viewed with growing unease: the rapid bureaucratization of the party, social inequality, the gradual suppression of free speech, etc. The storm broke in the spring of 1920, at the 9th Party Congress. Its deliberations tend to shrink in importance beside the drama of later congresses, such as the 14th and 15th, but in actual fact the 9th Congress stands alone: not only for the fury and the frankness of its debates, but because for once the centre of the stage was taken by fundamental questions of intraparty and Soviet democracy.

The oppositionists, the so-called 'democratic centralist' group, minced no words when describing the realities of 'proletarian democracy': 'Between congresses the people remain silent, and in their place the Central Committee develops feverish activity. For a whole year the Central Committee has been conducting its own policy'; 'The Central Committee is guilty of bureaucratic centralism. This is the heart of the matter. This centralism is flourishing here in all its beauty. They say that fish stinks from the head, and it is from the head that the party is falling under the influence of this bureaucratic centralism'; 'Our centres are trying very hard to kill, to diminish, to weaken any independent thought in the provincial party organisations.'[8]

Sapronov, the leader of the 'democratic centralists', launched a violent personal attack, unparalleled in Soviet history, against Lenin's leadership and policies:

> However much you may talk about suffrage, about the dictatorship of the proletariat, about the Central Committee working towards the dictatorship of the party, in actual reality it all results in the dictatorship of the party bureaucracy ... Then why talk about the dictatorship of the proletariat, about the workers' initiative, when there is no initiative! You are even transforming the party members into docile gramophones, who all receive orders from their bosses: go along and agitate, but as for electing your own committee, your own body— you have no right to do that.
>
> I should like to ask Comrade Lenin a question: and who is going to appoint the Central Committee? But what does it matter—there is one-man leadership there too. A single leader has been appointed there also. I hope we never reach that stage, but if we do, then the revolution will have been defeated ... Nevertheless, permit us

[8] *Deviatyi syezd RKP(b). Protokoly*, Moscow, 1934, pp. 51, 54, 67.

ignoramuses to ask you a question: now that you have adopted this system, do you believe it to be the salvation of the revolution ? Do you think that the salvation of the revolution is to be found in machine-like obedience? We shall fight to the end against the system being implemented by the Central Committee.[9]

To the wealth of facts quoted by the opposition, to their indignation and passion there could be only one rejoinder, and it was to be repeated over and over again, with decisive effect upon a great many communists with troubled consciences: acceptance of these demands would fatally undermine the dictatorship of the party, open the floodgates to the enemies of the revolution, and lead to the defeat of the proletarian cause. It was an unanswerable argument, and in the years to come it never failed to achieve its aim of depriving any oppositional grouping of support within the party. In the name of the single overriding object of preserving the party's dictatorship, every principle was gradually discarded, one after the other, until finally nothing remained that was worth preserving: only the means left to justify the means. But by then it was too late.

This crude argument might not have had its unerringly deadly effect had it not been overwhelmingly borne out, soon after the 9th Congress, by one of the most traumatic events of Soviet history—the revolt of the sailors of Kronstadt, the 'pride and glory of the revolution'.

In February 1921, the communist regime had reached a decisive stage in its development. The Civil War had left the country in ruins. The ill-conceived policy of 'war communism' had broken down. Disaffection and anti-communism were rampant, and nowhere more than among the industrial proletariat. The workers of Moscow and Petrograd were out on strike, and martial law had been introduced in the northern capital. The bolsheviks, having defeated their armed enemies, suddenly saw themselves surrounded by an ocean of popular hostility. It was at that moment that the Kronstadt sailors raised the banner of revolt.

Few events have been exposed to such massive and vicious falsification as the Kronstadt rebellion. It has been variously described by Soviet sources as White Guard, Menshevik, monarchist, anarchist, and counter-revolutionary, and some of the calumny has been repeated by Western historians who should have known better. The true nature of

[9] *Deviatyi syeze RKP(b).*, pp. 56–8.

the Kronstadt rebellion can be best ascertained through its programme, adopted by a mass meeting on I March 1921. The most important of its fifteen points were: the election of new Soviets by secret ballot, with a free pre-election campaign; freedom of speech and press for workers and peasants, for anarchists and Left socialist parties; freedom of assembly for trade unions and peasant organizations; the liberation of all political prisoners belonging to socialist parties; a review of the cases of all other persons held in custody; abolition of all propaganda bodies devoted to the exclusive propagation of communist ideas; the disbandment of 'road-block detachments', established for the confiscation of agricultural produce, and of the elite communist fighting detachments; the equalization of rations of all working people; full freedom of production for all peasants and artisans not employing hired labour.[10]

These were the equalitarian, libertarian, socialist demands of a revolutionary people, profoundly disillusioned by communist despotism, and unwilling to exchange one form of oppression by something that was even worse. For a brief moment in history the men of Kronstadt stood as the embodiment of a nation's will: inchoate, unorganized—but unmistakable in meaning. Of the popularity of their spontaneous demands, even among rank-and-file communists, there can be no doubt according to figures revealed to the 10th Party Congress at the time of the events, in Kronstadt itself about 30 per cent of the communists took an active part in the uprising, another 40 per cent remained neutral, and only 30 per cent opposed the rebels.[11] Therein lay the exceptional threat posed by Kronstadt for the communist regime, as Lenin was quick to perceive; he bluntly declared, and was many times to repeat, that Kronstadt, and the problems it typified, 'represent for the dictatorship of the proletariat a danger many times greater than that of all the Denikins, Kolchaks and Yudeniches taken together'.[12]

The peril was not allowed to spread. The Kronstadt rebellion was put down with brutality; hundreds were executed, thousands more sent to concentration camps. Ironically the final crushing of the uprising fell on the day of the anniversary of the Paris Commune of 1871, celebrated by the Soviets with great solemnity. Alexander Berkman, the famous American anarchist and early supporter of the bolshevik revolution, was

---

[10] George Katkov, *The Kronstadt Rising*. In St. Antony's Papers No. 6, London, 1959, pp. 23–4.
[11] *Desiatyi syezd RKP(b)*. *Protokoly*, Moscow, 1933, p. 255.
[12] Ibid., p. 31.

a witness of Kronstadt's defeat. Sick at heart, he wrote in his diary:

> *March 17.*—Kronstadt has fallen today.
>
> Thousands of sailors and workers lie dead in its streets. Summary executions of prisoners and hostages continues.
>
> *March 18.*—The victors are celebrating the anniversary of the Commune of 1871. Trotsky and Zinoviev denounce Thiers and Gallifet for the slaughter of the Paris rebels . . .[13]

For Berkman Kronstadt was the final milestone in the process of disillusionment with the communist dictatorship. The conclusion he drew from it was a forerunner of hundreds of similar tragic human documents in the years to come:

> Grey are the passing days. One by one the embers of hope have died out. Terror and despotism have crushed the life born in October. The slogans of the Revolution are foresworn, its ideals stifled in the blood of the people. The breath of yesterday is dooming millions to death; the shadow of today hangs like a black pall over the country. Dictatorship is trampling the masses under foot. The Revolution is dead; its spirit cries in the wilderness.[14]

In his monumental *History of Soviet Russia* Mr E. H. Carr has devoted three volumes, 1,400 pages in all, to the period of the Bolshevik Revolution 1917–23. Eight lines and two passing references is all Kronstadt gets. This is as it should be, for the rebellion was manifestly a failure, and thus irrelevant to the majestic march of history. But the communists themselves understand far better what it was all about. Years of explanations, interpretations and falsifications have not laid the fearsome ghost. And when, thirty-five years later, the Hungarian people rose against despotism, under strikingly similar slogans, it was the startled cry 'Kronstadt!' that reverberated through the pages of the Soviet and world communist press.

> If charnel-houses and our graves must send
> Those that we bury back, our monuments
> Shall be the maws of kites.

Kronstadt was crushed, but the experience left a permanent imprint upon the Soviet system. The lasting effect of the fright it administered to the communist leadership was expressed in their momentous decision

[13] Alexander Berkman, *The Bolshevik Myth*, London, 1925, p. 303.
[14] Ibid., pp. 318–9.

to extirpate any possibility of disunity, argument or differences of opinion within the party. The enforcement of monolithic uniformity was carried through in the tense atmosphere of the 10th Party Congress.

Lenin set the tone in words that allowed for no ambiguity: 'No more opposition, comrades—the time for that is past! Either here—or there, either with a rifle—or with the opposition. This, I am afraid, follows from the objective situation. No more opposition, comrades! And I believe that the party congress will have to draw this conclusion, will have to decide that now it is the end, that now it is curtains for the opposition. We have had enough of oppositions!'[15] And that was precisely what the congress decided.

The 10th Congress witnessed the moral fiasco of anti-totalitarian communist opposition, represented in this case by the so-called 'Workers' Opposition', with its near-syndicalist platform of autonomy for the trade unions, and privileges for the working class. Faced with the grim spectre of anti-communist revolt, it was reduced to justifying its actions and to protesting its immeasurable loyalty to party unity and discipline: 'There is no one among us who would deny the necessity for maximum unity . . . We have never once infringed party discipline, and when the Central Committee gives us an order, we reply: "As you say!" We accept this formula of discipline and unity, and believe it to be indispensable . . . Should the Central Committee direct all our Soviet institutions, keep them to the correct ideological tack, guide them in a class spirit? Certainly it should!'[16] Unity had to be preserved, whatever the cost, and the most that Shliapnikov, the usually courageous leader of the 'Workers' Opposition', could bring himself to do was utter a pathetic warning: 'If you wish to lose contact with the masses, if you wish to dissociate yourselves from the revolutionary elements—very well then, just go on acting as you have been doing until now . . . Here you can crush and defeat us, but you will be the losers for it.'[17]

The infuriated delegates howled for dire retribution against the opposition, and anyone else who might in future endanger the party's monopoly of power. Sensing the favourable atmosphere, at the very last meeting of the congress, when a large part of the delegates had already departed, Lenin sprung his surprise: a draft resolution prohibiting the disruption of party unity and the formation of factions, and empowering

[15] *Desiatyi syezd RKP(b)*, p. 121.
[16] Ibid., pp. 73, 74, 104.
[17] Ibid., p. 78.

the Central Committee if need be, to expel offenders, including its own members, from the party by a two-thirds vote. (Characteristically, this last provision was kept secret for a number of years.) One of the speakers in the hurried debate was Karl Radek, who made a remarkable declaration:

> I feel that we are here establishing a new rule, and no one can really tell whom it is going to be used against in the future. We do not know yet how the situation will develop, and how the rule is going to be carried out, but the comrades who propose it regard it as a sword directed against dissenters. I am voting for the resolution, but I have a feeling that it can well be used against us, too. Nevertheless, I support it . . . When danger arises, let the Central Committee adopt the harshest measures against our best comrades, if it considers this necessary. The Central Committee must have a definite line. Better that the Central Committee make mistakes—this is less dangerous than the present confusion.[18]

Fifteen years later, awaiting trial on charges of conspiracy, treason, espionage, terrorism and wrecking, Radek doubtless had ample opportunity to ponder on these words.

Another resolution, also adopted by an overwhelming majority, laid down the single guiding principle towards which the communist movement was always to remain faithful:

> Marxism teaches us . . . that only the political party of the working class, i.e. the Communist Party, can unite, educate and organize a vanguard of the proletariat and the toiling masses that would be capable of resisting the inevitable petit bourgeois vacillations of these masses, the traditions and the inevitable relapses of trade unionist narrow-mindedness and trade-unionist prejudices among the proletariat, and that would be capable of directing every aspect of the proletarian movement, or in other words—of directing the toiling masses themselves. Without this there can be no dictatorship of the proletariat.[19]

Needless to say, Marxism never taught, or even implied, anything of the kind. It was the single-minded determination of the Communist Party to ensure its own power at all costs, to preserve its dictatorship even

[18] *Desiatyi syezd*, p. 540.
[19] Ibid., p. 588.

against the will of the proletariat on whose behalf it purported to act, which inspired this profession of faith, this one principle of 'Marxism–Leninism' to which it has tenaciously clung long after jettisoning everything else.

The resolutions of the 10th Congress spelled, in effect, the end of meaningful *political* opposition inside the party (the famous controversies of the twenties centred almost exclusively on economic and international issues, and on personalities). Here and there stifled political debates continued for a time, discontent was still expressed—sometimes sharply, but this was only a series of rearguard actions, conducted in a strange twilight atmosphere, between freedom of discussion and complete suppression of political dissent.

Greatly encouraged by the 10th Congress, Lenin soon made it clear that he was not prepared to stand any nonsense. At the next congress, in 1922, he issued a harsh warning to all heterodox elements: 'If people create panic—even for the best of motives—at a time when we are conducting a retreat of unprecedented difficulty, and when everything depends on the preservation of complete order, at a time like this it is imperative to punish sternly, cruelly, mercilessly the slightest infringement of discipline . . . For any public expression of menshevik views our revolutionary courts must impose death by shooting—otherwise these would not be our courts, but God alone knows what!'[20] Lenin might not have meant it literally—his bark was often worse than his bite —and he could hardly have foreseen that the state of siege now proclaimed would last for forty-five years, but he certainly meant business: he demanded the immediate explusion of Shliapnikov, one of the oldest and most respected communists, from the party—for having criticized some aspects of economic policy at a local branch meeting.

It is a matter for surprise—and admiration—that despite these intense pressures attempts were still being made, although only semilegally and ineffectually, to stem the tide of uniformity and compulsion. Twenty-two leaders of the defeated opposition were even so naive as to apply to the Executive Committee of the Communist International with a comprehensive indictment of the situation within the Bolshevik Party: its complete suppression of democracy and dissent, its bureaucratization, divorce from the masses, etc. They were rapidly disabused of the quaint notion that the international communist movement represented a forum independent of the Russian leadership. But their ardour

[20] V. I. Lenin, *Sochineniya*, 3rd edition, Vol. XXVII, pp. 239–40.

survived even this blow, and we soon see the Vladimir group of the
'Workers' Opposition' preparing their 'theses', in which they declared
that 'the Central Committee is proceeding from the implementation by
the party of the dictatorship of the proletariat, towards a dictatorship of
the party over that very class whose dictatorship it is supposed to
implement'.[21] Retribution was not slow in coming, although it was as
yet mild, compared with what the future held in store.

It was in this period that we find practically the only case of a communist demanding democracy not just for members of the party, or even
for the proletariat alone, but for the whole population of Soviet Russia.
In 1921 an old bolshevik, Myasnikov by name, addressed a letter to
Lenin, advocating the re-establishment of genuine Soviets, the organization of a non-party Peasants' Union, and the introduction of freedom
of speech and of the press 'for everyone, from monarchists to anarchists
inclusive'. The idea was one of such startling originality that Lenin felt
constrained to reply more in sorrow than in anger; his letter illustrates
one of Lenin's cardinal virtues, so refreshingly different from the dis-
tasteful public personae of all his successors, namely the complete
absence of hypocrisy, the belief in calling a spade a spade: 'Freedom of
the press in the RSFSR, surrounded as it is by its enemies—the world
bourgeoisie, is equivalent to freedom of political organization for the
bourgeoisie and its most faithful servants—the mensheviks and the
S-R's . . . We have no wish to commit suicide, and therefore we shall
not do this.'[22] Myasnikov, however, was not to be put off. He established
an illegal organization, the 'Workers' Group', which in 1923 was broken
up, and its members arrested.

Myasnikov was not quite alone: at the same time there briefly existed
a larger illegal group, calling itself the 'Workers' Truth', and comprising
both communists and non-party people. It professed the view that the
revolution had been defeated, that a new ruling class had arisen, made
up of the party bureaucracy and the technical intelligentsia, that the
party had severed all its ties with the working class, and that the only
solution lay in a new, genuinely democratic workers' revolution. In later
years similar ideas were to achieve widespread currency, but at the time
the 'Workers' Truth' received short shrift.

Ironically, it was immediately after the final defeat of the libertarian

---

[21] *'Rabochaya Oppozitsiya.' Materialy i dokumenty.* Compiled by M. Zorky,
Moscow–Leningrad, 1926, p. 87.
[22] V. I. Lenin, *Sochineniya*, 3rd edition, Vol. XXVI, p. 473.

communists that some of the party leaders began to take alarm at the way things were going. The great conflict with the Trotskyite opposition, which was to last for four years, was opened in October 1923, by what came to be known as the Platform of the 46:

> Free discussion within the party has practically vanished, the public opinion of the party is stifled. Nowadays it is not the party, not its broad masses, who promote and choose members of the provincial committees and of the Central Committee of the RKP. On the contrary the secretarial hierarchy of the party to an even greater extent recruits the membership of conferences and congresses, which are becoming to an even greater extent the executive assemblies of this hierarchy.
>
> The regime established within the party is completely intolerable; it destroys the independence of the party, replacing the party by a recruited bureaucratic apparatus . . .[23]

The real struggle began when Trotsky joined the fray with his famous article on The New Course. But Trotsky, the apostle of discipline, the advocate of militarization, the subduer of Kronstadt, did not inspire great trust among the old oppositionists. With the controversy getting into full swing, Shliapnikov pronounced: 'A plague on both your houses!' In a *Pravda* article he wrote the following:

> Where is the guarantee that the clamorous fight that has now been started against the '*apparatchiki*' will bring genuine political results, and not lead merely to the substitution of one lot of *apparatchiki* by another? . . . In the present discussion the sole object of Comrade Trotsky and the opposition is the capture of the *apparat*.[24]

A somewhat prejudiced view, no doubt, but not entirely remote from the truth. Many years later Max Eastman, formerly a close colleague and supporter of Trotsky's, made a reasonable assessment of the Trotskyite attitude to intra-party democracy:

> In his famous fight against Stalin in 1923 and after, Trotsky was defending intra-party democracy, not because he believed in it as a programme, but because he believed the rank-and-file as then inclined would support the programme he advanced. The framework

[23] E. H. Carr, *The Interregnum 1923–1924*, London, 1954, pp. 368–9.
[24] '*Rabochaya Oppozitsiya*,' pp. 150, 156.

of democracy, if extended at least to the bottom layers of the party, happened to coincide with the framework of his programme. Or, in plain United States, the party if they had a chance to vote would vote for him. Had that not been so, he would, according to this doctrine, have been justified in replacing Stalin's 'centralism' with his own.[25]

Seldom, if ever, has a political enterprise failed as lamentably as the struggle waged by Trotsky and his new-found allies, Zinoviev and Kamenev, against the party machine. Outmanoeuvred, outwitted and outfought at every step, they were doomed to defeat from the start, their every effort paralysed by the deadening fear of infringing party discipline, undermining party unity, and thus 'objectively' aiding the class enemy. For them the Leninist principles of communist party dictatorship and 'democratic centralism' were sacrosanct; they fought their battle on the platform of a more consistent and faithful implementation of these principles. The Trotskyites neither sought, nor received popular support—it was the last thing they could have wished for—and they went down to defeat and disgrace, unmourned by anyone.

As a form of resistance to totalitarianism, Trotskyism was a non-starter. Less glamorous, but of far greater intrinsic importance, were the genuine popular movements of the twenties: the anti-communist peasant armed uprisings and guerilla campaigns, such as the Antonov movement in Tambov province, and the long drawn-out struggle of the Central Asian *Basmachi*. The Soviet authorities have seen to it that the outside world knows hardly anything about this aspect of modern Russian history; we actually possess far more information about, say, the city-states of ancient Greece, than we do regarding these desperate movements, bitterly fought and savagely suppressed, that often involved tens of thousands of men and covered enormous territories—and which took place a bare forty years ago. How could it be otherwise: the illiterate peasants who fought and died in steppe, desert or *taiga* kept no records and left no chroniclers; no commissions of inquiry were set up, no protest demonstrations organized, no signatures gathered and no funds raised by the otherwise so alert Western humanitarians; an impenetrable curtain—both physical and mental—was dropped on everything connected with these tragic events. This applies even to the popular resistance movement of the *Basmachi*—'perhaps the most persistent and

25 Max Eastman, *Stalin's Russia and the Crisis in Socialism*, London, 1940, p. 124.

successful in the entire history of Soviet Russia'[26]—a movement which held out until the early thirties, and which could only be extinguished by a series of large-scale military campaigns, fought by regular army formations, using tanks and airpower.

The *Basmachi* movement derived its exceptional powers of endurance from the strength of national, i.e. basically anti-Russian, feeling in Central Asia. Indeed, much to the surprise of the communist leaders and their trained Marxist glossators, with the passing of time it became ever more evident that nationalism constituted the most formidable and unyielding obstacle to the complete imposition of the uniform totalitarian pattern. National feeling flourished within the party itself, influencing even tried and tested old bolsheviks, and no sooner was one 'nationalist deviation' wiped out than another appeared to take its place. The list seems unending: *Georgia*, where the veteran party leaders— Mdivani and others—were removed by Stalin in 1922, and later disgraced and executed, for taking too serious an approach to their newly Sovietized country's autonomy; the *Tartar* republic, whose first communist leader, Sultan-Galiev, advocated the creation of a separate Moslem Communist Party that would embrace the whole Moslem population of the USSR, and who as a result of this became, in 1923, the first head of a Soviet national republic to undergo arrest and, a few years later, execution; the *Crimea*, which had its first communist leader, Veli Ibragimov, arrested for nationalism in 1927 and executed the next year; the *Ukraine*, by far the largest of the national republics, and a veritable hotbed of 'nationalist deviation', where one mass purge followed another culminating in 1933 with the suicide of People's Commissar Skrypnik and the wholesale liquidation of the ruling communist establishment; and a long line of similar cases, stretching until the present. Every Soviet republic, every national region has its own demonology of prominent communists who at one time or another fell victim to the dread sin of nationalism.

Barely stifled discontent flared into open resistance with the launching of collectivization in 1929. Not even our turbulent times can provide another event to compare, for scope, intensity and sheer accumulation of horrors, with this outright war unleashed by a government against its own people. Widespread famine, the death or deportation of millions, untold suffering, and the ruin of Russian agriculture were the price the

[26] Richard Pipes, *The Formation of the Soviet Union*. Revised edition, Harvard, 1964, p. 178.

country paid for this experiment in social engineering. Resistance was hopeless, yet all over the country there were desperate men who attempted a last stand. In 1929–30 the Chechen, Ingush, Kabarbin and Balkar peoples of the Caucasus, and the Crimean Tartars, rose in revolt.[27] Every one of these uprisings was drowned in blood.

This was not a matter that concerned the Moslem minorities alone: throughout the Ukraine, the North Caucasus, and other parts of the country dispossessed peasants, singly and in groups, tried to stop the monstrous onslaught. Once again, we know very little of this in detail. But some inkling of the truth can be gleaned even from the mendacious writings of official authors like Sholokhov. The general picture is borne out by the documentary evidence of the Smolensk archive, which the fortunes of war deposited in the West. In this, traditionally one of the most docile Russian provinces, 'a pall of terror enveloped the villages'. Reports of arson and murders of communists, together with pleas for military reinforcements, were dispatched to Moscow in an unceasing stream. The statistics of terrorist acts carried out by the villagers in 1929 were grim: 34 in July and August, 25 in September, 47 in October.[28]

The full imposition of totalitarianism in the countryside went hand in hand with the final elimination of opposition, discussion and freedom of thought within the party. The last formal opposition, that of the Right wing under Bukharin and Rykov, had been defeated—in strict secrecy, behind closed doors—early in 1929. A year later it became apparent that the first all-out drive for collectivization had failed, and that discontent was fast growing inside the party and in the country at large. It was at this moment that the Rightists decided to close ranks behind the party leadership—and thus sealed their own doom.

Paradoxically it was the very accuracy of their warnings and the popularity of the ideas associated with them that proved their undoing. Of all the opposition groups that had appeared within the party, theirs was the only one to put forward a genuine alternative programme of building socialism. At that critical juncture, when Stalin's plan of instant collectivization had collapsed, when the whole country was seething with unrest, a publicly promulgated Right-wing communist programme would have rallied around it not merely the malcontents inside the party, but millions of peasants, and every non-communist and

[27] Robert Conquest, *The Soviet Deportation of Nationalities*, London, 1960, pp. 85–7.
[28] Merle Fainsod, *Smolensk under Soviet Rule*, London, 1958, p. 241.

anti-communist in the land. The threat of a great peasant uprising hung over the party, and the old bolsheviks Bukharin and Rykov had no stomach for leading it. Bukharin himself made this quite plain at the 17th Party Congress, in the somewhat extravagant language that had become *de rigueur* by 1934:

> Our grouping was unavoidably becoming the focus for all the forces fighting against the socialist offensive, and primarily for the strata most threatened by the socialist offensive—the kulaks and their urban intellectual ideologists. In the light of later events it has become clear that the victory of this deviation would inexorably have opened the way for *the third force*, it would have weakened to the utmost the positions of the working class and led to an untimely foreign intervention.[29]

Bukharin and his followers were defeated by their own communist selves even before Stalin turned his heavy artillery against them. Entangled in their beliefs, imbued by the Leninist mystique of absolute, unconditional loyalty to the party, they laid down their arms, like so many others who had preceded them or who were to follow.

The years between 1930 and 1933 were the last in which small groups of communists—headed by Syrtsov and Lominadze, Ryutin and A. Smirnov—made forlorn attempts to turn back the victorious onrush of totalitarianism, to win support in the party and bring about a change in policy. They never got off the ground: the secret police were faster. After that, the silence of unanimity reigned, broken only from time to time by the sound of shots from the Lubyanka.

On 22 June 1941, Germany invaded the Soviet Union.

The war provided the nationalities of the USSR their one opportunity to display their genuine attitude towards the Soviet regime—and they seized this opportunity in no uncertain way. A number of armed national uprisings took place in the rear of the Red Army even before the Germans had arrived. Lithuania, for instance, was largely liberated by her own insurgents in the first days of the war, as were parts of Latvia and Estonia. Most remarkable of all was the record of the peoples of the North Caucasus and the Crimea. In this area the Wehrmacht reached or approached the territory of ten minority nations, and in almost every case it was supported by large-scale rebellions, guerilla actions, and

---

[29] *Semnadsatyi syezd VKP(b)*. *Stenograficheskii otchet*, Moscow, 1934, pp. 124–5.

volunteer units. Mass disloyalty here reached such an extent that after
the Germans had been driven out the Soviet government took the
hitherto unheard-of step of forcibly deporting the entire population,
men, women and children, of six national groups—the Chechens,
Ingushes, Karachai, Balkars, Kalmyks and Crimean Tartars—over a
million in all, in conditions of unspeakable horror, and of wiping their
names and the very fact of their existence from the records. Another
1,400,000 Soviet Germans were also deported, to prevent them from
going over. As for the Ukrainians—we have it on the unimpeachable
authority of Mr Khrushchev himself that 'the Ukrainians avoided
meeting this fate only because there were too many of them and there
was no place to which to deport them. Otherwise, he [Stalin] would
have deported them also.'[30] Here was genocide on a stupendous scale—
yet not one voice of protest was raised by the usually hyper-sensitive,
humanitarian and 'progressive' public opinion of the West!

As for the Soviet myth, it is only possible to concur with the late
Walter Kolarz: 'The liquidation of the republics amounted to a
practical as well as theoretical bankruptcy of the Soviet nationalities'
policy.'[31]

Strangely enough, most Western historians, engaged in their sum-
mings-up of the Soviet achievement, continue to this day to turn a blind
eye to the well-documented facts of the widespread and bitter anti-
communist struggle of the peoples of the USSR in the Second World
War. In the latest and most authoritative work on the Soviet–German
war, Mr Alexander Werth devotes a few pages—out of more than one
thousand—to discounting the extent of nationalist anti-Soviet resistance.[32]
The accepted version, as expounded in a recent American book on
Russian history, is that 'one of the most important elements contribut-
ing to Hitler's defeat in Russia was the loyalty of the people. The world was
surprised when the nazis found no fifth column here as they had found
it everywhere else.'[33] One stands awe-struck before this magisterial
dismissal of the reality of mass treason on a scale unparalleled in any
other occupied country, of the existence of a 'fifth column' embracing—
officially!—whole nations.

---

[30] N. S. Khrushchev, *The Crimes of the Stalin Era*. Special report to the 20th
Congress of the CPSU. New York, 'New Leader', 1956, pp. 44–5.

[31] Walter Kolarz, *Russia and her Colonies*, London, 1952, p. 67.

[32] Alexander Werth, *Russia at War 1941–1945*, London, 1964.

[33] Melvin C. Wren, *The Course of Russian History*, New York, 1963, p. 686.

Treason doth never prosper: what's the reason?
For if it prosper, none dare call it treason.

But the men who had fought on the enemy's side were no more than a small minority. However hard and cruel life had been under the Soviets, the great bulk of the Russian people defended their land as valiantly and stubbornly as ever. They had been sustained by elemental patriotism, and by hope: everywhere people believed that after the war the government would recognize their immeasurable sacrifices, and seek a reconciliation and a new start.

The intoxication of victory was soon over, and hope faded and disappeared. In its hour of triumph the communist regime showed itself to be as small-minded, vindictive, ungrateful and distrustful as before. This was the only country in the world where war had brought a relaxation, and peace a tightening of controls. Here there was no question of a land fit for heroes to live in: rather, it was the heroes of the partisan movement and of battles on foreign soil who were themselves suspiciously interrogated, to establish whether *they* were fit to exist in the country they had saved—for had they not been exposed to contamination by dangerous bourgeois ideas? Normalcy returned with a vengeance: shorter rations and longer hours, less houses and more labour camps.

In the Arctic night that now enveloped the Soviet Union even the thought of resistance or of simple heterodoxy seemed stone dead. It was of these, the last years of Stalin's iron rule, that Orwell wrote: 'If you want a picture of the future, imagine a boot stamping on a human face —for ever.'

Yet although in the post-war years the system of communist totalitarianism seemed changeless and fixed for eternity, the actual nature of the Soviet empire had been drastically re-cast. The Red Army had occupied half-Europe, and behind their protective shield Stalin was hurriedly imposing his system upon nations which had never belonged to Russia, and which possessed long histories of independence, and often strong democratic traditions as well. Only this time there was to be no slip-up, and the Sovietization of Eastern Europe was entrusted not to the revolutionary orators and barricade fighters of 1918–19, who had proved fallible instruments, but to the ever-reliable NKVD and their newly established branches. A new form of social transformation had been discovered by Stalin: revolution by police purge and rigged trial.

Events took their mournful course. A sequence of developments which in Russia had required a whole generation to achieve fulfilment was in Eastern Europe telescoped into three or four years. By 1950–51 Stalin's hand-picked minions had destroyed the democratic 'bourgeois' parties, executed or imprisoned both 'Right-wing' and 'Left-wing' leaders of social-democracy, emasculated the trade unions, extinguished all parliamentary institutions, abolished freedom of speech and of the press, cowed the churches and incarcerated their leaders, established one-party states, liquidated independent- and nationalist-minded communists, instituted five-year plans, and collectivized agriculture. And all this was done purely by police action, without ever once taking the risk of appealing to the toilers, or descending to the unutterable petit-bourgeois vulgarity of mass action (which might have put unwarranted ideas into people's heads). Altogether, an outstanding political achievement—particularly if we remember that Eastern Europe, to start with, had a much longer road to traverse before reaching the communist Golden Age than had backward Tsarist Russia.

Uniformity now reigned throughout the Soviet empire. True, it received a nasty shock when Yugoslavia broke away in 1948, but the long-term effects of that momentous event were only felt a few years later; at the time it had been countered by a highly successful series of purge trials. Yet beneath the surface of cheering demonstrations and escalating production figures all was not well: the very haste with which an alien and inhuman system had been imposed upon unwilling populations ensured the artificial and anti-national character of the 'People's Democracies'. Eastern Europe was to become the Achilles' heel of Soviet communism.

Stalin's death was announced on 5 March 1953. And with the old dictator's passing some invisible spring, that for years had kept institutions and men tautly fixed to their allotted positions, snapped. The successors were the first to sense it. To forestall trouble, they hurriedly embarked upon an ill-conceived round of reforms, re-organizations, and half-hearted concessions. Time was gained, but not much else besides: a slow process of decay set in, a gradual running-down of the machine. Taking the terror out of totalitarianism while otherwise keeping the system intact has become the political equivalent of squaring the circle.

It took longer for the peoples of the empire to realize that change was now possible. In Russia itself the first to move were those who had least to lose: the slaves. Without any co-ordination revolts broke out in

Vorkuta, Karaganda and other far-flung outposts of the monstrous kingdom of the slave-labour camps. They were savagely suppressed, they were probably more successful than any other previous form of anti-Soviet resistance movement, for within two or three years almost all the camps were closed down and the wretched prisoners released. In the West—cut off, as usual, from the facts—this measure was taken as decisive proof of the benevolent intentions of the new leadership: Russians know better.

Ironically, the Germans became the first of the East European peoples to revolt. Ironically—because among the many admirable qualities of the German nation rebelliousness and dislike of authority have never been particularly prominent. 1848 and 1918 were lukewarm revolutions at best, while Hitler, unquestionably the most evil of Germany's rulers, was never faced by a popular challenge, and enjoyed his subjects' support to the bitter end. A communist regime was the first government in Germany's history to evoke a spontaneous popular uprising. Never has failure been more dismal.

The most surprising and significant aspect of the East German rising of 17 June 1953, and of the simultaneous revolt in Plzen (Czechoslovakia), was the fact that these were essentially movements of the young people—the pampered, privileged, brainwashed favourites of the regime. These boys and girls had been regarded by their governments as the mainstay and the future of communism. The older generation were all infected by the capitalist rot, but only give us a chance to educate the youth . . . Well, they had had their chance—and lost. The communists' manifest failure to indoctrinate their young people is the most telling defeat of all. The developments of the next few years were to prove it to the hilt.

The floodgates of opposition, slammed shut by Lenin in 1921 and firmly locked up by Stalin several years later, slowly began to creak open. For a time, after the 20th Congress, it seemed as if nothing could withstand the raging torrent of criticism. Soviet intellectuals had started questioning the very tenets of the faith, while members of the Communist Party Praesidium were being shouted down at workers' meetings. Nothing like this had been seen for over thirty years.

In Eastern Europe Stalin's posthumous degradation rapidly led to the worst crisis in the history of the communist autocracy. The situation here was—and remains—in many fundamental respects different from that prevailing in the Soviet Union. The standard of living was, on the whole, considerably higher than in Russia—but it was commonly compared, unfavourably, either with pre-war days, or with life in the West, whereas Russians had long lost any standard of comparison. Again, the full weight of totalitarian terror had only been felt for a relatively short time, and its scope had been nothing like as comprehensive as in the Russia of the thirties—but this also meant that the processes of atomizing society and of reshaping the individual had not yet gone very far, and that society itself was much healthier and more vital than in Russia. Finally, overriding all other issues and welding them together into a single explosive mass, was the feeling of outraged national pride. Nationalism became the common denominator of East European resistance to communism.

The extraordinary events of 1956 require no re-telling: they are still very much part of the times we live in. The tide of revolt rose at Poznan, swelled in Warsaw, and, finally, erupted in Budapest. Since then communism has never been the same, nor could it be. The central development of the past ten years has been the continuing retreat of totalitarianism.

This has been by no means a rectilinear process. Communism, irresistible during its period of advance, has shown itself to be vicious, cunning and tenacious in decline. A totalitarian system possesses formidable recuperative powers. Every withdrawal has been followed by a fresh counter-attack. Fear still remains a potent weapon. Paradoxically, the communist regimes are sometimes strengthened by the very successes of the opposition: the concessions they are forced to make result in the most hideous features of the system being toned down, or even eliminated altogether, thus making life more bearable for their subjects.

The communist rulers have been considerably comforted by prevailing attitudes in the West. This is best illustrated by the immense contrast between the emotional reactions of Western progressive public opinion to two simultaneous, and roughly comparable events: Suez and Hungary. Where the first has become a synonym for unspeakable infamy, invariably brandished at the appropriate occasions, and remaining very much in the forefront of people's minds, the second and immeasurably more heinous act of aggression has been completely forgotten. Over the past few years the frenzied obsession with problems of race and colour has grown to an extent where every other issue is excluded from the purview of enlightened Western public opinion. The only form of injustice that excites wide public indignation is racial discrimination; any other type of persecution, whether for reasons of religion, class, or political belief, is impatiently shrugged off. The granting of independence to an unviable patch of African jungle is a matter of incomparably greater import than the continuing thraldom of half a dozen ancient and famous European nations. And in this great struggle against the remnants of Western colonialism progressive people the world over warmly welcome the tireless efforts and fervent anti-colonial devotion of the greatest and most cruel colonial empire of them all—the only empire that has expanded in the last twenty years, and that shows not the slightest intention of divesting itself of its booty.

The peoples of the Soviet empire have no lobby at the United Nations. No marches, demonstrations, public meetings or collections are organized in support of their cause. The problems that face them receive scant attention abroad. They fight, as they have fought for almost fifty years, alone.

In its latest, post-1956 phase, resistance to totalitarian uniformity has taken on varied shapes: from the intricate manoeuvring by which some party leaderships have contrived to gain a marked degree of independence for their 'socialist' countries, to the publications of nonconformist literary works; from spontaneous agricultural go-slows to the widespread cynical irreverence of the youth. The progress achieved by all these and many other methods would have been unimaginable a bare ten years ago. For, despite all the zigzags of Soviet policy, the retreats and come-backs, the alternation of liberal and repressive lines, the single fact that stands out above all else is that each new counter-attack by the forces of totalitarianism stops somewhat short of the preceding one. Each round ends with the juggernaut finding its absolute freedom of action curtailed still further. It is a long arduous process, but every new imperceptible advance by the forces of greater freedom and diversity is added up to what is already an impressive total.

The tiny cracks in the surface of the communist monolith have widened and joined up into gaping fissures. For all the grandiloquent boasting and the blood-curdling imprecations that still continue to be mechanically cast at the outside world, today the communist empire is in utter disarray. Not only has China set up in business as a rival power centre, not only has Rumania acquired a demonstrable independence, with the other satellites noisily chafing at the bit, but within Holy Russia herself despotism has been more and more openly defied. Within the past few years an astonished world has seen (when it did not prefer to shut its eyes) incredible happenings in the heartland of communist totalitarianism: popular uprisings—notably in Novocherkassk and Temir-Tau, student demonstrations in Moscow, workers' strikes in a number of industrial centres, and finally, a political trial in which the accused actually braved the fearsome might of the Soviet state to affirm openly their libertarian convictions.

Surveying the half-century of resistance to monolithic communism, we are entitled to draw some conclusions. One concerns the immense power of the most basic ideas and concepts evolved by civilized man in the course of his history: concepts of freedom and liberty, of truth, national feeling, moral rectitude, compassion, humanity, common decency. For fifty years these simple beliefs have plagued the communist rulers. The greatest concentration of naked power that the world has ever known was ruthlessly applied to crushing these ideas and wiping them out from human memory—for ever more. But again and again they reappear from under the ashes, in one form or another, proclaiming the indestructibility of the human spirit: in the speeches of the 'democratic centralists', in the manifestos of the doomed sailors of Kronstadt in the desperate terroristic acts of a ruined peasantry, in the reckless uprisings of minute mountain tribes, in the heroic resistance of the workers of Budapest, in the manuscripts of an ever-growing number of courageous writers.

'Ideas become a material force when they take possession of the masses,' said Marx. How right he was, and how wide of the mark the facile reasoning of people bemused by the transitory manifestations of governmental power. Imre Nagy and Pál Maléter, Boris Pasternak and Milovan Djilas, Andrei Sinyavsky and Yulii Daniel: they have all lost their battles. They will yet win the war.

FRANÇOIS FEJTŐ

The Two Sides of the Coin

DE-STALINIZATION AND DISINTEGRATION

'We must remain depositories of the truths of Budapest.' EDGAR MORIN in *Introduction a une Politique de l'Homme.*

'Socialism? Yes. A single party, obligatory unanimity? No . . .' IGNAZIO SILONE: La Leçon de la Révolution Hongroise. *Express*, November 1956.

'In the long run, life without utopia becomes unbreathable.' E. M. VIORAN: *Histoire et utopia.*

REVOLUTION OR COUNTER-REVOLUTION?

WE MUST remain depositories of the truths of Budapest, says Morin. What truths? The truths of the revolution or those of the counter-revolution? There has been much arguing about it after the event, and there still is, in Hungary and elsewhere. The argument itself deserves careful study for it reveals much confusion about the meaning of the very terms employed.

'Events ripen and we have revolutions,' wrote Montesquieu.(1) According to Littré, the term 'revolution' which has its origin in the vocabulary of astronomy, describes in a figurative sense a sudden and violent change in the politics *and government of a state*.(2) It is in this sense that Montesquieu often uses it, for instance when he states: 'All our histories are full of civil wars, without revolutions; those of the despotic states are full of revolutions without civil wars.' According to him the prophetical Jean-Jacques had said: 'We are approaching a state of crisis and the century of revolutions.'

Joseph de Maistre brings us closer to the truth, or, the truths of Budapest. In his view, what distinguishes the French revolution—and later, for the Stalinists, the Hungarian revolution—is that it is 'bad, radically' . . . a certain 'inexplicable delirium' . . . 'an atrocity of a novel kind . . .' a 'conspiracy against the cult'. Let us add: the *personality cult*, and we are fully in the present.(3)

For the Hungarian and foreign Stalinists the 1956 events were 'radically bad', intolerable, incredible, for they conflicted with the Marxist—if not Marxian—dialectics of history. Marx has undoubtedly deepened, sociologized, our understanding of the revolution which to him appeared, in the first place, an act by which the proletariat abolishes the status of the wage-earner and, simultaneously, private property. The industrial revolution sparks off the great social revolution, the task of which is to take over the conquests of the bourgeois epoch; it is a permanent revolution which never ceases until the new society is founded.(4) The revolution which we are to experience should be not merely permanent but also global: social, political, economic, cultural ethical. Not merely national, but world-wide. The Marxist revolutionaries from Lenin to Mao Tse-tung turned leadership by the Communist Party into a *conditio sine qua non*, the criterion of the authenticity, the orthodoxy of a revolution. A revolution or insurrection directed against a communist government became for them an absurdity. It seemed self-evident to them that communism equalled revolution, anti-communism —counter-revolution. A movement, an uprising, directed against no matter what sort of communist government could, *a priori*, have no other purpose than to 'turn back the wheels of history'.

In October and November 1956, Budapest demonstrated the falsity of this tenet. At the same time the Hungarian insurrection confirmed the correctness of certain analyses of Trotsky and Bruno Rizzi— analyses adopted by James Burnham and re-invented later by the Yugoslavs, notably Milovan Djilas—of the 'bureaucratic degeneration' of the Soviet regime. Trotsky foresaw that the economic and cultural progress of the countries bureaucratically dominated would necessarily undermine the foundations of that domination, and would lead, as he wrote in *The Betrayed Revolution*, to a second revolution. This second revolution would, in a certain sense, indicate a regression, not to the preceding regime but to the first Leninist (why not pre-Leninist?) phase of the revolution. According to Trotsky, it would re-establish democracy, the right to criticism, 'authentic' electoral freedom, the freedom of the parties, of the trade unions, free discussion of the economic problems, freedom of the arts and sciences, and a foreign policy more in conformity with the original principles. We see, thus, that even in a strictly Marxist vocabulary, 're-establish', 'restore', 'reconstitute', do not necessarily mean, and in the present case do not mean at all, 'regression'. What was really regressive, an impediment, an obstacle to the development of the forces of production, the development of human energies, was precisely the bureaucratic, oppressive, police-controlled socialism the Hungarian people had to suffer after the Russians. Even the orthodox—though not Stalinist—communists like Kádár and Mao, who branded the 1956 insurrection counter-revolutionary, have to admit that it was the outcome of a wrong policy, of the innumerable crimes and excesses of a bloody-handed and ineffective despot.

Trotsky's (and Rizzi's) scheme applies also to the Hungarian revolution. This event marked the beginning of, and supplied the model of this *second revolution*, of which de-Stalinization and de-satellization are the two most significant aspects in the popular democracies.

DE-STALINIZATION AND DE-SATELLIZATION

To speak of a second revolution is all the more appropriate since the agents of the evolutionary process come, in the first place, from the ranks of the intellectuals and communist politicians who had no wish to destroy the results of the foregoing revolution but, rather, desired to save them, restore them, carry them forward.(5) We have abundant proof of this both in Hungary and in Poland. In order to illustrate this continuity I want to mention only one example, the tragic case of Imre Nagy. In all his writings, in all his acts, Imre Nagy revealed himself as a communist to whom it was essential to safeguard 'the purity of Marxism–Leninism', to preserve that which was achieved, and ameliorate it.(6)

In reality, Nagy's revisionism—like that of Gomulka—took shape, before it burst the framework of the party in power, as a set of reforms dictated *from above*.(7) For, before the rising, Stalinism had already been found unbearable by the communist clerks and salesmen, the majority of whom had, for a great number of years, sacrificed their intellects and closed their eyes to the widening gap between principles and reality, ends and means, between the truths of which they believed themselves to be the depositaries and a system obviously built on lies and outrages.

It needed the collapse of the idol before doubts could be translated into acts. It was necessary that in Berlin, in 1953, then in Pilsen and in Hungary the workers and peasants should give voice to their discontent and that the leaders, until then believed to be infallible, show signs of hesitation and internal division. What we had suspected since the Moscow trials and since the Rajk affair(8) was then confirmed, namely, that Stalinism was the product or rationalization of a kind of political neurosis. The role voluntarily assumed by the bolsheviks and by those who followed them, from conviction, from opportunism or a mixture of both, involved the repression of moral qualities (friendship, humanity, love of people, concern for the welfare of ordinary men) and gave birth to an authoritarian, fundamentally contemptuous mentality.

The Yugoslav communists, and after them Imre Nagy, often quoted Engels who said that a nation oppressing other nations cannot be free. The same is true of individuals. The oppressor can never be free. He is a slave of the power to which he clings, he is a persecuted persecutor, he is no longer the man he was at the beginning of his quest. This is what is meant by alienation, or at least, its origin. This Hegelo-Marxist term, after the Hungarian uprising, as Jean-Marie Domenach noted, was promoted as one of the 'key concepts' of our age.(9) A psycho-sociologist of Hungarian extraction, Joseph Gabel, a pupil of György Lukács, was the first to enrich this notion by systematically elaborating the links existing between economic, political and social alienation on the one hand, and individual psycho-pathology on the other.(10) There is ample material for research into the psycho-sociology of communism, where Jules Monnerot has done pioneer work.(11) Jean Marque has enlarged the sphere of application of the concept of integrating into it the problems of de-personalization, of the material and spiritual de-possession of colonizers and colonized.(12)

The *theoretical* contribution of the 1956 Hungarian revisionists to the elucidation of the socio-genesis of alienation proper to the communist dogmatics, agents and victims of the Stalin cult, is certainly less than that of the Poles or the French.(13) The latter have been greatly inspired by the analyses of the young Lukács (who, at an advanced age, regained his youthful *élan* and became one of the promoters of the struggle against Stalinism); but in words and acts, in verse and in prose, and, principally, in experience, Hungarian writers, like Déry, Háy, Tardos, Zelk, have offered valuable contributions to our knowledge of the communist psycho-pathology. The Hungarian writings we assembled in January 1957, for a special issue of *Temps Modernes* (14), form an anthology of documents which spectacularly illustrate the tumultuous, painful, exalted awakening of men who have suddenly become aware of their aberration of conscience, of the fact that the party has abused their good faith. Many among them (I am speaking of the best) have, believing that they were serving the good of humanity, become accomplices in the rape of integrity, honour, security, in the crimes against the lives of the 'enemy' but also friends and comrades. By approving the persecution of the 'kulaks', the execution of Rajk, by spreading slander against Tito, against the West, they have themselves dispossessed themselves of their humanity; they lost contact not only with outside, but with inside reality as well. Dictating the thoughts of a people reduced to servitude they themselves lost the freedom of thinking, acting, being.

In connection with colonized peoples who have been robbed of their culture, Jean Berque speaks of an 'insurrection of the elemental' provoked by successive humiliations. In the spiritual and material happenings in Hungary and Poland in 1956, and later in the crisis experienced by the Czechoslovak intelligentsia since 1962, one recognizes this 'insurrection of the elemental', the resurgence of fundamental aspirations, like the need for fraternity, equality, genuine authority, liberty and above all, most frequently, the need for truth. To communicate with truth, to be possessed by it, speak it, shout it from the housetops. (Or, in the negative form: to stop lying.) To stop yielding, in the capacity of writer, journalist, historian, etc., to any censorship. To be, to become *oneself* again, by means of the language of truth.

One distinguishes in the subconscious preparation (for no one prepared it consciously) of the 1956 insurrection a moral passion that astonishes and commands respect. In explosions of this kind, in all violent crises, one generally finds the best and the worst among the revolutionaries; but here it was the best that dominated; the passion for purity and authenticity, often in a childish, romantic, I am tempted to say, anachronistic form. The battles of Budapest reveal a youthful, almost unrealistic *élan* and an idealism that compares with Petőfi's revolt a hundred years before. What exploded here was a violent desire for moral purification and of rebirth, the wish to restore an ethical foundation to politics and to society. Man, atomized, completely destructured by the suppression of almost all his organic and traditional relationships, sought to draw up a new social contract, to re-create on the basis of a national and humanistic *mystique* (I find no other word) a new community. He wanted to substitute a new confidence for the gravest of moral diseases: suspicion and all embracing fear.

I have enumerated the elements of de-Stalinization that survived it to re-emerge (the same causes producing the same effects) in the ranks of Russian, Czech and Slovak youth.(15) But nowhere do we find the will to overcome the moral nihilism of Stalinism(16) expressed with

such sincerity and clarity as in the writings of Imre Nagy in whose soul—
and this was undoubtedly the cause of his defeat—the ethical impera-
tives had, well before the uprising, gained mastery over the politician's
needs. Imre Nagy blamed Stalin and Rákosi in the first place for having
provoked a moral degeneracy which extended to each part of society.

> People's preoccupation with the material things [he wrote] their fear
> for their daily bread, destroy the most noble human virtues, virtues
> that, in a socialist society, should be cultivated with love: I speak of
> courage, of steadiness, of sincerity, of fidelity to principles, of con-
> stancy. Instead of these, cowardice, hypocrisy, servility, falsehood and
> opportunism are praised as virtues. The degeneration and corruption
> of public life lead to the corruption of hearts and the degradation
> of character. The debasement of the soul to be observed in
> society is one of the gravest manifestations of the ethical and moral
> crisis taking place at this moment. It has to be said that the debase-
> ment of character and of our entire public life reflects itself in the
> domain of our social life and precipitates the de-composition which
> has begun as the result of an increasingly acute economic and political
> crisis. Lies proliferate; careerism spreads destroying honour and
> honesty, an atmosphere of distrust, suspicion and vengeance weighs
> on the minds; humanism, which should be the characteristic trait of
> socialism, is repressed and its opposite, a cold inhumanity, reigns in
> public relations. Our social life presents an astonishing picture.(17)

Imre Nagy here pronounces the severest and most final judgement
possible on the moral effects of Stalinist despotism.

POLITICAL, ECONOMIC AND SOCIAL ALIENATION

As we are dealing here with better-known facts we shall touch more
briefly upon the economic, political and social effects of Stalinism
against which Hungary rose in 1956 and against which the progressive
elements of the other communist countries never cease to battle. It
would, of course, be impossible to separate these from the moral climate
described above.

Political alienation was the inevitable result of the omnipotence of the
state(18), of the totalitarian organization, of the suppression of democracy within and without the party, of the establishment of a single
party, of the suppression of free trade unionism, of the smothering and

uniformization of all political, social and cultural organizations including the churches. 'The AVH, the political police (wrote Imre Nagy in 1955) was raised above society and above the party and became the top organ of power.' In fact, Stalinism was, more than anything, a system of police and terror, arbitrary arrests, fake trials, the suppression of legality.

It is understandable that one of the first objectives of the 1956 de-Stalinization in Hungary was the limitation of the power of the police and the restoration of legality, and this is still one of the foremost demands in the other communist countries. But they did not stop here. In their *Manifesto* published on the eve of the uprising, the intellectuals of the Petőfi Circle demanded the introduction of a socialist democracy. Later, in the course of its development, the movement gave precision to the term 'socialist democracy': with an elementary force and spontaneity, receiving directives from nowhere else, the revolutionaries began to demand a 'turning back' in the sense that Hungary should continue *'the democratic and popular evolution begun in 1945'* and *'discontinued at Moscow's orders in 1948'*.(19) What they wanted was not to bring back a capitalist, bourgeois, feudal and clerical system but to re-establish a democratic, parliamentary and socialist regime such as they had known immediately after the liberation. It was to this regime that Hungary owed the agrarian reform, the nationalization of the key industries and banks, and which corresponded—and it seems to me still corresponds—both with the fundamental aspirations of the population and to the degree of intellectual, technical and material evolution of Hungarian society.(20)

Economic alienation was the consequence of the total control of the Hungarian economy by a political and dogmatic apparatus which applied in their totality the methods of centralized planning and excessive bureaucratism characteristic of the Stalinist regime in Russia.

Together with the dictatorship of the proletariat the Russians introduced in Hungary excessive bureaucratism that is one of the principal cancers of their own regime. In Hungary, the growth of the bureaucratic apparatus has, in a way, overcompensated for the growing loss of confidence of the people in the government. The so-called state administration comprised 280,000 persons out of a population of 9,500,000. To this number we must add the effective of the Army— some 250,000 or 300,000 soldiers,—the regular police, the 100,000 members of the political police (AVH), the officials of the party apparatus—over 40,000—the functionaries and employees of the industrial and agricultural administration. These figures give an approximate picture of a regime which was worse than a caricature of the 'inexpensive state' desired by Marx. Almost a million adults, 90 per cent of whom would have been capable of productive work, were employed to record, control, calculate, indoctrinate, spy on, and sometimes kill the Hungarians actually accomplishing the productive work.(21)

On this level also, de-Stalinization was entangled with decentralization, de-bureaucratization, with a planning taking into account the national possibilities. It is not surprising that in its *Manifesto*, of which we have spoken before, the Petőfi Circle should have demanded the revision of the 1956–1960 plan (as well as the economic treaties concluded with the Soviet Union).

The fact that the Stalinist system of collectivization has completely disorganized Hungarian (and not only the Hungarian) agriculture is so well known that I shall not dwell on it here.

Social alienation. It is the irony of fate that no regime known to modern history has ever been as fundamentally *anti-social*, that none has ever done as much as to mystify, destroy or deform *class-consciousness*, the key concept of the Marxist conception of history, as the regime of Stalin, imposed by him in the name of socialism. At the 6th Congress of his party, Tito declared that 'the situation of the workers *there* is worse than in even the most backward capitalist countries'. His friend, Moshe Pijade, revealed that in the countries calling themselves dictatorships of the proletariat and preaching the alliance of the proletarian and peasant classes, the latter are 'excluded from any participation in power'.(22)

In general, one believes the Hungarian uprising to have been the result of agitation mainly by the intellectuals, in spite of the massive participation of the youth of Budapest. But the revolution was not merely to the Petőfi Circle, the *Literary Gazette*, the University and the School of Technology, but first, and foremost, the workers of Csepel and Ujpest. It was not merely a moral revolution but also the rebellion of poverty. An official inquest of the Hungarian trade unions has put forward precise and astonishing information on the condition of the workers on the eve of the uprising:

The subsistence minimum which had been established as the basis of this investigation was very low. Thus, it includes one suit of clothes per person every three years, one pair of shoes every two years, one sheet and one shirt every year, etc. In this way we arrived at the figure of 1,400 forints per month as the subsistence minimum of a family of three. It turned out in the course of the investigation that only about 15 per cent of the worker families of three had an income above this minimum in 1956; 30 per cent earned approximately 1,400 forints, while 55 per cent of the families did not attain this figure. 15 per cent of the workers had no winter coat, in a country of continental climate . . .

The discontent of the working class which burst forth with such elementary force in the first hours of the uprising seems all the more justified as, contrary to the promises given by the regime, the standard of living, which had rapidly augmented between 1945 and 1949, took a downward curve after that date to show, in 1953, a 17 per cent decline (official data).(23)

The extremely low living standard of the workers and the majority of peasants contrasted sharply with the luxury or semi-luxury in which the privileged members of the 'new class' lived. 'What is the value of life when one earns 600 forints?' said a wounded revolutionary to the physician who treated him and asked him the reasons of his participation in the movement. At the same time the privileged journalists—an impressive number of whom participated in the revolution for reasons other than economic—earned then 4,000, 5,000 forints a month and the high-ranking party officials, even better remunerated, lived like aristocrats. It is certain that the general indignation provoked by the way of life of the privileged bureaucrats, their villas, their American armoured cars, their exclusive beaches, their servants and their dissoluteness played an important part if not in the unleashing but at least in the generalization, I could even say, *proletarization*, of the uprising.

But beyond the Hungarian revolution, even beyond the famous workers' council movement which embodied the conscience of *the Hungarian wage earners*, the pressure for the amelioration of the workers', peasants' and technicians' living standard, for the suppression of the privileges enjoyed by the new class, for the restoration of the right to strike, the right to professional organizations, remain part and parcel of the process known under the name of de-Stalinization. Perhaps the bases of socialism have been eroded in the socialist countries (just as in the capitalist countries); but socialism has still to be achieved.

NATIONAL ALIENATION AND DE-SATELLIZATION

There is an essential difference between moral and intellectual alienation on the one hand, and the forms of economic, political and social alienation on the other, that should not remain unmentioned. In the first case, alienation is, in a way, the work of the alienated. He has alienated himself. In the second, alienation is suffered, its effects resemble those of any dictatorship imposed by a minority. In Hungary this dictatorship was aggravated by the fact that the ruling minority—the party—was itself deprived of almost all the attributes of national sovereignty for the benefit of a foreign power. Having to bear the effect of what the Yugoslavs and later the Chinese, called 'great-power chauvinism', that is, the *sui generis* imperialism of the USSR, the governing party became, after having been purged of its most authentic elements, the instrument of a satellization, the consecutive phases and consequences of which I have discussed elsewhere.(24) After the defeat of the revolution the new leaders imposed on the country have in great haste repudiated the past, admitting that by the 'automatic application of the Soviet experiences, the erroneous interpretation of Soviet–Hungarian friendship, the suppression of the national interests and the ignoring of traditions' the Rákosi regime 'has deeply wounded the national sentiments of the population'.(25) The uprising was the outcome of these 'errors'. The explosion of national feelings and resentments has reinforced, exalted and exasperated the *elementary* character of the uprising. The Hungarian revolution, first intellectual, then worker and national, grew into a grandiose and spectacular manifestation of national unanimity against foreign domination.

Undoubtedly, on the level of 'satellization', Hungary's fate had neither unique nor exceptional features. All European people's democracies suffered at the hands of Stalin, in 1949, the same process of centralization which eliminated at one blow all the differences of their evolution. 'It made no difference whatsoever (we read in the "Clandestine Hungarian Document") that Poland had been a victim of Fascism, that Bulgaria and Rumania made war on fascism, or that Hungary remained loyal to Hitler to the end.'

Some of these countries possessed deep-rooted democratic traditions, others did not. Czechoslovakia was one of the most industrialized countries of Europe while Albania was still at the stage of goat-breeding. Who cared? All these countries became 'dictatorships of the proletariat' and at one blow 98 per cent (neither more nor less) of the population voted communist with a sincerity of which the Hungarian revolution was a staggering illustration. The system applied to international relations was the same as that applied in the Soviet barracks for recruits: whether one was brown, the other blond, whether one was curly-headed the other not: henceforth everyone will be bald. Bald, yes. You will all be shaved on the same day, in the same way, with the same enthusiasm.(26)

But in none of these countries, including Poland (perhaps with the sole exception of East Germany) did this foreign domination violate the national interests and traditions as much as it did in Hungary. Poland needed the USSR to protect her western borders. Czechoslovakia and Bulgaria were traditionally pro-Russian. The Rumanians, though deprived of Bessarabia, owed the retention of Transylvania to the good will of the Russians. Fear of a German renaissance drove the Slavic countries into the arms of the Big Soviet Brother. The case of Hungary, however, was special. Reason commanded them to be on good terms with the Soviet Union but their eyes were turned, traditionally, towards Vienna, towards the West. In addition, nowhere was the preoccupation with national survival, which, according to Bibó, characterizes all the small Eastern European peoples (27) as powerful as in Hungary. In this once great people, who were subsequently dismembered and humiliated, nationalism has taken a particularly radical form, oscillating between heroic feats and a defeatist realism, between feelings of superiority and feelings of inferiority, between Byzantium and Rome, East and West.(28) Literature and historiography have always held up before the Hungarian people a mirror in which, alternately, they saw Epinal's image of oriental knights lost in the outskirts of the West, and that of an exiled, orphan people, without brothers or sisters, but which assumed the exalting role of defender of the West against the barbarian Turks and Russians.

Everything predisposed this people to the rejection of submission to the Russians whom it considered a crude multitude, less developed than themselves and from whom they could learn nothing. Yet, as stated by the 'Clandestine Document', during the Rákosi regime the Hungarians were compelled to:

accustom themselves to the fact that any editorial of the *Pravda* had a greater influence on their country than all the speeches pronounced in the Budapest House of Parliament, always supposing that these speeches contained any reasonable suggestion. Everywhere one encountered Soviet experts who walked around with the arrogance of colonial officials among the natives. It was these experts who commanded the Hungarian soldiers and policemen to be clad in Soviet uniforms; it was they who organized the trials while the Soviet information services spread their network everywhere. And this *de facto* domination had to be supplemented, nobody knows why, by humiliating ceremonies. József Révai, to whom, by the way, we owe an excellent analysis of the 1848 revolution and Kossuth, carried this fawning to such extremes that, at the unveiling of Stalin's monumental statue, he declared that the figure of Hungarian history was none other than . . . Stalin. And when, in the autumn of 1955, a Soviet delegate of secondary importance called Pegov spoke in Budapest at a public meeting to pay homage to the 'productive zeal of the Hungarian worker', István Kovács, one of Rákosi's collaborators, replied: 'We thank our comrade Pegov and we assure him that the Budapest workers will continue to do everything in their power also in the future to deserve his praise.' The workers present at this meeting shook with suppressed fury. It was, in the first place, against this national humiliation that the uprising of October 23 was directed.(29)

We know that after Stalin's death the Soviet leaders realized that excessive satellization (coupled with economic exploitation) had been a mistake and that the empire had to be reorganized. Mao Tse-tung was also urging them since 1954 to reform.(30) Thanks to a Polish absconder, Seweryn Bialer, we now have the authenticated minutes of the July 1955 session of the Soviet Central Committee at which, referring to Mao, Mikoyan criticized Molotov's policies and denounced the 'inadmissible forms of interference' in the internal affairs of the satellite countries. On the same occasion Kaganovich upbraided the Soviet ambassador in Poland for behaving like the 'governor of the country' and for treating Bierut, head of the Warsaw government, 'like a valet whom one summons when one wants to give him an order'. It is well known that Rákosi was treated in the same way.(31)

Unfortunately the Soviets took too long to draw practical lessons from this self-criticism. There was a big gap between the promises made, the hopes engendered by the June 1955 Belgrade declaration about which, in his *Political Memoirs*, Imre Nagy stressed the 'historical importance', and the acts of the Soviet leaders who helped Rákosi to overthrow the first (and very mildly reformistic) Imre Nagy government, and subsequently replaced Rákosi by Ernő Gerő, a Stalinist as much compromised as his predecessor. Moscow hesitated too long before giving the green light to an opposition which, though it would no longer accept a 'humiliating, subordinate role', and though it demanded that Soviet-Hungarian relations be based on the five Bandung principles: national independence, sovereignty, equality of rights, non-interference, self-determination,(32) did not even dream of breaking off relations, and later yielded only to the almost irresistible pressure of the popular masses provoked by Soviet intervention when proclaiming Hungary's neutrality and her withdrawal from the Warsaw Pact.

Before this happened, however, the people 'had made itself independent of the opposition',(33) the movement abandoned the rails of *historical realism* to plunge headlong into a 'messianic utopia'.(34) Yet, this utopia seems to have expressed the genuine Hungary, it reflected her deepest tendencies and aspirations. Thus, what appears to have been the hour of delirium was, in reality, the hour of truth.

Moscow, at any rate, was quick to grasp this. Proof of it lies in the unfortunately tardy declaration of 30 October 1965, which admitted that 'excesses and errors have reduced the significance of the principles of equality in rights in the relations between the socialist states' and proclaimed that 'the countries of the great community of socialist states can build their relations exclusively on the principles of equal rights, observance of territorial integrity, political independence, sovereignty, and non-interference in each-others' internal affairs'.

Despairing of a concord between words and acts the Hungarian people demanded, in October and November 1956, the right of secession, a demand rejected by the force of arms which could not be defeated in the international situation of that epoch. However, the centrifugal forces that manifested themselves so tempestuously in Hungary in 1956 were not completely exhausted. At the time, the Rumanian, Czechoslovak, Bulgarian, Albanian and even Chinese leaders hastened to join the USSR in the condemnation of Imre Nagy's 'national communism' and agreed that the Magyars had to be disciplined. But in 1960 the Albanians defied the Kremlin; in June 1963 Mao Tse-tung published a twenty-five point proposal which was to be the New Charter of the Socialist Countries; in December of the same year a Slovak author called Mnacko, protested against the 'monstrous custom of treating nations like human material(35); in April 1964 the Rumanian Central Committee published a resolution which could be described as a declaration of independence. In these documents one discovers almost word by word the formula used by Imre Nagy and the Hungarian opposition in 1956 to denounce foreign domination. Since then, national communism has become general, patriotism has been rehabilitated and pluralism admitted. The people's democracies are no longer 'put in the same bag', they are no longer compelled to a forced march. Polycentrist evolution justifies *a posteriori* the ideas that led Imre Nagy and his companions to the scaffold.

After her attempt at neutrality had been crushed, would Hungary at least be permitted the consolation of becoming, as it was wryly predicted by the conquered of 1956, 'the most liberal of the Soviet provinces' ?(36) This is another story which will have to be discussed elsewhere. The Hungarians, at any rate, believe that in spite of the defeat they suffered and their continued condition of satellite, their sacrifices were not completely wasted.

NOTES

(1) The Spirit of the Laws, XXVIII, 39.

(2) E. Littré: *Dictionnaire de la langue francaise*, T.6.

(3) Joseph de Maistre: *Textes Choisis*, et présentés par E. M. Cioran; Ed. du Rocher.

(4) Karl Marx: 'Addresse du Conseil géneral de la Ligue communiste', in *Les Marxistes*, présentation de Kostas Papaioanou, p. 231.

(5) According to Littré, counter-revolution is a 'revolution that tends to destroy the political achievements of the preceding revolution'.

(6) See my portrait of Imre Nagy, Introduction tó the French edition of Imre Nagy's *Political Memoirs*, published under the title *Un Communist que n'oublie pas l'Homme*. Plon, 1957.

(7) See Imre Nagy's speech of 4 July 1953, the acts of his government

between 1953 and March 1955, his *Memoirs*, op. cit. above.

(8) See our analysis of the trial in *Esprit;* November, 1949.

(9) J. M. Domenach: Pour en finir avec l'alienation; *Esprit*, November 1965.

(10) Joseph Gabel: *La fausse conscience*, Edition de Minuit, 1962; by the same author: Formen der Entfremdung, Fischer Verlag, 1964.

(11) J. Monnerot: *La sociologie du communisme*.

(12) J. Berque: *La dépossession du monde*, Seuil, 1965.

(13) See, notably, Adam Schaff's remarkable book: *Marxisme et l'Individu*, 1965.

(14) *La Révolte de la Hongrie*, with an introduction by Jean Paul Sartre.

(15) Here are a few random examples from the 'revisionist' literature of that country: 'You have produced a general psychosis of fear . . . everyone is afraid of something, of someone.' (L. Mnacko in *Kulturny Zivot*, 8–6–1963); 'We are building a collective society but we are creating lonely people.' (L. Dobozy, *Literarny Noviny*, 12–9–1964); 'The feeling of security, integrity and freedom, the duty to be brave and to think, the task to form one's own opinions, one's own personality . . . have not been authorized.' (P. Stevcek, *Kulturny Zivot*, 21–12–1963).

(16) See Michael Polanyi: *Beyond Nihilism, in History and Hope*; collective work edited by K. Jelensky, London, 1962.

(17) See Imre Nagy's *Political Memoirs*, quoted above, p. 115.

(18) 'Socialist society (says Adam Schaff, ex-Stalinist, then Golumkaist converted late to revisionism) knows various forms of alienation . . . if only as a result of the existence of the state. And what a state!'

(19) See 'Hungarian Clandestine Document', drawn up in late 1956 and quoted by F. Fejto in *Les Lettres Nouvelles*, June 1957.

(20) On this subject the 1946–47 analyses of the foremost Hungarian sociologist, István Bibó, too little known abroad, retain all their validity, a premonitionary validity. After the Liberation 'the paralysed forces of Hungarian society became activated for the first time since 1514, aiming at a greater freedom'. 'The more the Communist Party insists on annihilating the so-called reaction, the more it isolates itself in the country.' 'It is a question of life or death for Hungary that the collapse of the "ancien régime" be, or rather, become a genuine freedom and that the oppressive factors of the *pathological* social structure threatened by the appearance of the Red Army be eliminated: aristocrats who spent their life

hunting, officers and officials leading the exclusive life of a caste, gendarmes and Germano-maniac educators, should never return.' Between 1939 and 1945 Hungary had become ripe for a revolution that would turn it into a democracy comparable to Finland or Austria. The best sons of the country would always be nostalgic for the 'ouverture' that had to be re-created.

(21) See 'Un Document Clandestin Hongrois', in *Les Lettres Nouvelles*, p. 888.

(22) This fact was expressed by a joke which circulated in Hungary during the dark years: 'What is the difference between capitalism and socialism? Capitalism is the exploitation of man by man. Socialism is the reverse.'

(23) Clandestine Hungarian Document, cited above, pp. 886–7.

(24) François Fejto: *Histoire des Democracies Populaires*, Paris, Seuil, 1952; and *La Tragédie Hongroise*, Paris, 1956.

(25) Resolution of the Socialist Workers' Party, *Népszabadság*, 10 December 1956.

(26) Clandestine Hungarian Document, cited above, pp. 884–5.

(27) István Bibó: 'The Great Poverty of the Small Countries of Eastern Europe', in *Válasz*; 1946.

(28) 'Because in the past they were so skilled at playing the master, in our time they were less disposed than any other Central European nation to put up with slavery; if they had a taste for leadership would they not also have a taste for freedom?' E. M. Cioran in his admirable *History and Utopia*.

(29) *Les Lettres Nouvelles*, p. 885.

(30) See my book: *Chine-URSS. La fin d'une hégemonie*, Plon, 1964, chap. XI and XII.

(31) See my analysis of these minutes in *France-Observateur*, 11 July 1957.

(32) Imre Nagy's *Political Memoirs*, op. cit., p. 98.

(33) We mean Imre Nagy's followers. Clandestine Hungarian document, p. 886.

(34) Peter Veres in *Kortars*, 1964.

(35) *Kulturny Zivot*, 21–12–1963.

(36) Clandestine Hungarian Document, op. cit.

(37) I dealt with the subject for the period of 1957–63 in 'Hungarian Communism', essay published in the collective volume *European Communism*; ed. by W. E. Griffith, M.I.T., 1964.

PART II

Hungary Ten Years After

Hungary 1956

JOURNEY TO BUDAPEST

SEEN AGAINST the eastern sky on the late afternoon of the 26 October 1956, the frontiers of Hungary at Nickelsdorf were wide open, as they had never been in ten years—beckoning us to cross. The insurgents had taken over the customs house, chased away its occupants, and cut out the Red Star from their national flag hanging outside; it now had a gaping hole in the centre. There were about twenty of these young men, ragged, unshaven for the most part, wearing the red, green and white armbands of their national colours, with Tommy-guns slung over their shoulders. They were full of confidence, and said the road to Budapest was in their hands; they claimed to be destroying the Russian tanks in the city.

'Come!' they cried. 'Come and see what we have done! And what we are going to do!'

They offered to take us (two Austrians curious like myself, and a Swiss photographer) in one of their lorries to Győr fifty miles away, where they said we would find another food-lorry bound for Budapest. All other means of communication had ceased, so we accepted the offer; I sat in front with the driver and a German-speaking girl who also wore the armband of the insurgents.

Although winter was in the air, it had been a day of bright October sunshine, and the hills and woods ahead, the undulating countryside of Transdanubia, lay under a blue haze. The sun was setting in a cloudless sky, and the long fingers of elm and poplar, pointing eastward with giant fingers, already fell across field and meadow. Not far to the north gleamed the line of the Danube, parallel with the road we followed.

As we drove, the girl told me that she and her friends had been travelling up and down this highway several times a day since the revolution began, taking food to the nearby town of Győr. They had had little sleep, and her face was drawn; but it broke into smiles when she spoke of the revolution. 'I work in a factory in Győr,' she said. 'Ten years ago we all believed in the new system. There is not a soul in Hungary who does so now. All our workers have taken up arms. We shall not put them down until there is not a Russian soldier left in the country.' She was a heavily built, good-looking girl of about twenty-eight, with strongly-lined, almost masculine features, and dark hair already showing a few traces of grey.

Most of the villages we passed through in the dusk seemed deserted; but at the entries there were groups of insurgents who stopped us to examine our papers. Where the situation was clearly controlled by these men, the examination was rapid and cursory; but where, as in Magyaróvár, Russian troops or the AVO secret police were thought to be in the neighbourhood, a careful examination took place.

For about thirty miles we passed at least fifteen of these improvized road-blocks, at each of which the insurgents lowered their Tommy-guns when they saw us slowing down; they then looked carefully inside the lorry for members of the fleeing AVO. In one of the villages we passed some cars on whose windscreens large Hungarian writing had been daubed in red—*Ruszki Haza!* 'That means "Russians go home!"' the girl told me. 'Those cars have come from Budapest, and that writing is in blood. The blood of wounded patriots.' There was something sincere about her, and I did not feel she was trying to dramatize the situation.

At one of the road-blocks, we were told that Russian tanks had been seen ahead, and that we must wait until the scouts reported that they had been destroyed. These people did not seem to have the slightest doubt that *they* would destroy the Russians; they could not envisage that the Russians might destroy them. Their confidence and optimism were infectious; and I felt I was present at some world-convulsing event, some cataclysm like the French Revolution.

While waiting for this information, we went into a small café where we drank *barack* and listened to the wireless. The girl said that the patriot station *Kossuth* was now operating, and that the government radio in Budapest could not be trusted. A babble of opinions were being voiced in the café, all obtained from the conflicting wireless reports, Hungarian and foreign. The Russians were leaving—they were not leaving—Nagy had left the government—Nagy had committed suicide—the students in Budapest were demanding a public trial for Gerő, the first secretary of the party—Tildy, the old president, had taken Nagy's place—Tildy had resigned—Cardinal Mindszenty was forming a

Catholic Democrat party—six newspapers representing all the parties of the new democracy were coming out tomorrow. . . .

Half an hour later, two insurgents came in to say that the Russian tanks had withdrawn to the north, towards Czechoslovakia, and that our lorry might proceed to Győr. We were then escorted by a small Hungarian army-carrier, with a machine-gun mounted in the back, on the road to this town. It was straight, with wide open fields on either side, so that there was little danger of a lurking tank; but the soldiers kept a sharp look-out. The Hungarian roads here are quite well surfaced but narrow, and because there is not much traffic, the peasants allow their famous ducks and geese to pasture freely on the verges. These animals enjoy the roads, strut on them, waddle on them, doze on them; we often had to pull up abruptly at corners to avoid running them down.

Győr is the first sizeable town in Hungary, fairly well-to-do in normal times, a kind of Hungarian Maidstone. Its inhabitants were in a state of euphoria, dancing and singing like dervishes in the main square. Some were waving Hungarian flags (again with the Red Star cut out of the centre), while outside the town hall a powerful amplifier was broadcasting Beethoven's Third Symphony. On many of the walls and shop-windows were the words 'Russians go home!'; and hanging by a cord from a lamp-post in the middle of the square was a life-size marble bust of Rákosi, the former dictator of the country. Children were pelting it with stones.

Here I learned that the insurgents had taken the AVO barracks by storm that morning and broken into the prison, where they had freed two hundred political prisoners. I was told that the Prefect, Szigethy, was inside the town hall at this moment, with his military commander Szabó, organizing a government independent of the one in Budapest. An orator in the middle of the square was saying, 'This morning the Soviets have started firing in Budapest again, after a two days' truce, pretending they were retiring. We cannot trust our government in Budapest. We will march there with all western Hungary, and make Nagy keep his words . . .' Whenever he mentioned the name of Nagy, the head of the new government, there were cries of scorn. This man, who was later to become so popular, was not yet trusted.

Various opinions were held about him. Some said it was Nagy who had called in the Russian tanks two days before. Others remembered when he stood up for the peasants against the communists three years ago. Others pointed out that he was still a communist. Some wanted him to govern only when he had insurgent representatives in his cabinet. It was impossible to form any opinion in this 'fog of war'.

Our lorry had by now unloaded its potatoes, and was returning to the Austrian frontier for more; so that we had to find another bound for Budapest. We found one fairly soon, but had to wait some time for petrol. There was only one pump operating in the city, and at least forty vehicles were queueing before it. But at the sound of the magical word 'Westerners', everyone in the queue began cheering us, and our lorry was sent ahead, to be filled from an aged hand-pump.

When we set out on this, the last stage of the journey to Budapest, the western sky was a deep carmine red, while in front of us to the east all was dark and grey. On the left still lay the Danube, nearly a quarter of a mile broad, reflecting the lights from the cottages and villages which lined its northern, Czechoslovak bank; on the right, were the flattening fields and gently undulating landscape which marked the beginnings of the great Hungarian plain. Here was a splendid sense of loneliness, silence and space.

But twilight time, at any season of the year, is a little sinister, when trees in copse and spinney seem to come alive in a manner quite unlike that of their daylight, static friendliness; and tonight it was easy to confuse them, in one's imagination, with movements which might be human. It was therefore even more important to stop promptly at the road-blocks, where half a dozen insurgents stood behind lanterns. At one of these was a group of armoured carriers of the *Honvédség* (the Hungarian regular army), and some men with bloodstained bandages round their heads. 'We have come from Budapest,' they said. 'There is fighting at Esztergom, forty miles ahead.'

The last stages of the journey took place in pitch dark, although the sky ahead was occasionally lit up with flashes; and as we neared Budapest we heard the sound of firing. Although I had not been aware of Russian troops in any numbers on this journey, they surrounded Budapest. They were allowing vehicles with food, such as ours, to enter the city, but were attacking any armed vehicles of the *Honvéd ség*. They had withdrawn from the roads and villages, and were living in the woods and fields around us, in tents and tanks. The fact that we were an isolated lorry, clearly unarmed (although we flew the insurgent flag with the hole in it), probably saved us from attack. The only vehicles that now came towards us were Red Cross trucks bringing wounded from Budapest, and once at a cross-roads, a tank lumbered by, its cannon wagging ominously, its wireless antennae high. A soldier in a steel helmet was standing in the turret; but because both Hungarian and Russian armies wore the same uniform, it was impossible to tell whether it was friend or foe. Nor had we any idea of what we might find in Budapest—a battle going on or, as some had said in Győr, calm partly restored. A half an hour later we came over the big hill, and Budapest lay before us in the valley of the Danube.

We went down the hill into Buda and entered a deserted city. On the big quay which lines the right bank of the Danube, the street lamps were alight, but no human beings were about. Most of the city lay in darkness, but electricity was still being produced for the undamaged quarters. We passed an isolated tram, standing empty and forlorn in the middle of the street, its windows shattered, but its lights on.

The only sign that human-beings inhabited these houses were little candles placed in all the windows, thousands of them. For today was All Souls Day, when Catholics place candles in the windows in memory of their ancestors. These little flames were flickering, but not only in the windows, sometimes at road level, on the pavements, and at the street-corners. In this way, the driver said, they were honouring their newly dead as well as their ancestors, at places where a day or two before they had fallen in the fighting. In those streets without electric lighting, this was the only form of illumination, thousands of little flames flickering on the ground, a weird Walpurgis night atmosphere amid the enveloping blackness.

I had asked the driver to take us to the British Legation, which I knew was somewhere in Pest. But he appeared obsessed with the idea of first showing the 'Westerners' what had happened to his city in the last four days; and he refused to take the slightest notice of our suggestions. He was a thuggish-looking man with a close-cropped skull and a somewhat aggressive manner; we were little disposed to argue with him. Whereupon, he took us over the big bridge near the Margit island, and instead of going along the left bank, he took us to the Üllői út and the Kilián barracks in Pest, scene of much of the recent fighting. He slowed down occasionally to gesticulate at a fallen facade, torn-up tram-lines, burnt-out tanks and—most grim sight of all, in the Köztár-saság square—four bodies hanging by cords from lamp-posts. These, he said, were members of the AVO who had been hanged that morning outside the party building. Before these corpses he became almost lyrical; and although we suggested again several times how convenient it would be for us if we could be deposited at the British Legation, he still refused. One of the Austrians then pointed out to us that this man had brought us safely to his city; we should not complain if, in his pride, he wished to show us what he and his fellow-countrymen had achieved.

Anyway, we were completely in his hands and so, for nearly an hour, we made a conducted tour of the damaged parts of Pest—a place of unlit streets and lanes and small shops, some with lamps in the windows which lit the facades flickeringly. But in other places, there were dark patches through which a solitary wayfarer came and went mysteriously. Sometimes in the dark we met armed patrols at street corners, who leapt out in a disconcerting way with guns and torches. We suggested to the driver that he should at least put the light on inside his driving-cab, so that they could see from a distance that we were unarmed.

He took us to the Stalin square, where the vast monolithic statue of the dictator had been overturned. Between the fractured stumps of the legs now flew the red, green and white flag of Hungary. '*Stalin kaput! Stalin kaput!*' he kept on repeating; and I began to wonder if he was demented, and if we would ever persuade him to stop. His heavy face with its burning eyes and slight veneer of sweat as he became more and more indignant, was animated and expressive. Each time when he pulled the lorry up abruptly in front of some new 'sight', he would wave his arms and let out a flood of oaths which, although I could not understand one word, except the repeated, '*Communismus kaput! Communismus kaput!*' will long remain in my memory.

Occasionally from behind a tree, or the corner of a house, a figure would detach itself and leap into the street, pointing a Tommy-gun—sometimes a boy not more than fifteen years old. We would stop with a grinding of brakes, and the child would advance and demand our passes. I confess—and the Austrians agreed with me afterwards—that these children were more frightening than all the insurgents. They clearly regarded it all as a grand adventure, and I felt that their fingers were easy on the trigger.

At last the driver began to tire too, and asked us what we wanted next. 'The British Legation!' we said with one voice. Surprisingly, he knew the way, and five minutes later, to our relief, we saw the Union Jack hanging over the doorway of a vast, four-square building made of granite—the entry, it seemed, to a beleaguered garrison. The two great iron doors were chained and padlocked. A member of the staff peered out suspiciously, while I shouted and we brandished passports. At

11.30 p.m., with a clanking of keys and chains, we entered the British Legation.

★   ★   ★

In the Stalin square the next morning, the people of Budapest had not only pulled down the dictator's statue, they were feverishly chopping it up into little bits, so that not a trace should remain. Outside the Communist Party headquarters was a mountain of cinders, consisting of burnt communist books and pamphlets. A ceaseless hail of these came hurtling out of the windows, together with paintings and photographs of Stalin, Lenin and Rákosi, to keep the fires alight. Even gramophone records of the leaders' speeches added to the blaze.

When these busy people realized who we were, they clustered around, beseeching us to let our countrymen know the truth, suggesting that we should take photographs of a big oil painting of Stalin which had just been hideously defaced. They slapped us on the back and shook our hands a dozen times, until we felt that we, not they, had liberated their city. An old woman in tears kissed my hand as if I were a Monsignore; and one of the Austrians suddenly found himself clasping two babies.

Meanwhile inside the building, a grim AVO hunt was in progress. A number of AVO men had just been caught in the sewers and hanged, I was told. Would I care to step inside and take some photographs of them, for the benefit of the West? But the sight of the hanged men the night before had been enough, and I refused this invitation. The AVO men had evidently imagined that their Russian masters would quickly dominate the situation, and they had been waiting underground (literally), for this to happen. But when the lull came and they appeared in public again, they found to their dismay not the Russians, but the population of Budapest, in control. Their cruelties of the past were now expiated. After execution, their bodies were left hanging for an hour or so, for all to see; then the dust-carts came and took them away, and more were displayed. The Hungarians never seemed to tire of looking at the corpses of their late masters. To see the hate combined with glee on the faces of some of these people as they gazed on them was to realize what communism had done in ten years to the Hungarian mind.

It might be supposed from this audacious behaviour that the Russians had left, or had at least evacuated, the city. This was not so. They still surrounded it, and some were in the suburbs. The next day an English-speaking Hungarian who had offered to act as my interpreter said, 'In the barracks I will take you to, you will see that the Russians are still here. Nagy is lying when he says they have gone. Several thousands. With their families.'

For perhaps twenty minutes we walked towards the eastern part of the city, into an area which seemed like some shelled village from the Second World War. Russian tank artillery had been employed against large apartment houses; tram-wires were lying tangled on the ground; barriers of overturned trams and burnt-out armoured cars had been erected in the streets. At length we came to a long white wall about six feet high. 'The barracks,' he said. 'The thing is to walk past as if you were indifferent. Don't stop at that gate, just glance in quickly.'

We joined a small file of people hurrying past the barrack gates, which were guarded by a sentry and a group of Russian soldiers.

'As long as they stay in the barracks, our people don't mind,' he said. 'But yesterday when two armoured cars came out wagging their guns, everyone came into the street and threw stones at them.'

As we passed the gates, we saw some armoured vehicles inside, with Russian soldiers working on them. At the end of the street we stopped and looked back as an armoured car of the *Honvédség*, waving the new Hungarian flag with the hole in it, lumbered slowly down to the barracks. People scattered quickly into doorways, and it seemed as if trouble was about to begin again. But the car stopped at the gate, and a soldier with a Hungarian armband got out, carrying two large metal cans which he handed over to the Russians. 'Milk,' explained my interpreter. 'Milk for the Russian babies in the barracks. They have come to an agreement. Every day our people bring fifty litres for the Russian children.'

This was typical of the curious relations existing between the populace and the Russian troops during this twilight period of the revolution. In some parts of the city they were still firing at one another; in others, giving one another milk, or throwing stones. Once we came upon a Russian armoured car at a street corner, with a crowd around it, half-hostile, half-curious. The Russian soldiers were grinning as if embarrassed, trying to talk, even to exchange cigarettes. It was not hard to believe the story that some of these men had defected to the Hungarians whom they had been ordered to fire upon—nor to realize this was a further sign that the revolt was working-class. Even the soldiers of the Russian proletariat knew it.

In short, relations between the populace and the Russian troops—who were often loath to open fire—was better than is generally supposed in the West. I was told later of a young Hungarian woman, visibly pregnant, at whom the Russian soldiers in the street cried 'Baby! Baby!—and insisted on her accepting their food and rations. And this at the height of the revolution.

All the same, it was clear the next morning that the Hungarians were intent on effacing every sign of communist influence from their city. It was this courageous, if perhaps imprudent, Hungarian violence which distinguished this revolt from that of their neighbours, the Poles who, a week before, had been prepared to advance to independence by easier stages. The people of Budapest seemed to have gone mad, intoxicated with their new liberty. Almost hourly for the next two days, the unfortunate Nagy, the new Prime Minister, found himself forced to make democratic concessions on Western lines. Here was a typical demand from the workers of the town of Komárom—which I was shown—crudely written and printed:

> We, the students, workers and peasants of Komárom have always shown our faith in Imre Nagy. This faith was weakened when he called in the Soviet forces to destroy us. We know now that it was not Nagy who did this; he was made to act and speak with a pistol at his throat. We therefore restore to him our faith; but we do not hereby give him a blank cheque. Imre Nagy knows we are watching him. He must immediately expel the Russian paid criminals from the government, as well make the Russian troops leave our country. He must immediately announce free elections, with secret ballots, under an international commission from the UNO. Within the limits in which he achieves this, we will support him. Otherwise, we reject him.

*   *   *

That afternoon I met Cardinal Mindszenty who had been released in the morning by Magyar soldiers from his prison fifty miles away, and brought back to his old palace in the Uri utca of Buda. Outside this building I found a crowd of people, many praying on their knees in the rain, some of the women weeping. Above the balcony hung the Cardinal's blue and white flag, with the new Hungarian flag beside it.

I rang the bell and asked if I could interview the Cardinal, claiming that I represented the well-known English *Sunday News* (which was untrue, for I am not a journalist). A fat, well-nourished monk appeared and examined me carefully; he held the fingers of one hand in the cord around his stomach, and with the other graciously indicated a courtyard behind the big doorway. Inside I found a number of men with the faces and manners of Western journalists. One of them told me that he represented the Vatican Television, and that they were about to have an interview with His Excellency. As representative of the *Sunday News*, I was naturally entitled to a place in this group.

It appeared that the Cardinal was, at this moment, eating his first meal as a free man for five years; and we were shown into an ante-room to wait until he had finished. Here were gathered a score or so of foreign journalists who had managed to reach Budapest; the Italian Vatican representative immediately began erecting his cameras. Thus, when the Cardinal spoke to the public for the first time after eight years, he had before not only press representatives of most of the Western countries, with their flashlamps and microphones, but also a complete West German cinematographic apparatus, and a Catholic television camera. The almost medieval atmosphere of this part of the city, the ancient houses of Buda with their coats of arms still above the doors, the whole setting of the past in which the interview took place, was thus rudely brought into the twentieth century—as if Hollywood had invaded a cathedral.

Through a barrage of electrical cables, bulbs and reflectors, the Cardinal entered the room. He was a stoutish man of middle height, and he wore a long black soutane with red buttons down the front, a purple cape and a scarlet skull-cap. His face was large and massive, but on the whole dignified, the eyebrows knit, the nose acquiline; bulging, close-set eyes and heavy mouth suggested a certain peasant cunning. These fierce, somewhat bewildered, eyes now looked out upon the world he had not seen since 1948. He had a beard of about three days' growth.

A German reporter in a teddy-bear coat with a hand-microphone now began asking questions into it, and then thrusting it in front of the Cardinal's mouth. Had not the Vatican shown its approval of all this by sending its own television representative (the man I had spoken to, Signor Ruggero Faido), the scene might have seemed irreverent. But it was one of the great moments of post-war history, and the world was to know of it. Whatever happened now, even if the Cardinal were killed tomorrow, he had returned at the end of his life to preach to his people from the pulpit. This was a moment of triumph for the Catholic Church which, true to its tradition, was propagating the triumph with the most modern means available. (This is in the thousand-year-old Catholic tradition; while castigating the discoveries of science, the Church will use them ruthlessly enough if they yield material advantage.)

Cardinal Mindszenty had been sentenced eight years before for espionage, high treason and currency offences. He is a Hungarian nationalist, believing in the myth of St Stephen, that is in Hungary's divine mission to defend Western Christendom against Eastern paganism of all kinds. Although a man of faith, integrity and courage, he was (as later events proved) too purblind and uncompromising to be of much use to the Hungarian people at this crisis in their history.

As he sat there breathing heavily, he seemed bewildered. The journalist who thrust the microphone into his face caused him to withdraw involuntarily, as if he had been presented with a pistol. And when he spoke, it was slowly and with effort, with none of the accomplished ease of the pulpit orator; between each of his words there must have been a pause of nearly a second. He said his country was suffering again for civilization, and that the civilized world should do something about it. Pious expressions of sympathy from the United Nations were of little help against Russian tanks. He explained what had caused the revolt, the economic reasons which had brought his country to the verge of bankruptcy; the poor pay of the factory workers; the collectivization of the peasants, which was contrary to the temper of an individualistic people.

'I am tired now,' he said, 'and I would like a little sleep before I address myself to the new tasks tomorrow. I must find my priests again. Many of them have been imprisoned or killed. But with God's good grace, we will take up our work again.'

He raised his hand in blessing and walked slowly from the room; he seemed completely exhausted, physically and mentally. The five Magyar soldiers who had released him from prison, and who were now acting as his bodyguard, stood to attention as he passed.

I went sadly down the hill into Pest, realizing that his request for help from the West would never be answered. England and America would do nothing for Hungary. We were at war in Egypt, the USA was occupied with her elections at home; neither would risk a third world

war. This small nation of nine million would have to fight on alone, if
the Russians decided to crush their revolt. That they would fight was
certain. Anyone who had seen these improvised soldiers, from the
factories, universities, fields and shops, with out-of-date weapons in
their hands, prepared unaided to face the greatest land power in the
world, could not doubt that.

*   *   *

By 2 November it was clear that the most delicate phase of the revolution, diplomatically and politically, had been reached. Either the
Russians would withdraw and democracy on Western lines would
return—or the most rigid form of communism would be imposed to
redress the situation. Imre Nagy was acting as a kind of middle-man,
between the insurgents and the Russians, moderating the demands of
the former, persuading the latter that he was master of the situation.
His wireless appeals, contrasted with those of Radio Győr which was
still in the hands of the insurgents, revealed the dilemma:

'. . . let us finish with this flow of blood!' he said that morning. 'Let
us finish with these murders! Let us finish with this destruction!
The new government has been formed on the broadest basis, with
the various parties represented. We have firmly decided to achieve
profound economic, social and political reforms. We guarantee that
the demands of the Hungarian people shall be satisfied. For this
reason, the revolt no longer has meaning. We therefore warn all those
in possession of arms that they must be laid down by 6 p.m., or they
will be treated as bandits . . .'

Meanwhile, at almost precisely the same moment, Radio Győr was
saying:

. . . we will not lay down arms, because we cannot believe in government promises. We will lay them down only when there is not a
Russian soldier left in the country . . .

The decisive day, when these two demands seemed for a moment to be
reconciled, was Thursday 1 November; and the time was 4 p.m. It was
precisely at this moment, too, that Budapest seemed to have returned
to something approaching normal conditions. People had come out

again this sunny afternoon, to walk along the Danube; the Sunday afternoon crowd had brought their children; there was even a pram or two. The insurgents with their Tommy-guns and arm-bands were for the first time less in evidence. I passed the Parliament buildings and stood by the Danube watching the last Russian civilians leave in the big pleasure steamers, bound for Rumania. There were bulky men in square-cut overcoats and trilby hats, and fat peasant-type women in ill-fitting suits, with their suitcases, parcels and children.

I was standing near the Chain bridge watching these families leave, when an English journalist I had met the day before ran up to me and said, 'If you want the story of your life, come to the Parliament buildings now! Nagy is about to make an impcrtant declaration about the Warsaw Pact.'

I followed him to this building where, by showing his journalist's pass, he was able to take me upstairs, through salons and corridors full of the Biedermeyer furnishings, marble-mounted and ormolu mirrors from the last century, to the door of the cabinet room. Here, he said, the government had been in session for two hours, arguing about the weighty decision they were about to take.

On the first landing we were told to wait in a reception room, in which other journalists were walking up and down with notebooks. Suddenly the big doors opposite opened and we saw, for a moment, Kádár the new first secretary of the Communist Party, seated at a table, and at his shoulder the Prime Minister, Imre Nagy. Near the wall was the President, Tildy, whose voice seemed raised in argument. On the other side of the table, out of view, sat (we did not know it at the time), the Russian ambassador, Andropov.

A quarter of an hour later, an official from the Hungarian Foreign Office, whom my friend evidently knew, came out of the cabinet room quickly. Taking him by the arm he said in English, 'Have you a motorcar? Well, leave Budapest immediately! Don't waste time here asking for more news. When it comes, you won't be able to leave.'

He said that the government had decided to withdraw from the Warsaw Pact, and had appealed for help to the United Nations. Whatever Nagy might feel personally about the wisdom of this step, he felt it was the will of the Hungarian people. Some of the cabinet, and of course the Soviet ambassador, were trying to dissuade him; 'And the pro-Russian forces in the cabinet will finally win,' he said. 'Nagy is now going to the radio building to make the announcement. But you see what will happen afterwards.'

Five minutes later we saw the Russian ambassador leave hurriedly; and a half an hour later, Nagy went to make the courageous statement about withdrawing from the Warsaw Pact, which meant that Hungary was no longer a satellite—which was responsible virtually, too, for the second Russian intervention. But in the streets that evening the Hungarians were elated. 'Nagy has cleaned his slate,' they said. 'We can support him, he's our man now.'

They felt that Hungarian honour had been saved, that whatever happened now, their revolution had not been in vain. But along with this feeling of relief, went one of tension. The pacific crowds of the afternoon soon melted away, as quickly as they had formed; the barricades went up again; the determined looking youths and workers with Hungarian armbands and Tommy-guns appeared on the streets again. When dusk fell, these streets emptied, and although the night was fine, an eerie atmosphere of waiting, as before a thunderstorm, possessed the city.

I returned that evening to the British Legation, where I was told that our Minister, Mr Fry, had just been called to the Hungarian Foreign Office. In the little restaurant which had been improvised on the top floor of the Legation (where all the families of the British officials were now living), an atmosphere of forced good humour prevailed. We sat drinking and talking till 9 p.m., when the Minister returned and said he had an announcement to make. He had decided to send a convoy to Vienna the next morning, with the less important members of the staff and all the wives (including his own). The convoy was to be led by Mr Russell, a third secretary. He said no more; but everyone knew what this meant.

When conversation again became general, he came up to me and asked if I would care to help Mr Russell, and accompany the convoy. As I had no work to do in Budapest, he saw no point in my remaining; the fewer Englishmen here at the moment, the better. He could not afford to send more than one of his diplomats, and would be glad of any help I could give. He asked the same of an Oxford undergraduate who had spent the last five days in Budapest, going about with the insurgents.

We agreed. But we went to bed that night wondering if the convoy would be able to leave. The tense hours before dawn when armies move, found us at the window looking out at the hill above Buda where the

Russians were supposed to be encamped. But all was still. And at ten o'clock that morning, our convoy of eight vehicles—mostly British and French diplomats' private cars—crossed the big Chain bridge, moving west.

If this drive was less eventful than my journey into Budapest surrounded by the insurgents, it was in some ways more informative, because we now met the Russians who were preparing their assault on the city. No longer at the road-blocks were the armed, determined young men; they had now been formed into units well away from the roads, so as to avoid contact with the Russians. Their places had been taken by old men and women; sometimes, sixty-year-old men stood beside machine guns, and often the road-blocks were guarded by boys. We showed our papers at these blocks, and were allowed to pass.

A wintry gale from the south-east was now blowing, stripping off the leaves and sweeping them along in slanting squalls of snow and sleet. Not far from Győr, we ran into a heavy snow-storm and then, through the falling flakes, we saw ahead a large tank going in our direction. 'A 50-ton Stalin,' said one of the British officials in our party learnedly. 'What splendid tanks the Russians have left the insurgents!'

It was difficult to pass this tank because it was moving west too: I blew the horn impatiently, to get it to withdraw to the side of the road. At length we managed to squeeze past, only to find ahead of it another Stalin tank of the same size. Again I blew the horn in irritation—and again at last we managed to pass. But there was yet another tank in front of this and then, as we rounded a corner, a whole line of them running out ahead, about fifteen, trundling along, wagging their guns and antennae.

'Really! These insurgent tanks ought to get off the roads to let us pass,' said the British official again. But then as we passed one of them, a face appeared at the turret and looked down—a Mongolian face. '. . . they are Russians!' he finished lamely.

Our car was in fact sandwiched in a long column of Russian tanks. More Mongoloid faces peered down at us as we passed, blank, expressionless, slit-eyed, beneath bell-shaped helmets. The Russians were bringing up their eastern troops. With these not particularly reassuring road companions we remained for nearly three-quarters of an hour, trying to pass. It is understandable that to men in such machines the ordinary, standard motor-horn means little or nothing.

After Győr, we saw more Russians in a maize field at the side of the road—armoured cars with tents around them, soldiers eating their mid-day meal out of mess-tins in the snow. Young for the most part, the term 'simple soldier' applied to these men admirably. Of the thirty or so I saw, twenty at least were Mongoloid, almost Chinese, in appearance; several had taken off their helmets and were scratching their shaven heads. These were the troops who were gathering around Budapest for the assault due to take place in two days' time. Although dirty and slovenly in appearance, there was a businesslike air about their equipment and vehicles. They could clearly move, fire and communicate with one another by wireless. And what more can you ask of the modern soldier?

We later learned that we were one of the last Western convoys these Russian troops allowed through. A few hours later, their tanks fanned out along the Austrian frontier, closing it completely, in preparation for the assault. To travellers from Budapest, Red Cross personnel, or journalists wishing to 'file' their cables in Vienna, they repeated the two words, '*Niet Wien!*' stubbornly, and forced them to return to Győr, Magyaróvár, or Budapest itself. In this way we came to Nickelsdorf again, and left the people, who, by liberating themselves, were soon to liberate Eastern Europe from the excesses of communism.

PAUL IGNOTUS

Hungary 1966

THE HUNGARIAN communism as we knew it after the Second World War had started under the rabidly anti-communist rule of Admiral Horthy in the inter-war period. It was our Whites who had set its patterns of behaviour. This would seem to contradict the assertion made by many students and/or sufferers of Stalin's Hungary, including the present writer, (1) that communist rule had been imposed on the Hungarian people by foreign arms and that all its features were blatantly strange to Hungarian taste, likings and traditions, good and bad alike. Indeed, there has never been a Hungarian ruler, whatever his blood and creed, birth-place and mother-tongue, with less attachment on the part of the indigenous population of that country than the Hungarian-born Russo-quisling Mátyás Rákosi, with his broad and juicy plain-country Magyar accent. No one doubted that, as a leader, he was of foreign make. This did not prevent him from appealing to patriotic emotions and national pride with a profusion that would make any parochial Kipling blush. History does breed such contradictions: the wider the cleavage between power and people, the more shameless the designs to camouflage it. The Hungarian Constitution ordered to be enacted on 20 August 1949, which replaced the customary Hungarian coat of arms with one hardly distinguishable from that of any Soviet republic, contained, in the meantime, militarist cries outstripping in jingo rhetoricism anything put into law by previous Right-wing governments. This was, of course, Rákosi's responsibility, and that of his masters and his lieutenants. But that they got away with it was largely due to Right-wing authoritarian conditioning. Or was this due to fear alone? Fear, fear for life and job, fear of torture and of the unknown; animal fear (2) was no doubt the cement of society. Rákosi was clapped, yet there was not a moment when his fat and bald head did not serve as a target for whispered jokes. Whatever the horrors involved, it was irresistibly comic. The same could not be said about his terminology.

His folksy and chauvinist verbiage was loathsome and degrading, and known to be utterly mendacious; but nobody laughed at it. People had learned to swallow any ideological rubbish without a grin. Sad as it is, sense of subordination defeated even sense of humour. Fear, fear; but what else was there to it?

★   ★   ★

There was belief in authority. To put it more crudely, there was the belief that someone holding public office, big or small, could not entirely be wrong. He could be a fool, a brute, a madman: he must none the less be more than an ordinary citizen. A *gendarme* may have been, personally, a nitwit and a bully—in fact he was trained to be one—but the steel of which his bayonet was made must have been a metal nobler than that of a surgeon's or butcher's knife; whatever the technologists said, its status transubstantiated it. It was an awe-inspiring instrument on the bottom rung of a ladder, from the top of which Hungarians were told how to be Hungarians.

Again, the reader may find this conflicting with what he has heard of Hungary. In 1848–49, as well as later, in 1956, Hungarians were a nation of freedom fighters. Even in earlier centuries, they were in the vanguard of religious liberty and constitutionalism; the late Professor R. W. Seton-Watson, who certainly could not be accused of holding a brief for Hungarian nationalist myths,(3) paid tribute to them as the protagonists of Parliamentarism in Central and Eastern Europe. They were, as a nation, wedded to liberalism, to the defence of the individual against central power, to the exaltation of tolerance in defiance of any overlordship and bigotry. How could *this* be reconciled with a vision of bureaucratic and military superiority?

History provides the answer. To find an explanation one has to go back in time; let us, however, control our temptation to go back too far. An appropriate starting point seems to be the Hungarian Reform era of the 1830s. Hungary and her sister province, Transylvania, were treated, within the Habsburg empire, as a glorified colony. There was a large Hungarian nobility, larger in proportion than any other nobility in Europe, estimated at about 5 per cent of the population of the provinces to which their influence extended. Writers on Hungarian affairs often mistake it for the aristocracy; they speak of old Hungary as a country modelled on the ideas and reflexes of maharaja-like landlords, dukes and counts and bishops of fabulous riches. Truth was better or worse but different; and to complicate matters, those huge landlordships did exist, right until 1945, and did make their mark on life. Yet, Hungarian history was less determined by them than it was by the strata of lesser noblemen, ranging from quite well-off country squires and quite educated county officials—they talked about public and legal matters, after all, more fluently in Latin than in their mother-tongue—to masses of privileged poor peasantry, the 'bemoccasined squirearchy', too poor to afford boots, and owning nothing but a *vox*, the vote which on election days they could sell to the highest bidder. They were, however, free, which mainly meant freedom from taxation. They were *the* Hungarian nation, irrespective of their mother-tongue which was overwhelmingly Hungarian (or Magyar) but not necessarily and not always so. Moreover, they were the 'people', *populus hungaricus*, as distinct from the rest of the inhabitants who were only 'populace', *plebs*, and 'non-Hungarian' at that, even if Magyar by mother-tongue (as roughly one-third of them actually were).

The privileged underdog is destined to be, alternately, the standard-bearer of subversion and the dedicated gaoler of a retrograde order, ultra-liberal and fascist. The Hungarian nobility, in the course of its history, often emerged as an army of liberty and often, without realizing it, as the praetorian guard of oppression. Even more often, it was both; and in any case, it was divided. In the mid-1830s, its division was most typical. Its aristocratic froth, though on exhibit in national parades, was linked to the Court in Vienna rather than to any institution in Hungary. The Habsburg high officials in that period, panic-stricken by Western developments, were keener to avert the liberalizing effects of social reforms than to try, as in some previous period they had tried, to increase their revenues and make administration more efficient by modernization; on the whole, therefore, the aristocracy opposed the Reform trend. As to the lesser nobility, its upper layer was prepared to give up its privileges, but its lowest layer stuck to them through thick and thin; suffering from poverty, and wish for improvement, were in inverse ratio. Which was quite a logical state of affairs; the educated and the well-off could more easily afford equality of civic rights than could those who had nothing but their miserable prerogatives to fall back upon.(4)

The Hungarian middle-nobility comprised an *élite* second to none in feeling of responsibility for the whole community, and in artistic and scientific curiosity. It was patriotic in determination and romanticism (and unprotected against the pitfalls of romantic patriotism), but humanist in learning and cosmopolitan in nostalgias, fascinated by English, French, German, Italian examples in social and natural philosophy, fine arts, poetry, economic and administrative reform, whilst cultivating the monuments of the Hebrew and the Hellene and, particularly, the Latin antiquity. An *élite* is always a minority, even within one class; but it was a compact minority, strong enough to make an impact on the majority. A minority within the minority was that of the *doctrinaires*, for which they were derided: the circle of Eötvös, Szalay, Csengery, Kemény, who went further in detecting the causes of squalor and torpor and misery than the lofty and self-deceptive nationalism of the epoch permitted. They pointed out that the interests vested in the caste-ridden counties, traditional bulwarks and symbols of national liberty, hampered social progress more fatally than did those embodied in the Habsburg dynasty and the central power. They recognized that an emancipated Hungarian nation could not 'go it alone' and were seeking to synchronize the elevation of the Hungarian peasantry with that of their subject Slav and Rumanian races. Outnumbered and outshouted though these 'doctrinaires' were, (5) they were not isolated; their humanist spirit was allowed to impregnate national life as a whole and to determine the course of innovations carried out or planned in legislation, to the benefit of generations to come. The Hungarian 1830s and '40s produced one of the few moments of history when *noblesse oblige* was almost valid.

Is there such a thing as unselfishness of a class? There is, occasionally, the determination of a class to integrate its own interests into a broader pattern of interests. The Hungarian noblemen knew from their own predicament as well as from their experiences about the *misera plebs contribuens* that if the country was to be saved, a great change had to be brought about. Széchenyi, Kossuth, Eötvös differed about what to do; but what they equally deplored was the absence of a middle-class, or *bourgeoisie*, or *tiers état*, or *Bürgerthum* or *Mittelstand*, of independent professionals and traders. Indeed, that class hardly existed in pre-1848 Hungary; and what there still was of it—mainly in the guilds—was overwhelmingly German (Schwabs or Saxons as they were generally called, with little regard to where they really had come from), only exceptionally Magyar by mother-tongue. It was the middle-nobility's determination to substitute for it. So long as that determination lasted, whatever the ordeal the nation had to weather, the Hungarian cause was wedded to that of liberty.

* * *

Let us skip now fifty or sixty years. The fear, or vision, of the liberal Hungarian lesser nobility had come true; most of them had lost their estates or plots. What was there for them, or their sons, to do? Rural life, beneath the level of landlordship, meant merging into the masses of a peasantry mostly very poor and treated *de facto* like serfs by the county magistrates, in spite of the abolition of serfdom in 1848; and merging into the turmoil of new industries and commerce, and the free professions thriving on them—well, that was the thing visualized by Deák and Eötvös as well as Kossuth, but when it came to putting the idea into practice, the psychological hurdles proved insurmountable. Snobbery, mental laziness, fear of humiliations and discomfort concurred in deterring noblemen from embarking on this road. The reluctance of the dispossessed landlords to go into trade has been a common-place subject, all over the more or less civilized world. But in Hungary with its huge nobility and practically no indigenous *bourgeoisie*, it had become the basic problem of the nation—at any rate, the most tangible one. Poor noblemen wanted jobs, and not very exacting ones at that; in the government offices, in the counties and municipalities, in the armed forces, and in that section of private enterprise sufficiently dependent on central power to be treated as 'official'. The aura of officialdom had come to make up for the vanished, or at any rate ragged, privileges of noble birth.

About half, or slightly more, of the population of Hungary were but 'nationalities', that is, non-Hungarians; and to keep them down was a special task, 'patriotic' as most Hungarians honestly believed. This was a national headache, but a godsend as well; a reason to inflate the county bureaucracy and to stack it with expert bullies and well-groomed idlers of all grades. Paternalistic oppression had become part of Hungarian nationalism. The class whose privilege it was to exert oppression was known as the 'gentry' or, in phonetic Hungarian spelling, *dzsentri*, a word incomparably more frequently used in Hungarian than in its English original, and in a different sense. What had survived of the 'landed gentry' did belong to it; so did, however, the broad kith and kin of the former landlords now cushioned in the higher grades of the public administration; and so did a large host of professionals and near-professionals linked to them. And so powerful was the magnetism of a gentlemanliness and security of (as a rule, modest) income expressed in officialdom that the former burghers' sons, 'Saxons' and 'Schwabs', if once Magyarized, and keeping their heads above water, also joined in and far from acting as the core of a Hungarian *tiers état*, swamped the masses of the *dzsentri*. After a while, the question whether someone could prove his nobility, and that of his grand-parents, had become, if not ignored, yet secondary in the Hungarian scale of snobberies;(6) the upper middle-class youngsters absorbed by the squirearchy were considered almost equal to the offsprings of ancient nobility. A sort of slightly racialist and upper-class equalitarianism prevailed in this arrangement; 'a *dzsentri*(7) is' said the author, the late Kálmán Csathó, who knew this layer of society intimately, 'any gentleman if not a Jew.'

In the meantime, Hungary was Liberal—or belatedly Whiggish would perhaps be the more precise word. Her cities, particularly Budapest, were on the whole free; so were most branches of commerce and industry; religious tolerance, if not unblemished, was still more observed than it was in the French Republic of the Dreyfus Affair or in the Vienna of Lueger, to mention only examples from advanced countries. Freedom of the press—that is freedom to write and print, if not the freedom to distribute printed matter everywhere—was comparable to that in any democracy; schools and other sources of knowledge were accessible to anyone able to spare time and money, and even to some sections of the poor. Liberalism seemed to most of the *dzsentri* still an integral part of Hungarian national tradition. The memory of the wars for freedom provided the moral reason to keep to it: but there was a practical reason as well. That bureaucracy, or squirearchy, had after all to be financed. Money could only come from where it was made; that is, from the *entrepreneurs* and the whole un-paternalistic network of people woven round them. And free enterprise was Jewish. Outside Jewry (and converted Jewry) everybody was either too squirearchic, or too poor, or too squirearchic *and* poor to try his hand at it. Simultaneously with capitalism, modern anti-capitalism became Jew-ridden, 'un-Hungarian'; and so did, in turn, modern art and science and journalism, except only the papers specializing in extreme nationalism and anti-semitism, and often not even those.

In other words, two upper middle classes existed side by side: one, the diluted petty squirearchy, the *dzsentri*; and another, that of the traders and intellectuals, the new *bourgeoisie*, tolerated, even pampered in a way, and still kept out of the 'national' community, isolated in a ghetto. It was in this atmosphere that a second Reform era, headed by the 'second Reform Generation',(8) dawned on Hungary. It brought about, like the one of some eighty years before, a combination of artistic and scientific experiences only of interest to the initiated few, with a drive for the improvement of the peasants' and proletarians' lot. As the First Reform Generation had been embedded in the middle-nobility, so was the Second in upper middle-class Jewry; the 'dzsentri' layers had become intellectually barren.

This did not mean the desiccation of the source of genius in any class or radical community of the Hungarian population, and least of all in the Hungarian nobility. The greatest Hungarian scientist at the turn of the century, the physicist, Baron Loránt Eötvös, happened to be the son of the leader of the *doctrinaires* in the 1830s, József Eötvös; the leading poet of the 1910s, Endre Ady, the symbolic figure of both modern ways in literature, and Radicalism in politics, came from the impoverished county squirearchy; and to mention only those of the young artists emerged in that period who have since then achieved world fame, the composers Béla Bartók and Zoltán Kodály were sons of middle-class families which, under Kálmán Csathó's definition, would also have qualified for 'dzsentri'. Talent was far from being a Jewish monopoly; but its appreciation had become one, for nobody but Jews cared about either Jewish or gentile talents.(9)

Middle-class Jews, emancipated and de-Judaized Jews, are a strange lot all over the world. They show gifts far above the average in matters both practical and spiritual; but they are capable of producing the most spectacular failures where the two meet, notably in statesmanship. Einstein has changed man's vision of the invisible universe, and Chagall that of the visible universe, and Lord Marks that of visible Britain; but their opposite numbers as shapers of national policies would, outside Israel, hardly be found amongst people of family backgrounds similar to theirs. Again and again and again, beware of generalizations—there are plenty of exceptions (Disraeli), debatable cases (Blum), and reasons to qualify such a classification of abilities. But recalling the triumph and fall of the Second Reform Generation in Hungary, I could not resist a melancholy sigh about the way my country saw business-mindedness and scholarly intellect merge into political blunders in 1918–19. The end of the First World War made Hungary's fate slip into the hands of the Left, including its intellectuals. True enough, it was a diabolical challenge; called to govern over a heap of shambles, surrounded by victors anxious to see Hungarian democracy disgrace itself before its birth, they would have needed a giant of manoeuvring to lead them into consolidation. The head of the government, Count Michael Károlyi, a controversial character even in retrospect,(10) could in my view be credited with historical merits but was not a fortunate choice by Providence for the job at that moment. And of the intellectuals in high posts, the two most typical of the Reform Generation, Jászi and Kunfi,(11) panicked when faced with the unsavoury tasks without which there has never been a government, especially in revolutionary times. Their blunders certainly did not invalidate the truth in their advocacy of land reform, social reform, electoral reform, and the reform of local government and the necessity for Hungarians to come to terms with their neighbouring nations. But the beneficiaries of old abuses succeeded in twisting the moral of the tragic story, and feudalism in Hungary was granted another lease of life. Added to ancient inequities was the mania to make Jews and liberalism and intellectuals the scapegoats for all evils. By the autumn of 1919 White Terror was rampant in Hungary.

★   ★   ★

Let us skip fifteen or sixteen years this time. Hitler had come to power in Germany, and Gyula Gömbös in Hungary. Gömbös was acclaimed by one set of his supporters as the Hungarian Hitler; and by the other as the man sent by Providence to avert the Hitlerite danger from Hungary. What he really was after was diluted Hitlerism, clemency and palliness towards non-obstructive Jews, courteous observance of Parliamentary, aristocratic and religious rituals, but moulded by nationalist Führers. In foreign affairs his outlook was oversimplified, nebulous, and well-founded. His determination to 'base Hungary's future on the Rome–Berlin Axis'(12) earned him contemptuous grins at a time when the *Duce* and the *Führer* were ready to cut each other's throats; but he trusted them both as *Kerle*, 'fickók', 'guys', and that was that. When one morning, as usual, the political correspondents called at his office, he took one of them, a reporter of a Liberal daily, by his shoulder and made him turn towards the map of Europe. 'Why talk so much balls to me, mate? About a secret vote and the rest? Who cares? There are other important things. Look here. There's [he jokingly imitated German accent] Hitla'! There's little Dollfuss! There's Benito! And [pointing to Budapest] there's me! France is *fuccs!*'—pronounced *footch*, a German-Hungarian slang word meaning kaput, 'done' or the like. He, Gömbös, was, like Hitler, violently anti-Legitimist; whereas Mussolini was sympathetic to the Habsburg pretender, and Dollfuss unmistakably for him. Nobody could have foreseen either Dollfuss's assassination or Mussolini's capitulation on the *Anschluss* issue. It would be wrong to attribute to Gömbös hopes to that effect; he simply vested his hopes in a Guys' International which he felt was *national* whatever the language it talked, unlike the Pope and the Habsburgs and the Bolsheviks and trade unionists and cosmopolitan bankers and undisciplined writers who carried disloyalty to their nations in the fibres of their being.

Kingsley Martin has several times recalled the interview he had with Premier Gömbös at that time. When asked by Mr Martin what he considered was Hungary's most important problem, he answered without hesitation, 'The middle class'. Mr Martin first thought the answer to be a hint at the absence of any Western-style middle class; but this, as it turned out, did not occur to Gömbös. The trouble was, he explained, that there were not enough 'jobs' for the sons of the dispossessed landowners and of the civil servants. 'Middle class for him was the swollen bureaucracy.' Kingsley Martin was amazed at the sight of gala dresses and pageantry: 'It was the last I saw of pre-French Revolution Europe.'

This account is correct; at the same time, Gömbös and his lieutenants advertised their government as 'the people's', *népi;* 'Mind you, not *one* count is in it', was the comment most frequently heard on it after swearing-in;(13) and it promulgated an Era of Reform, though in rather obscure language. It was typically the government of what the Premier, to the astonishment of a Western observer, called middle class—of the 'dzsentri', even more diluted and inflated than before. There were no longer 'nationalities' for them to administer; the country's size and population had been reduced to roughly one-third by the Treaty of Trianon; and it was on this rump that the ancient county squirearchy fell back. Bureaucracy had bred bureaucracy; the privileged, government-appointed 'middle-class' man, as the sleeping partner or the sleepy patron of private enterprise, became a dominant figure in the economy. The *numerus clausus* in the universities(14) and the *de facto* almost total ban imposed on persons of Jewish extraction in new government and municipal appointments made the cleavage between the 'dzsentri' and the 'bourgeois' middle classes wider than it had ever been. As a result, the 'dzsentri' became completely bureaucracy-ridden in his mind; and the 'bourgeois' followed suit obediently but with more and more chips on his shoulders. In the cauldron of a nationalism kept boiling by caste needs, gentiles and Jews were equally conditioned to swallow anything if declared with Authority.

★   ★   ★

The hundred years of liberal intellectualism thus came to an end. Nationalism took over. Whether 'nationalism' is the right term may be questioned. It depends on what we call nationalism. Professor Luethy (15) pointed out that this word as applied on the Continent and in English scientific literature has quite different meanings: in Continental use, it stands for a quasi-religious ideology, attributing to the interests of the nation, as embodied in the state and its hierarchy, the moral right to take precedence of all other laws and considerations; whereas in the English use, it means the epoch when nations became aware of their existence, and the currents of thought and feeling springing from it. Indeed, in the analysis of Professor Hans Kohn,(16) a native of Central Europe but in his terminology typical of the Anglo-American approach, 'nationalism is inconceivable without the ideas of popular sovereignty preceding', and is, therefore, linked to representative government and other institutions known as democratic; and Professor Carr considers that the era of European nationalism which had started with the French Revolution reached its climax with the outbreak of the First World War, and that its subsequent jerky postscripts, from the proliferation of nation-states in the early 1920s to the frenzy of 'National Socialist' genocide in the early 1940s, were transitions into a new age.(17) On the other hand, in France, no one would be astonished to read that nationalism—as distinct from patriotism which had certainly been at its high tide during and immediately after the Great Revolution—first got an articulate expression in the utterances of Maurice Barrès who opted for the company and guidance of the 'dead in the French soil' as against the living Frenchmen who voted (let alone the non-French for whom he did not care at all). The monarchist, Maurras, went even further when he glorified the perjury and forgery committed by a French officer because it had been meant to serve French military prestige. Simultaneously, in Germany, Treitschke's *Staat ist Macht* supplied the theoretical foundation, if such was needed, for a nationhood vested in power which placed itself morally above human rules. There were analogous trends in the English-speaking world as well, ever since 'My country, right or wrong' had been pronounced; but, for good or evil, they were more blurred, more hypocritical, more self-deceptive and therefore, on the whole, by far less inhuman. Kipling, amongst the writers of importance, certainly stands out not only as a believer in British Imperialism but also for his smug candour of admitting that he prefers lies if coming from his 'own stock' to whatever true and kind things he may be hearing from a 'stranger'; yet, he would never have turned cruelty and lying into virtues to be extolled in a national mythology. His nationalism was that of a Royalist Jacobin. One may call it the last, sharp flicker of nationalism as it had emerged when medieval Europe was going to pieces; or else the faint reflection, in the spirit of British compromise, of new forces heading for victory over liberal Europe, first monarchist, later fascist, ultimately 'National Socialist.'

I could not spare the reader this excursion into political semantics after pointing out that, in the Hungary of the middle 1930s, it was nationalism which eroded the values of intellectual liberty and conditioned the population to brook any ideology if proclaimed by the state hierarchy, whether Hitlerite in 1944 or Stalinist in 1949.

Surely if the word 'nationalism' is used to mean what, e.g. Professor Kohn means by it, this is pure nonsense? (18) Hungarian liberalism had always been conscious of Hungarian nationhood; it had even been wedded to it. Patriotism and liberalism could not be antagonized. Moreover, both Hitler's occupation of Hungary in 1944, and the subordination of Hungarian to Russian interests in 1949 were by all traditional standards, Royalist and Republican alike, an insult to Hungary as a nation. To assist them, for a Hungarian, amounted to treason: at any rate, in the code of conduct of a liberal patriot, either jingo or moderate and cosmopolitan. But nationalism as it arose implied the worship of power and its hierarchies; it was a mystical and utilitarian creed which made ample use of patriotic emotions but was by no means identical with them. In its extreme form, its nature revealed itself when the man who amongst the many Hungarian would-be Hitlers proved to be most appealing to the masses, the retired Army major (previously on the General Staff), Ferenc Szálasi, introduced himself to the public. Up to then, he was completely unknown, just one of the many idlers of swollen 'dzsentri' (incidentally, of its lowest stratum, being an NCO's son). Overnight, little roneoed—at that moment not even printed!— scraps of paper were showered on the people of Budapest with the text:

My aim is to take power: Szálasi.(19)

This formula wrought miracles; though, unlike Mussolini or Hitler, Szálasi was an extremely bad speaker, the masses raved about him; mainly but not exclusively those of the lower strata of the 'dzsentri' middle class, with their host of NCOs, *gendarmes*, government office commissioners, track-watchmen and the like who, however poorly paid, felt themselves members of a superior caste for being cells in the organism of authority.

Was there no intellectual resistance to this trend? In fact, it was minute. The 'bourgeois' (by origin Jewish) upper middle class had by then lost its intellectual integrity almost to the same extent as had the middle-nobility (the upper 'dzsentri') by the early 1900s. In some respects, no doubt, intellectual life was progressing; books, often of high quality, sold better than ever before. There was vivid interest in literature and sociology, and even more in their border country. But the intellectuals and writers themselves were vying with the illiterate in currying favour with the captains of the nationalist era; if not with such crude specimens as Szálasi, or his Arrow Cross fascism movement, then with blurred varieties, some of them smacking of aristocratic Catholicism, the other of Communazi plebeianism. Jews could not, of course, be anti-Jewish racialists (though some did try) but the *Zeitgeist* affected them no less than it did those clamouring for their extermination. There were amongst them, as there were amongst gentiles, some very few intellectuals opposing the fascist-nationalist-racialist world trend *in toto*,(20) but their majority only drew the lesson that national interest was an ideal nobler than truth and justice and that whoever was holding power, or had the *guts* to grab it, was representative of the 'nation', no matter who had helped him to be so. Szálasi's quisling administration, though only lasting for some months, proved that the mystic rituals standing for 'nation' could carry on undisturbed by the obvious fact that foreigners were the masters.

★   ★   ★

We have to skip comparatively few years to see how this continued under Russian overlordship. The People's Democracy under Rákosi's leadership (1948–56; but with the peak period, when his power was unchallenged, lasting from mid-1949 to mid-1953) was the continuation, after a short interval of qualified freedom, of the nazi practices. It was not national communism; but national*ist* communism. Play with words? Maybe another term should be required but the way 'nationalism' has often been used does warrant this application. I am not the first to feel like this. George Orwell, who can certainly not be accused of obscuring what he had to say by juggling with technical terms, wrote:(21)

> By 'nationalism' I mean first of all the habit of assuming that human beings can be classified like insects . . . But secondly . . . the habit of identifying oneself with a single nation or other unit, placing it beyond good and evil . . . Nationalism is not to be confused with patriotism . . . Nationalism . . . is inseparable from the desire for power . . . I am using the word 'nationalism' for lack of a better. Nationalism, in the extended sense in which I am using the word, includes such movements and tendencies as Communism, political Catholicism, Zionism, anti-Semitism, Trotskyism, and Pacifism. It does not necessarily mean loyalty to a government or a country, still less to one's own country, and it is not even strictly necessary that the units in which it deals should actually exist . . . The nationalist does not go on the principle of simply ganging up with the strongest side. On the contrary, having picked his side, he persuades himself that it is the strongest, and is able to stick to his belief even when the facts are overwhelmingly against him. Nationalism is power-hunger tempered by self-deception. Every nationalist is capable of the most flagrant dishonesty, but he is also—since he is conscious of serving something bigger than himself—unshakably certain of being in the right.

Pacifism, as a variety of nationalism? However annoying some of the 'Stop bombing . . .' parrots may be, I would not go *that* far. Yet,

Orwell had his good reasons to use this word 'for lack of a better'. It was the Treitschke–Maurras philosophy which had made the world— including, most alarmingly, its intellectual *élite*—safe for 'power-hunger tempered by self-deception', Right, Left and Centre.

Rákosi's was Left. This fact introduces another semantic difficulty in dealing with it: for him, and for Stalinists in general, 'patriotism' was a laudatory qualification, and 'nationalism' a pejorative one; in this, if in nothing else, they were at one with George Orwell (and for that matter, with the present writer). Yet, Rákosi was as much of an *unpatriotic nationalist* as had been his last Right-wing predecessor, Szálasi. The two men were not of the same stuff. Rákosi was infinitely cleverer: a quick-witted vulgarian who would have achieved some sort of career under any social order—if not as a prophet, then as a chain-stores' organizer or a press lord—whereas it is difficult to imagine Szálasi in any predomi- nant role without history's special bend to conform with the paranoiac vision he most uninhibitedly expressed. But 'power-hunger tempered by self-deception'—tempered or rather strengthened?—worked equally in them. They both were willing without a qualm to put at the disposal of a foreign power all resources of their country and then to perform, in deadly earnest, rituals suggesting their own mystical oneness with the Hungarian soil and its unspoilt working and fighting people, as against the cosmopolitan parasites just removed, deported, extermina- ted. Both combined the betrayal of their country with appeals to her instincts of tribal seclusion and aggressiveness, national self-glory, xenophobia, and a vision of racial purity.

Rákosi's record of treason is well known. Of the other, that is, the nationalist side of his rule, some conspicuous features have also been noted: his eagerness to strengthen the Iron Curtain; his pleasure in cam- paigning against everything international (except when Soviet spon- sored), from Roman Catholicism through Freemasonry to Social Democracy; his kindling of anti-semitic hatred by staging raids on 'Zionists' and offering them as targets for fun to the 'Arrow-Cross small fry' in reward for their conversion to communist partisanship. The grotesque sight of a purely Jewish party leadership guarded by pogrom- happy AVO personnel and followed by crypto-nazi masses has already received some publicity, *inter alia*, in accounts by the present writer.(22) Yet, since the protests and revolts against Stalinism and its surviving buttresses took the shape of national movements against foreign domina- tion, people tend to forget that a variety of nationalism, and one not very different from that encouraged by Hitler, had been in force under Stalin's aegis as well. As the whole life was covered with its manifestation, a whole volume would be required only to enumerate the most important of them. At random, however, let me mention these:

'National sovereignty' was to be worshipped. So was 'national independence'. 'Federation' was a dirty word; even 'socialist federation' (it will be remembered how already during the war Tito and, until his recantation, Dimitrov had aroused the suspicion of the Soviet leaders with their Balkan federation planning).(23) The Iron Curtain had to be maintained in regard to the sister satellites in the Soviet camp almost to the same extent as towards the non-communist world; eulogies of neighbouring non-Soviet Slavs had always to be fitted in the general frame of Peace Camp rhetoricism; the idea that communist Hungary should develop special links of her own with, say communist Poland and Czechoslovakia was as inadmissible as that she should do so with Austria (the Yugoslav heretic was of course worst of all). In a word: save direct subservience to the Kremlin, *any* international link was considered a greater evil than was national self-sufficiency.

Some may think it far-fetched to lump together Szálasi's and Rákosi's reliance of racial purity images; the former, after all, was a declared racialist, 'Rassenschützler' *fajvédő*, which was on the list of dirty words with the latter. But the word, if it was to mean what it literally does, made no sense in Hungary at all. Everybody knew that the population of the Danubian basin was racially—that is, anthropologically—an indissoluble motley; and that, should one accept the absurdity of equating anthropological races with language groups, as the nazis more or less consistently did, even then, Hungarians with their 'Turanian', Ural Altaic language, ought to have been excluded from the 'Aryan', Indo-European community. To Szálasi's crowd 'racial defence' therefore only meant two things: (*a*) a high-sounding excuse to plunder, torture and kill Jews; and (*b*) a climate of *Volksknecht* martiality, a quasi-tribal solidarity of *guys*, distinguished in handling jugs and knives and clubs. Of the two, (*b*) carried on unabated under Rákosi. Newspaper reports on political trials (when not suppressed altogether) bore a striking resemblance to what they used to be in the nazi press of Right-wing Hungary: foreign-sounding surnames, or ex-surnames, of persons singled out for vilification, repeated and rubbed in on any possible occasion, whether Jewish, Serb or German minority or any other non-Magyar 'blood' had to be denounced as corruptive: this applied to the presentation of the case of Cardinal Mindszenty (formerly Péhm) as to that of the communists Rajk, Szőnyi, Szebeni (since Rajk had come from Transylvanian 'Saxon' stock, and the other two were Jews). In the meantime, it was a patriotic duty to ignore the foreign 'blood' in whoever was acting as the *vezér*, leader or, rather, chieftain, whether 'Schwab' like Gömbös, Armenian like Szálasi, or Jewish like Rákosi. In the homegrown Zhdanovite fictions, the villian was preferably given a foreignsounding name; virtue under communism, like under nazism, grew from Blood and Soil.

This may give an idea of how much of the (*a*) aspect of nazi 'racial defence' could carry on in the Stalinist years. Not everything could, of course; since part of those who would have been massacred under Szálasi were actually in power and busy massacring others. But this was the whole difference. A number of Jewish middle-class men and *petits bourgeois* took special pleasure in flaunting their cruelty with fellow Jews, and irrespective of either the social standing or the political allegiances of their victims. Young men returned from Auschwitz had special gusto in torturing others who had just been saved by the skin of their teeth from Auschwitz;(24) in the same way as Rákosi, personally, took pleasure in arranging the beating to death of his former cellmate, old comrade in illegality.(25) (One of his reasons for doing so may have been that he disliked eye witnesses to survive.)

The belief in authority and in the ennobling magic of officialdom thus won its final battle. The new, 'Marxist–Leninist', squirearchy postured with relish as the inverted successor of the 'dzsentri'; 'revolutionary rule' equalled snobbery plus vindictiveness. In the summer of 1949, shortly before my arrest by the AVO, I had a drink with a former farmhand, now secretary to a parochial party organization, who as his tongue loosened up, confided, 'There is but one thing I feel unfair today: those old-time big shots were all addressed Sir and My Lord,(26) and for us Comrade Secretary will do . . . well, are we so much worse than *those* were?' Others may not have been *that* naive, even when tipsy. But fundamentally, their feelings were similar. Let me return, because it is the most delicate aspect of the question, to the part played by Jews in the show. It was but a minority of Jewry of course, but quite a substantial minority: an *anti-élite* of theirs comparable to the rabble-gentry wielding power under the leadership of the Hitlerite quislings some years before. In the new ruling class, under Rákosi, they made the hard core. In so far as this goes, it was indeed 'Jewish dictatorship', that of the anti-semitic Jews; typical of those ex-commercial middle classes most deeply penetrated by the sentiments prevailing over the previous twenty-five years of White and Brown anti-liberal and pro-racialist rule.

★ ★ ★

Let us make now the last skip: from Stalin's death until the months when the tenth anniversary of the Hungarian October of 1956 is approaching.

How much has the nature of nationalism, anti-nationalism, and authoritarianism, changed since then?

To a large extent, this is an international question; it applies to the whole of communist Central and South-eastern Europe. 'Multicentrism' and 'liberalization' or 'let-up' have become common facts of life; all countries concerned have been given a chance, not though of baling out of the Marxist–Leninist stargazers' *ensemble*, yet of becoming more national, more international, and more human.

Much may be said—and is being said, presumably, in other contributions to this collection—about the varieties of political patterns which subsequently emerged in various states; at this point, it will be sufficient to stress that the progress towards recovering national independence (as freedom of diplomatic manoeuvring is generally called), and that aiming at the restoration of personal liberty, though on the whole enhancing each other, are by no means always linked together. In Rumania for instance, the establishment of what is generally known (perhaps with reason) as a national communist order has hampered rather than precipitated liberalization(27); and the renewal of old-fashioned, pan-Latin nationalism, welcome though it be from some literary aspects, received an ugly climax in the persecution of minorities, mainly of Hungarians. (The word 'persecution', to be precise, should be applied to practices in use mainly in 1957–60; today's practice is only 'discriminatory'; but the ruling spirit has not substantially changed since.)(28) In Hungary, on the other hand, where Soviet rule re-established after the crushing of the revolt was more direct and more blatantly a violation of the popular will than anywhere else, liberalization has out-paced that in most other communist countries.(29)

Hungary's economic nationalism and Russo-centrism have been moderated during the last nine years—not in spite of Soviet friendship but rather as a result of it. This applies to her attitude both towards her Comecon partners and towards the West. What Stalin had established with his satellites was 'a trading system of a radial bilateralism, with the Soviet Union symbolizing the hub and the dependent countries the spokes', a trusty Hungarian (by now, British) student of Eastern European economics pointed out; but 'Stalin's heirs recognized the immense waste inherent in the Stalinist method of intra-bloc relations and were determined to replace this economic insanity with a rational programme of co-operation'.(30) Comecon is still far from being a success; it was less able to act as an economic unit than was the Common Market. But multi-lateral planning was given the green light. Efforts to seek fields of special co-operation with Western-bloc and non-aligned countries have also been encouraged; whereas, for instance, Professor Imre Vajda is active as a champion of projects affecting mainly Britain (31) and Austria, other economists are concerned with other Western countries.(32) In fields less directly practical (history-writing, for instance), interest has been growing for the European and Danubian schemes of the past and for their deceased heroes who had been buried long enough to be praised as 'progressive in their own time' without greater risks today. The political hopes of the intelligentsia, whether pro- or anti-government, are crypto-federationist.

Whilst Soviet-sponsored nationalism has given way to its hybrid with co-existence, popular feeling has also been mellowed with regard to both the irritation at Russian overlordship and the jingo daydreams. The wounds of the Stalinist years and of November 1956 are still sore but the Russians do not rub salt in them, and their moderation is greatly appreciated—by conservatives and crypto-semi-fascists (33) even more than by Left-wingers. In the Russo–Chinese controversy, non-Stalinist Hungary is altogether pro-Russian and rejects the Maoist alternative; the pro-government ideologists denounced Mao's 'Trotskyism' but really nobody cared what sort of 'ism' it was—the one thing every Hungarian realized was that it was a spoke in the wheel of liberalization. This, again, assuaged anti-Russian resentments. Furthermore, the country in Eastern Europe fraternizing with Peking (apart from Albania which is treated as a joke) happens to be Rumania, the very country whose nationalism causes most hardship to Hungarians under her jurisdiction, and most irritation to Hungarians in Hungary. In 1965, practically no week passed without Rumanians interfering with Hungarian affairs by protesting against films, fiction, recollections that had contained, in their view, unfair references to Rumanians; and the Hungarian government, although known to be unhappy about Rumanian nationalism, mostly gave way lest Hungarians be accused of estranging Rumania from the Soviet camp. Most notable of the literary scandals of this nature concerns the author, Gyula Illyés, who, whilst in Paris, made a moderate but unequivocal statement about the renewal of nationalism in countries such as Rumania. Subsequently, his two plays inspired by and partly dealing with László Teleki,(34) the liberal and independentist reformer of the last century, have not been admitted to the Hungarian stage. Illyés enjoys enormous reputation in Hungary, in government and opposition circles alike; 'but', a high official confidentially told the present writer when on a visit in Budapest in April 1965, 'we simply cannot afford a public performance of those plays; it would degenerate into an anti-Rumanian demonstration'.

Would it be right to regard such 'anti-Rumanian' and kindred feelings, even when exuberant, as 'nationalist'? Not *per definitionem*, if 'nationalism' stands for an ideology. On the other hand, it would be wrong to think that the authoritarian and bureaucracy-ridden psychical climate of 1919 and after, which could hardly ever be separated from nationalist ideology, should now have disappeared. It has definitely survived but with the attributes of apparent normality reconquered. The Stalinist regime was 'revolutionary' in the same way as the Hitlerite used to be; the present one is more akin to the Consolidation as Count Bethlen's decade had been called, or to the Reform Era of unknown destination under General Gömbös in the mid-thirties. Such analogies must not, of course, be over-stressed but do hold good in essentials, that is, concerning the general state of mind. Under Hitler and Stalin, an average citizen lived day and night in terror; today, like thirty or forty years ago, it is enough for him to *behave* so as to have his sleep undisturbed.

The quality of conformism has accordingly very much improved. The ideal of an ambassador in the West under Rákosi was a James Bond villain; today, it is a salesman. As market economy has to an increasing extent been allowed to modify the functioning of state-owned industries and Kolkhoz farming, the skills of *entrepeneurs*, merchants and unpolitical engineers have regained the esteem in which they used to be held before socialism was declared. In fact, they are higher in the social scale of merits than they have ever been. Thirty years ago, the banker or industrialist, however rich, was subordinated to a caste-ridden bureaucracy; today, his successor, the economic top official, is part of the governing bureaucracy himself. The caste spirit has gone; the members of the ruling set-up may be recruited, as far as their social background is concerned, from practically anywhere. Yet, the 'dzsentri' cult of titles and established hierarchies has also had its come-back, facilitated by the abundance of honours and rituals with which society is regulated. In culture, a new mandarinism prevails which in both spirit and personnel has much in common with the old. The Hungarian Academy of Science,(35) invested with powers greater than it has ever wielded before, combines overt dedication to Marxism–Leninism with the preservation of some mainstays of the nationalist and conservative scholarship nurtured in the Horthy era.

Such pacts between 'Red' and 'White' are as a rule concluded at the expense of 'Pink'. Liberalization has gone a long way but not long enough to forgive liberalism, even less liberal socialism which is not supposed to be existing. Wherever non-communist hues are required in the cultural landscape, the shadows of some former authoritarian ideology are preferably used. A key figure of present-day Hungary is the enormously multi-sided and prolific author, László Németh who, in the thirties, was the most ingenious supplier of formulas enabling Hungary to fit in the Hitlerite world order without giving up her own racial and humanist idiosyncrasies. For the last six or seven years, Németh has been dedicated to supporting the Kádár regime, and mainly its Soviet orientation, so zealously that on at least one occasion it was a moderate cultural *apparatchik* who cautioned him not to indulge in anti-Western jeers which may spoil the planned ventures in co-existence.(36) The interesting thing is that Németh could perform this without in so many words recanting any of his previous beliefs; he was allowed, indeed, encouraged peacefully to blur his former *fascisant* authoritarianism into the *communisant* one of today. Another able Right-wing author of the thirties, Endre Illés, head of the most important publishing concern today, crusades in his essays against liberal traditions—'impressionism' is one of his bugbears—outstripping in rigour many a communist doctrinaire; which may be calculated to vindicate what survived of Zhdanovism, or what survived of the equally 'anti-impressionist' officialdom of thirty years ago, or both.

Mutual assistance of Left- and Right-authoritarian sagas is a constant feature of Hungarian academic and literary life, at times getting out of hand and appearing like an attempt to exonerate the representatives even of unrespectable extremes. In the connotations of volumes comprising documents by (and on) the late Michael Károlyi,(37) as a reviewer in Budapest pointed out,(38) both the leading publicist of nazi Hungary, István Milotay, and the ex-dictator of personality cult and mass murders, Mátyás Rákosi, were treated with conspicuous tact and forbearance, whilst a social-democrat, even if fallen victim to his protests against White terror would be denigrated as much as possible.(39) This was, in all likelihood, due to clumsiness and ignorance rather than to a sinister plot but is still revealing of the confusion of ideas and moral degradation prevailing in the Hungarian mind, as a result of more than forty-five years of hardly ever interrupted, authoritarian pressure. Should, then, in Russia the 'Stalin image' be restored to 'its former pedestal' as (in connection with the Sinyavsky–Daniel trial) some British press commentators forecast,(40) such silly lapses may once again prove to be no lapses at all.

Yet, it seems more likely to the writer that the development will tend towards further liberalization, although on a difficult, tortuous road and rarely with enchanting scenery. The 1956 rising seems in retrospect, partly on account of its defeat and partly despite it, the moment when the lid was put on a Stalin who could in many ways be equated with Hitler, so as to prepare the ground for something more traditional, more eclectic, more 'normal'. In this sense, it was indeed a 'counter-revolution', the one since consolidated under János Kádár's leadership. Let us hope for further progress backwards, for an evolution towards reviving the gentlemanly liberalism before 1919. Let us venture a further dive into utopias and imagine that in Hungary—and in her neighbouring countries—the educated ruling classes will be able to surmount nationalist interests and superstitions, recognizing what seemed commonsense to Baron József Eötvös and other 'doctrinaire' reformers 120 or 130 years ago. Add to this the marks of technological, financial, hygienic amelioration, not due to communism, but rarely hampered, often even furthered by it; all this brought about in a hybrid motley; and if you don't insist on truth and justice prevailing, you may as well call the prospects bright.

NOTES

(1) *Political Prisoner*, Collier Books, New York, 1964, especially Chapter 4, 'In Slavery at Large'.

(2) cf. Tamás Aczél, *The Ice Age* (novel), Simon and Schuster, New York, 1965; Secker and Warburg, London, 1966.

(3) As in *Eastern Europe Between the Wars* (1945).

(4) This was not, of course, a hard and fast rule. The initiator of the Reform era, Count István Széchenyi, came from the high aristocracy; its leading poet, Mihály Vörösmarty, from the crested and lettered proletariat, 'bemoccasined' as it were; and even learned non-nobles could be found, sons of merchants and artisans and peasant serfs, particularly in the priestly orders. But the best scholars and liveliest intellectuals, such as Ferenc Kölcsey, Károly Kisfaludy, József Bajza, Baron József Eötvös, László Szalay, Antal Csengery, young Baron Zsigmond Kemény, and Gábor Kazinczy, Ferenc Pulszky, or men like András Fáy, equally well known as a novelist and an Aesopian fabler and the founder of the first Savings Bank, as well as the most dynamic and gifted politicians of the epoch, Baron Miklós Wesselényi, Ferenc Deák, Lajos Kossuth, belonged to the strata generally referred to as the 'middle nobility'. More important still, it was this layer that provided the bulk of the readers. By the mid-forties, with the wind of the coming revolution in the air, and the Radical poet Sándor Petőfi in the vanguard, the scene had turned somewhat more 'plebeian'; but in the preceding two decades, the habitat of Hungarian culture was definitely the middle nobility.

(5) Again, beware of generalizations: the Transylvanian leader, Wesselényi, drafted plans for federating Hungarians and Rumanians, with remarkable (albeit, alas, fruitless) far-sight. In 1848, Kossuth's envoy in Paris, Count László Teleki, was one of the first to advocate a Danubian Federation (cf. Zoltán Horváth, *Teleki László*, Budapest, 1964). Other progressive Independentists, e.g. Kossuth's rival and Premier, Bertalan Szemere, came round to such ideas later, and so did in exile Kossuth himself (most competently set forth by the late historian, Béla G. Iványi, especially in his articles for *Irodalmi Ujság*); but in 1848, the leaders of the rising, particularly Kossuth, refused to consider any such solution; and the enthusiasts of world revolution, such as the first socialist deputy in the National Assembly, Mihály Táncsics, or, for all his magnificent visions in other fields, the poet Petőfi, had equally little understanding for the fact that not everybody in Hungary wanted to be Hungarian. It was one of the

cases to which many analogies could be found today, when revolutionary extremism slipped into retrogradeness, and only some of the middle-of-the-roaders had the intellectual courage to face facts of social life.

(6) For one thing, the use of invented titles of nobility had become so widespread that it would have been impossible to go by them in classifying people.

(7) Used in Hungarian *per analogiam*, e.g. 'a magnate'—that is, not a collective noun.

(8) Thus named by one of its leaders, Ervin Szabó, (cf. Zoltán Horváth, *Magyar Századforduló—A második reformnemzedék története*, 1896–1914; 'Hungarian Turn of the Century—History of the Second Reform Generation, 1896–1914'; Budapest, 1961).

(9) In natural sciences this was less marked since the University harboured them with only mild discriminations against some social layers and/or trends of thought; although what was additional to officialdom, was even in that field linked to 'Jewry', that is, to the industrial concerns that ran laboratories and subsidized research. In arts, humanities, and social sciences, however, the mental exhaustion of the 'dzsentri' had become visibly ubiquitous and fatal; with the absolute rule of stick-in-the-mud conservatism and parochial exclusiveness in the official institutions, any spirit of adventure and experiment, whether high or lowbrow, esoteric or profit-making, and irrespective even of the performer's religion and race, was branded in public as 'un-Hungarian', and in private as '*too* Jewish'. Business was tolerably Jewish, intellect was intolerably so. Hungary, in the meantime, entered a new golden age of her artistic and scientific life, with a fantastic eruption of creative geniuses. The two foci of cultural renewal were sociology and *belles-lettres*; the former embodied in the Sociological Society (Társadalomtudományi Társaság) and its monthly *Huszadik Század* ('Twentieth Century'), and later in a more extremist setting, the Galileo Circle of undergraduates; the latter in the fortnightly *Nyugat* ('West'). The scholar of greatest authority amongst the sociologists, Professor Gyula Pikler, a legal philosopher who later concentrated on physiology and psychology, was politically a moderate who only provoked the misgivings of the Church and the government by urging that scientific methods should be allowed to be applied to any subject. The editor of

'Twentieth Century' was Privat-Docent (later, as an exile in the US, Professor) Oszkár Jászi, a Victorian-style Radical, whose most shocking heresy consisted in urging equal rights for the national minorities in practice (as it was supposed to be the case in theory). The editor-in-chief of *Nyugat*, Hugó Ignotus, was a fine poet and an original political thinker (searching for a sort of liberal middle-class socialism—unaware, alas, of what Keynes was to put his finger upon, some twenty-five years later!) but made his mark on the epoch in a third capacity—as the leading aesthete, the fighter for the recognition of literary and artistic values which staggered or bored the philistines. He was one of the first to recognize the importance of psychoanalysis, in close friendship with Dr Sándor Ferenczi, Freud's 'Archbishop of Budapest'. His associate editors were Ernő Osvát, the dedicated digger in manuscripts, appreciative of all morsels of poetry but too high in ultimate standards to be creative himself; and Miksa Fenyő, the efficient organizer and lively polemist, (in his non-literary capacity, Secretary, later Director, of the Industrialists' Association, 'Gyosz'). Their main patrons were first Baron Louis Hatvany, himself an author, and later Baron Móric Kornfeld, a leading industrialist (both sliding away by the time of the Horthy *regime* in opposite directions: Hatvany as a political *émigré* in Vienna, Kornfeld as the patron of Roman Catholic and conservative literature, a friend of the Minister of Education, Count Kunó Klebelsberg). Of the intellectual leaders of social-democracy, Zsigmond Kunfi was the most fascinating personality, an enthralling orator; and the most accomplished theoretician of revolutionary socialism, combining Marxism with syndicalism, was the historian and librarian Ervin Szabó, too extreme to be tolerated in the Social-Democratic Party but accepted as the Director of the Municipal Library by the liberal Budapest Town Hall. All of these were of Jewish extraction, as was the Polányi family, perhaps the most lively social centre for fine arts and political science to meet, with a daughter famous for beauty and sophistication, and sons some of whom have since made their name in the English-speaking world. Another *habitué* of those circles was young György Lukács, echoing new German Idealists, with only grains of the Marxist-to-be in him—coming from the enobled bankocracy. These are but random examples to illustrate how in the two last decades of Habsburg Hungary, middle-class Jewry ('middle class' ranging from industrial barons to white-collar proletarians, and 'Jewry' from Christians to atheists) filled the intellectual vacuum left open since the ancient middle-nobility had ceased to comprise such a compact *elite* as the one, particularly of the 1830s and '40s. Needless to say that it was not, even in that broad sense, exclusively Jewish or exclusively middle class; it was the very opposite of anything socially, racially, or even ideologically exclusive; it was a mixture of all social and racial strata of Hungary in a concert of all trends opposed to mental sloth and complacency, and many of the middle-class Jews in it were not only willing but snobbishly keen to dissociate themselves from their own social and racial backgrounds. Yet that background must not be ignored; its own liberal era may perhaps be explained without it, but not the anti-liberal reaction that followed and is still on, however tarnished it has often been.

(10) Never has yet an attempt been made to describe his unique career with anything approaching scholarly detachment. In Britain, Professor A. J. P. Taylor, has often made enthusiastic references to him, motivated by the ideas and passions they shared rather than by the result of an enquiry into the techniques he made use of as a politician; whereas the University specialists on Hungarian history, Professor Denis Sinor and, particularly, in his admiration for some leaders of Axis Hungary, Professor C. A. Macartney, merely pour abuse on him without even an attempt to understand who he was and what he was up against. Altogether, outside the circles committed to his cult for some lyrical reason, I am sorry to say, his memory does not fare well with students of Hungarian history; e.g. in the well-balanced and factually accurate handbook on Hungary, *Ungarn*, by Denis Silagi, (Verlag für Literatur und Zeitgeschehen, Hanover, 1964), Károlyi is meted out harsh treatment, by summary jurisdiction. My own attempts in some of my publications quoted amongst these footnotes, were certainly too sketchy and impressionist to make up for a comprehensive work on the matter. The most important book on Károlyi is still his *Memoirs, Faith without Illusions*, published shortly after his death in 1955, by Jonathan Cape, London; a touching and basically truthful, personal account—although too emotional to be trustworthy and, in addition, scattered with factual errors which subsequent publications in Hungary did little to correct.

(11) Oszkár Jászi, leader of the Citizen's Radical Party, was for a brief period Minister of National Minorities. He was doomed to fail in negotiations with those 'minorities' who by then had developed into cores of new imperialist powers, however petty; but, less excusably in his position, he resigned, practically ran away and hid himself in phrases. Kunfi, Minister first of Public Welfare and then of Education, was haunted by the nightmare that there *might* by a bolshevik-like workers' revolt: 'that's one thing we can't do, we can't shoot workers!' he kept repeating. Embittered about the lack of sympathy for a democratic Hungary on the part of the West, he drove himself into the hope that 'We must seek Russian support'; and without ever trying to obscure the dividing line between the communists and himself, he plunged into the venture of a 'Hungarian Soviet Republic'. Jászi may have been the loftiest, and Kunfi the most sophisticated, of the Hungarians holding power in their time, but they could not be called successful. The two, together with the poet, Ady, may be regarded in their outlook as the cross-section of the Second Reform Generation. To their right as it were, hesitant to take the revolutionary course, Pikler and Ignotus had faded out of the limelight by the day when the republic was declared (in November 1918); to their left, Ervin Szabó was dead. Ady, though attending the republican celebration, was too sick to move (and actually died in January 1919): and the other leading authors of *Nyugat*, such as Babits, Móricz, Kosztolányi, Karinthy, Szomory, Arpád Tóth, Gyula Juhász, J. J. Tersánszky, Milán Füst, Ernő Szép, were rather effaced as public figures though some of them were made to do penance in the subsequent era of White Terror for their radical daydreams, pacifism or vague communist sympathies.

(12) The expression was actually coined by him (*Pester Lloyd*) 20 June 1934).

(13) 'Hungary's revisionism was spiced in 1932 by the appointment of Gömbös, previously Minister of War, as Prime Minister. This put an end to the predominance of the magnates under Bethlen in favour of a new man, a soldier who was half German and highly susceptible to nazi influence.' Elizabeth Wiskemann, *Europe of the Dictators, 1919–1945*, The Fontana History of Europe, Collins, 1966, pp. 120–1.

(14) About the crippling psychological effect of the *numerus clausus* on

Jewry cf. Steven Nádasy, *A Werner család* ('The Werner Family', novel, in manuscript).

(15) 'From the nationalist point of view the nation is a personality of a higher order with its own soul, will, consciousness, and mission. Every attempt to define "the nation", "the nationalist idea" or "national feeling" ends in mysticism or mystification . . . [But . . .] The assumption that Nationalism and Democracy are inseparable —and even practically identical—became a basic tenet of American political thought . . . Anglo-Saxon theorists never seemed to grasp the fact that in the Old World, nationalism was the extreme example of the destructive effect of "secularized religiosity" and of "misguided moral mission".' (Herbert Luethy, 'On the rehabilitation of nationalism', read by courtesy of *Encounter*, original draft submitted for discussion to a study group of the Congress for Cultural Freedom, in Berlin, 1960, in response to Professor Michael Polanyi's essay 'Beyond Nihilism'.)

(16) *The Idea of Nationalism*, The Macmillan Company, New York, 1945, p. 3.

(17) Edward Hallett Carr, *Nationalism and After*, Macmillan & Co., London, 1945.

(18) Professor Váli in his contribution to this anthology, draws conclusions very different from mine on the role of 'nationalism'. The difference of opinions between us is due mainly to semantics; he likes to use the term in another sense. I do not object to that; the ornithologist and the chess theorist are equally right when they talk of a 'rook' by which they mean very different things. I do not mean to play down the difference manifest in the preference for one or another use of the same word. But it reveals, I think, difference in general outlook rather than in our assessments of the realities and prospects in our native land. This, however, will be judged by a detached reader of our essays more authentically than by ourselves.

(19) In the original: 'Célom; a hatalom átvétele.—Szálasi'.

(20) cf. Paul Ignotus, 'Radical Writers in Hungary', *Journal of Contemporary History*, Number 2, 1966.

(21) 'Notes on Nationalism' (1945), *Collected Essays*, Mercury Books, 1961, pp. 265–7.

(22) e.g. in Chapters 5, 7 and 9, of *Political Prisoner*; and in the essay, 'Assisted by Thugs', in *Prison, A Symposium* edited by

George Mikes, Routledge, 1963.—See also Silagi, op. cit. p. 114).

(23) cf. Milovan Djilas, *Conversations with Stalin*, Rupert Hart-Davis, London, 1962, p. 157.

(24) Ideologically, the persecution of Jews by Jews was carried under three headings: (i) 'Anti-Zionism'; (ii) 'Class struggle'; the non-communist Jew was a 'class enemy', even if poor; and social democrats, as 'capitalist lackeys', were the worst of 'bourgeoisie'; and (iii) a Communist Party member if accused (with or without foundation) of deviating, was labelled 'Titoist-Trotskyist'. Added was, automatically, the charge of high treason (spying).

(25) cf. Chapter 8, *Political Prisoner*.

(26) These are but vague hints at the Hungarian equivalents; to explain what it really used to be in Hungary would take too long.

(27) Mr Patrick Gordon-Walker, reporting most appreciatively on the progress towards national independence which he had witnessed in Rumania, added that as a result of this development Rumanians 'have not enjoyed the liberalism of Khrushchev's Russia' (*Daily Herald*, 9 June 1964).

(28) From the administrative point of view, the decisive clamp-down on the Hungarian Autonomous Territory was made in 1962 (cf. George Bailey, 'Trouble over Transylvania', *The Reporter*, New York, 19 November 1964), and the measures taken then have not been revoked.

(29) There were moments, in the last few years, when Hungary seemed to have overtaken Poland, though not Yugoslavia; then suddenly Czechoslovakia gave the impression of making a bid for going ahead in freedom of thought and worship and commerce, though by no means in de-Stalinizing her leadership; whilst new waves of arrests in Hungary, and their announcement in ludicrous neo-Stalinist jargon (cf. article by László Szabó, *Népszabadság*, 19 February 1966), came in support to those professing scepticism about the durability of improvements. The order of comparative liberalism may change from season to season; but that Hungary is ahead of *most* other communist countries can safely be stated.

(30) George Kemény, 'Economic Integration in the Soviet Bloc', *Problems of Communism*, Washington, September–October 1964.

(31) cf. his article, 'Industrial Co-operation Between British and Hungarian Firms', *The New Hungarian Quarterly*, Spring 1965.

(32) Kádár in his 1966 New Year's message, emphasized that Hungary

had developed her economic ties with all types of countries, East and West and non-aligned. He put special stress on links with North Vietnam; with the USSR; with Comecon countries in general; and with 'Austria, France and England'. Actually, in the foreign trade estimates for that year (quoted by FEC, 21 January 1966), West Germany was the Western country with the largest volume of trade with Hungary foreseen; 150 million dollars—in spite of the lack of diplomatic relations between Bonn and Budapest. Other Western countries followed in this order: Austria, United Kingdom, France, Italy, Switzerland, United States of America.

(33) Apologies for this heavy neologism which accuracy demands.

(34) *Másokért egyedül* ('For Others, Alone'), Szépirodalmi, Budapest, 1963. One of them has been successfully performed in Paris.

(35) Ever since its foundation, initiated by Count István Széchenyi, in 1825, the Academy has comprised 'Arts' (in the British academic sense) as well as 'Science'; in fact, one of its main objectives was the development of the Hungarian language; and *belles-lettres* had always some representation in its membership, first rate at the outset, declining later.

(36) Commenting on Major Gagarin's flight (*Kortárs*, April 1962), he ridiculed congratulatory telegrams by presumably unhappy Western government leaders. He then received the confidential warning that he must not be facetious about mutual appreciation in the space race; indeed, by the next year, a series of cosmonaut stamps was issued by the Hungarian GPO, paying tribute to American as well as Soviet space heroes.

(37) *Károlyi Mihály válogatott írásai* 1920–1945. Budapest, 1964.

(38) Zoltán Horváth in the periodical *Kritika*, May 1965.

(39) Béla Somogyi, editor of *Népszava*, refused to serve under the Hungarian Soviet government, but later, under White Terror, stood up for communists as well as other persecuted categories. On 17 February 1920, together with his contributor, Béla Bacsó, he was kidnapped, killed and thrown into the Danube by 'Detachment officers'. The rude attack on his memory in the index of the book, objected to by Horváth, reveals appalling meanness indeed. What should be added is that the soap-box diatribes in the index against refugee social democrats such as the late Károly Peyer, or Anna Kéthly, are equally out of place in a work with scholarly pretences.

(40) Moscow letter, *Sunday Times*, 6 February 1966.

TIBOR MERAY

The Sources of Power

THE ORIGIN AND DEVELOPMENTS OF THE PARTY

THE SECRETS OF BIRTH

WHEN WAS the true date of birth for the Hungarian Socialist Workers'
Party, which is today Hungary's one and only, and consequently ruling
party?

This is what one can read about this question in the fourth volume of
The New Hungarian Encyclopaedia:[1]

> In the summer of 1956, Hungarian counter-revolutionary elements,
> supported by international reaction, succeeded in setting up against
> the dictatorship of the proletariat a broad-based political front which
> extended from the revisionist conspirators of the left to the Horthyites
> and the Arrow Cross men [Hungarian Nazis] and which launched
> on 23 October 1956 an armed counter-revolutionary uprising. In
> this difficult situation, Hungarian communists created a new revolu-
> tionary centre, the new Central Committee of the Party and the
> Revolutionary Government of Workers and Peasants. Until the new
> Party Congress, the executive Committee under the leadership of
> János Kádár, stood at the helm of the new Central Committee. These
> were the members of the executive committee: Antal Apró, Béla Biszku,
> Lajos Fehér, János Kádár, Gyula Kállai, Károly Kiss, György
> Marosán, Ferenc Münnich, Sándor Rónai, Miklós Somogyi.

The conclusion every attentive reader draws from this text is that the
party—turning against 'the counter-revolutionary danger'—was
founded around 24 or 25 October under the leadership of the above-
mentioned men.

On the same subject, however, the party's official literary periodical
gives somewhat different information:

> The defeat of the counter-revolution necessitated the establishment

[1] *Uj Magyar Lexikon*, Akadémiai Kiadó, Budapest, 1961.

of a new revolutionary centre which would give clear directions for the struggle and which would lead the revolutionary forces into the battle for the restoration of the legal order of the people's democracy, for the defence of national independence, for the safe-keeping and further development of our great accomplishments, for socialism and for peace. Under the leadership of János Kádár, Ferenc Münnich and György Marosán, this new revolutionary centre was set up, and on 4 November 1956 the revolutionary government of workers and peasants came into existence.[2]

Besides the noteworthy detail of this second list of leaders being much shorter than in the previously mentioned publication, the reader is given the impression here that the party was formed sometime around 4 November. 24–25 October or 4 November: the difference would appear insignificant if the question did not concern 1956 and those ten and some odd days, which, despite its shortness, represent the most important period in modern Hungarian history. Would it be possible that the leaders, ideologists and encyclopaedia-editors of the party did not know or perhaps forgot the exact date of the party's foundation? The opposite is true. They know full well and they remember perfectly; it is precisely the concealment of the truth which is the purpose of their publications' obscurities, apparent superficiality and sweeping inexactitudes.

The fact is that the Hungarian Socialist Workers' Party was not born on 24–25 October or around 4 November but exactly on 1 November, in the very midst of the revolution, built on the ruins of the Stalinist Hungarian Workers' Party. The party's birth was announced on Budapest radio by no other person than its present leader: János Kádár. Since then, Kádár's writings and speeches have been published in many volumes and in over a thousand pages, but to search there for this radio message—which had ten million ear-witnesses in Hungary—would be a futile exercise. And if somebody would start distributing in Hungary this speech of Kádár's—the foundation paper of the party now in power —he is unlikely to get away with less than a ten-year sentence in jail.

Let us be fair. It was a nice and sincere speech, and the new party was launched in a fine patriotic spirit. János Kádár began by saying that he had only contempt for the Russian and Hungarian versions of Stalinism and he welcomed enthusiastically the revolution of the people:

[2] *Társadalmi Szemle*, Budapest, October 1958.

In this crucial hour, we speak to those whom the fidelity to the people and to the country, and honest service of the pure ideas of socialism led to the party, which the Hungarian representatives of socialism, Rákosi and his clique, corrupted through blind and criminal policies into an instrument of tyranny and national servitude. This adventurism unscrupulously wasted that moral and ideological heritage which you collected in the old world with honest struggle and with sacrifices of blood, which you acquired during the battle for our national independence and democratic progress. Rákosi's men grossly insulted our national decency and self-respect when they ignored completely our homeland's sovereignty and freedom, and wasted light-heartedly our national resources. The glorious uprising of our people threw off the Rákosi-rule from the back of the nation, and won freedom for the people and independence for the country—without which there is no socialism and there cannot be socialism.

After he called attention to the necessity of turning against the danger of counter-revolution, Kádár announced the birth of the new party in these words:

In these critical hours, the communists who fought all along against the Rákosi-tyranny have responded to the wishes of innumerable true patriots and socialists, and have decided to found a new party. This new party breaks once and for ever with the sins of the past. . . . Its name is Hungarian Socialist Workers' Party.

Who were the founders of the new party?

To start the organization of the party, to handle its affairs and to call for a most urgent meeting of a party-founding national congress, a preparatory committee has been formed, the members of which are Ferenc Donáth, János Kádár, Sándor Kopácsi, Géza Losonczy, György Lukács, Imre Nagy and Zoltán Szántó.

As it is evident from the lists of *The New Hungarian Encyclopaedia* and of the periodical *Társadalmi Szemle*, János Kádár alone was *really* among the founders.

And finally: what was the first and leading idea in the new party's programme?

[The Party] defends and will defend the independence of our homeland, against anybody . . . Our people proved with their own blood that they support unshakably the government's demand for the complete withdrawal of Soviet forces. We don't want any more dependence! We don't want that our country should become a battleground! We speak to every honest patriot! Let us join hands for the triumph of Hungarian independence and of Hungarian liberty!

In the light of all this, it is rather obvious why the Hungarian Socialist Workers' Party is so secretive concerning the date and the circumstances of its birth. Even if today it resembles the other communist parties faithful to Moscow, in the hours of its birth it was, without exaggeration, a singular and exceptional member in the family of Marxist–Leninist parties. This was the only communist party which began its career by condemning its immediate predecessor, that other communist party which ceased to exist on the very same day. This was the only communist party which did not pledge unconditional fidelity to the Soviet Union, but independence from the Soviet Union. This was the only communist party which had not come into existence before a revolution but during a revolution, and immediately declared its complete solidarity with the revolution.

This 'singularity' continued, although under radically different circumstances.

It is not rare with communist parties that they should change their history as easily as they change their political line. But in this respect, too, the Hungarian Socialist Workers' Party beats the records of its predecessors and contemporaries: not even seventy-two hours were necessary for János Kádár to call 'the glorious uprising of the people' a 'counter-revolution', to change the demand 'for the complete withdrawal of the Soviet forces' to a request for 'the entry of the Soviet forces', and to modify his solemn promise to defend the homeland's independence 'against anybody' to the extent of his becoming the leading personality in Hungary's re-colonization by the Soviet Union.

It is not rare with communist parties that they should jail or even execute their leaders. The most remarkable accomplishment in this field too belongs to the Hungarian Socialist Workers' Party. Less than two years passed and among the founders of the party Imre Nagy had been hanged, Géza Losonczy murdered in jail, Sándor Kopácsi sentenced to life imprisonment, Ferenc Donáth sentenced for twelve years, György Lukács and Zoltán Szántó deported to Rumania for some time.

There was only one man in the seven-member leadership who was left unharmed: János Kádár.

After having rejected its own remarkable programme, the conditions of its founding and its first leaders, nothing is more natural than that the party should have come to accept that which it had first condemned: its ill-famed predecessors between 1919 and 1956.

In 1959, the Hungarian Socialist Workers' Party held its *first* congress, which called itself the *Seventh* Congress, so indicating its solidarity with the four decades of the Hungarian communist movement, and, moreover, expressing pride in the past and appointing itself its heir and successor. The party has thus come around to accept as its own tradition Béla Kun's communist dictatorship in 1919 as well as Béla Kun's execution in 1939 in the Soviet Union; the participation in the anti-fascist war in Spain of László Rajk and his associates as well as the execution in 1949 of the same László Rajk and his associates in Hungary; the ten-year reign of Mátyás Rákosi, which Kádár described on 1 November 1956 as 'blind and criminal' and as 'the instrument of tyranny and national servitude', but about which today Kádár feels that 'even if some mistakes did occur during those ten years, the party-line was fundamentally correct'. There was no need to do anything but to cloak the birth of the party in a thick fog, and the much-desired continuity was immediately restored: in the shadows of Lenin, Stalin, Khrushchev and Brezhnev, there stood everybody from Béla Kun to Mátyás Rákosi and Ernő Gerő, up to János Kádár.

THE MEMBERSHIP OF THE PARTY

It is, however, easier to restore this continuity on paper than in reality. The immediate predecessor, the Hungarian Workers' Party, used to have more than 900,000 members. Half a year after the Soviet intervention, despite all the advantages that a party-member held at that time, the party could cajole only 283,000 of its disciples back into the fold.[3] This number increased to 346,000 in June 1958, to 402,000 in December 1959 and to 478,000 by January 1961. Since then, no official figures have been published, but according to an article in the party's central organ *Népszabadság*, the number of party-members grew by 11·3 per cent between 1961 and 1964[4] which means that the figure is

[3] *Társadalmi Szemle*, June 1961.
[4] *Népszabadság*, 29 May 1965.

now about 550,000. It appears, then, that the *party failed in its efforts through more than ten years to reach 65 per cent of its former strength.*

The Hungarian party-press concerns itself with this problem on a virtually day-to-day basis. For instance, this is what the *Népszabadság's* already quoted article says:

Although we purified the idea of party-membership and discarded everything that was unworthy of it—the taking of personal advantages, first of all—yet there are people who ask: is it worthwhile today to be a member of the party?

This is how the problem is formulated in a provincial newspaper:[5]

Politically untrained people who are not members of the party but stand close to it ideologically, often ask themselves: 'Why should I be a party-member? It would only add to my troubles.'

The same paper writes on 22 January 1965:

Cases multiply which stand witness to the fact that people in important economic positions, persons not in the party and a part of public opinion begin to look down upon the party-organization and attribute less significance to it than before. It happened in a factory at Makó that a diligent, respected worker was told that he might join the party if he wanted to. This is what he replied to the communists: 'I won't go over to you, because you are about to disintegrate.'

If such is the picture among technical people, peasants and workers, things look even grimmer among the youth.

The Eighth Congress of the Hungarian Socialist Workers' Party was held at the end of 1962. The press, the radio and the television were full of the so-called 'Congressional Theses'—that is to say with the new party programme. Two university instructors, Mrs János Kardos and Mr Péter Hajdu, conducted a 'sociological poll' among students of a high-level technical school.[6] To the question, what is your opinion of the theses of the Hungarian Socialist Workers' Party's Eighth Congress, 'almost 50 per cent answered by revealing their complete ignorance of the theses, 25 per cent allegedly had some knowledge but knew nothing about the essence of the theses, a little less than 20 per cent had a rough idea and it was only about 8 per cent of the students who penetrated to

[5] *Csongrádmegyei Hirlap*, 30 October 1964.
[6] *Felsőoktatási Szemle*, July–August 1965.

the essence of the theses'. Not even cold-war propagandists could find more characteristic data for the complete or partial indifference of more than 90 per cent of the youth towards the Communist Party.

Who are the people making up the party-membership, about half a million in number? There is never any accurate information, and thus we must confine ourselves to rough estimates. The country has about 20,000 party organizations; if we modestly count only three functionaries to each unit, this adds up to 60,000 members. Among the approximately 300,000 trade union functionaries, 25 per cent belong to the party—another 75,000 men. This shows that *from the half a million members, more than 130,000 are professional functionaries of the party and the trade unions.* We must furthermore add to this number those functionaries of the state and the mass-organizations who work in the party's youth organization and women's subsidiaries, in government departments, local councils, other state offices, the armed forces and the police, etc. Their number should be between 3–400,000. It is clear then that the Hungarian Socialist Workers' Party has hardly any common soldiers: workers, peasants or intellectuals who do not occupy some official post. *The party as a whole is a party of functionaries.*

The composition of the delegations to the last, so-called Eighth Congress may be taken as a characteristic confession. (Characteristic even if one considers the high-level nature of this meeting and accepts the fact that because this was a party forum, party-functionaries outnumbered functionaries of the trade unions and the state.) The membership was represented at this congress by 612 voting delegates and thirty-six others with the right to participate in the debates. According to the report of the Mandates Committee[7] this was the composition of the delegations:

    41·6 per cent party-functionary
    13·4 per cent functionary of mass-movements
     6·0 per cent functionary of the state
     7·1 per cent member of the armed forces
     6·0 per cent manager.

Only 11·1 per cent of the delegates are described as workers, but even here one has to take into consideration that such statistics usually list as workers those who were *once* workers, but have been occupying over the last twenty years various high official posts.

[7] *Népszabadság*, 23 November 1962.

It would be nevertheless a mistake to suppose that these members—who actually live off the party and who live better than the average Hungarian—would react with interest towards everything which comes to them from the party and which links them to the party. Once it was unimaginable that members should miss a membership meeting—unless a serious illness or some other grave reason kept them back. Nowadays reports such as this can be found in the provincial press:

> At the entrance, my old acquaintance Ferenc Fancsali received me:
> 'I think you, comrade, came on the wrong day. It's the day before a holiday and it's pay-day as well. We aren't likely to have a membership-meeting.'
> 'It has never happened to me in the half-year of my career as a Party Secretary,'—Imre Papp, the Secretary of the Local Organization tells me with a sigh—'that so few people should come to attend. . . . We can't even bring a resolution, because only 25 members came out of the 65.'[8]

The publications of the party are received with complete indifference by the membership. A provincial newspaper complains for example that in the county of Vas, there are a little less than four members for one *Pártélet* (periodical dealing with everyday problems of the party), twenty-nine members for one *Társadalmi Szemle* (the ideological periodical of the party), thirty-one members for one *Nemzetközi Szemle* and forty-two for one *Béke és Szocializmus* (both party publications explaining foreign developments).[9]

What is it, then, that ties these people to the party? These phenomena —which cannot really be called isolated—indicate hardly a trace of enthusiasm and of ideological bonds. What remains is the possibility of *personal advantages*. As they are mostly functionaries, it is understandable that they cling to their desks and to the smaller or larger fleshpots— for which they can thank the party—and from the point of view they oppose changes—actually, all changes—which might not be advantageous for them. What once characterized the communist movement— enthusiasm for the new, extreme desire for the new—becomes with these professional functionaries an adherence to the old and the established. The result is a stiff conservativism.

---

[8] *Szolnokmegyei Hirlap*, 22 April 1965.
[9] *Vas Népe*, 12 November 1964.

THE PRESTIGE OF THE PARTY

Even if people do not change willingly, the times do change. This change presents the greatest problem for the Hungarian communists. The party —which Soviet tanks put back into their former privileged position—is today considered as perhaps the most reliable branch-office Moscow has. In supporting the Kremlin's more flexible attitude in the Moscow–Peking dispute, the Hungarian communist line corresponds to the national interest up to a point. Beyond this point, however, we see that Hungarian communists—unlike their counterparts in Rumania—do not act in the national interest, as they show no sign of intending to exploit the Russian–Chinese feud for wresting a greater measure of independence from Moscow.

Over and above these considerations of foreign policy, the following of the Soviet party-line has doubtlessly led to a certain liberalization in the country's internal affairs. From the point of view of the party membership, particularly one aspect of this process of liberalization is significant: the unquestionable fact that the top party leadership now tries to utilize those experts in the direction of economic and other affairs, who were previously ignored, demoted and often even persecuted. For the country, this process is useful and it could be more useful only if the political dogmas did not tie the hands of these experts. For the moment, however, one cannot even dream about that.

From the top party leadership, this process does not represent any immediate danger: they were given their positions by the Russians and they could be removed only by the Russians. No matter how many dilettantes there are among them—and there are plenty—their so-called positions of trust are not threatened even by the best experts.

This is, however, not the case on a lower level. The policy which begins to respect expertise—even if the person in question is not a party-member—undermines critically the prestige of communists. Perhaps it is not too much to say that in the long run—and this may not necessarily mean too long a time—this policy represents a mortal blow to the party. It is not a question of jobs—the chief engineer of a factory will not take over the post of the party secretary or of the trade union secretary—it is a question of *roles* and *actual influence*. In Hungary today, there is a peculiar 'class-struggle' which is fought on one hand between the party-members and the non-members, and on the other hand, within the party, between the top leadership and the members.

However paradoxical it may appear, the fact is that the top leadership joins forces in many cases with the non-members against its own party-membership. This does not mean that the party-members no longer have certain privileges—they do—but day after day, they feel their power and prestige decreasing. Anxiety about the future often throws them into panic and sometimes drives them to the verge of opposing their own leaders.

In the Hungarian press, there is an abundance of references to this new situation. Here is a sample:

> In a railway junction, there have been many complaints over the last few years that the central authority gives peculiar instructions when asking for the names of those who should be awarded prizes and medals: if possible, there should be no party-members among those receiving these distinctions. This is not an isolated mistake but a trend . . . which is proved by the fact that recently this central authority requested the same station to submit *another* suggestion for an award to an outstanding worker, because the person who was first proposed *happened to be* a party member.[10]

In the same article, one reads this a little further:

> A short time ago, the party secretary of a village with a strong kolkhoz said at a meeting: 'Before, when there was some kind of a discussion in the kolkhoz, I was invited, together with the chairman of the Local Council. After we finished—such is the custom—we drank some wine with the guests. Later on, they started to leave me out and they invited only the chairman of the Local Council, but nowadays neither of us is asked to participate in these meetings. You can imagine that I don't come up with this problem because I feel sorry about the wine—I have my own vineyard.

Another article on the same subject, from another provincial newspaper:

> One often hears intolerant opinions at membership meetings and in private discussion with communists. 'We are ignored when leading posts are filled,' somebody said. 'Against our recommendations, a chief engineer and a chief accountant were appointed,' another claimed.[11]

[10] *Veszprémi Napló*, 13 June 1965.
[11] *Vas Népe*, 13 December 1964.

Here is yet another complaint from a third newspaper:

> In many party-organizations of our county, what gives cause for anxiety is that lately, it seems as if here and there, economic experts and non-members were beginning to look down upon the party-organization. Several economic experts do not take into consideration the counsels and the criticisms of communists. This is what some people said at a recent course given for party secretaries: among workers, one can hear opinions that 'there isn't much that the party-organization is entrusted with; the word of communists no longer counts as much.[12]

The same article says a little further:

> Recently, it happened at Makó that an expert from the ministry suggested a significant reorganization in the work of an institution. The suggestion was not at all popular among the workers but the expert ignored this. Moreover, he did not even speak with the party secretary, because he knew that the party secretary would be against his ideas. When there was nevertheless some talk that it would be better to discuss matters with the party secretary, the expert replied: 'The party secretary means as much to me as a fleabite to an elephant.'

If the advantages decrease, the power is reduced, and if, more and more often, the right to advise and the weight of advice equal zero, the interest in being a party-member and the interest in not being a party-member will inevitably clash. It can hardly be doubted that it is the former that suffers in this conflict.

Thus, regardless of the intentions of those setting it into motion, the process of liberalization may rapidly reach a point where the 'proud title of party-member' (Stalin) will entail nothing but the scornful contempt of the non-members.

ON THE DEFENSIVE

What in any case has already come to pass in Hungary is that the Communist Party—which once advertised itself as 'the vanguard' and 'the motor of progress'—was forced into a defensive position, if not in the exercise of central power but on the ideological front. In the publications, articles and resolutions dealing with party life, one can

[12] *Csongrádmegyei Hirlap*, 27 January 1965.

hardly find anything else but the descriptions of this defensive position on one hand, and encouraging words on the other hand for those party-members who have been losing heart. Let us quote again a few articles which mirror the present conditions more convincingly and authentically than any analysis.

'Come out in the open!'—this is the title of an editorial which appeared in the *Veszprémi Napló*. The article tells the following story:

In a village of the district of Pápa, where a good number of intellectuals live and work, there was a movement afoot to organize a club for intellectuals. Although it was the party secretary himself who had thought of it and called the first meeting together, nothing came of the idea. A counter-argument was advanced: 'We won't form a Gentlemen's Casino, as in the old times.' However the real reason, if we are right in our suspicions, was the fear that one might have to go into battle and that one might have to come out in the open: perhaps there would be some people among the intellectuals not in the party, with whom one would have to argue . . .[13]

'Some people believe,' writes the central newspaper of the party, 'that our militancy has been flagging recently and the passion of the communists has gone slack. It is possible that there is some truth in this in some places.'[14]

A correspondent of another newspaper reports:

'We are not courageous, we dispute and argue little,' I heard the other day from a speaker in the membership meeting of the party-organization of Rábacsanak. Another said: 'We have been very quiet, as if we forgot how to make propaganda.' . . . The communists should make propaganda at work, when people talk about all sorts of things, among friends, acquaintances and at every conceivable opportunity. . . . Well, a significant part of the party membership in the villages have no courage to do all this.[15]

An article in the provincial daily *Délmagyarország* considers the problem of indifference.

At a trade union meeting, one speaker went so far after a long argument and several logical jumps that he claimed to 'prove' that there

[13] *Veszprémi Napló*, 23 April 1965.
[14] *Népszabaság*, d25 May 1965.
[15] *Kisalföld*, 18 September 1965.

was not really such a great distance between the two fundamentally opposite systems of materialism and idealism, and between their respective tenets concerning society, and it is merely a question of faith who calls which theory his own. The speaker demoted the Marxist world-outlook to the level of faith, confused those great conflicts, irreconcilable and fundamental theses which characterize the two philosophical systems and make up the differences between them. I am not angry at this man and I am not even blaming the regime which allows the expression of such ideas. On the contrary: I consider as one of the proofs of our democracy that there is an atmosphere which makes possible the competition of ideas. Only in the awareness of its power and of its truth can a regime permit such a 'luxury', and we believe in this power and in this scientific truth of ours. Then, what is my complaint? Quite simply that at this trade union meeting, there were materialists and communists, yet the speech was left unanswered and nobody rose to deny its points, as if they were true!

'More effective ideological work!'—demands the *Népszabadság*, as it tries to encourage disheartened party-members. Then it states sadly: 'A part of the membership is not sufficiently active in questions of outlook, they are unaccustomed to take the initiative.'[16]

The situation has grown so critical that it was found necessary to deal with it at the highest level. In April 1965 the Central Committee published its so-called ideological guidelines, under the title 'Some Present Tasks of the Hungarian Socialist Workers' Party'. There was nothing to do but to state:

> The ideological work falls short of the requirements. The leaders, the workers and the institutions of the ideological front were not prepared for the greater tasks of the present. In theoretical work, in *agitprop* activities, there has not been a sufficient development of the militancy which could have fought against harmful tendencies with the necessary strength and could have thrust back these tendencies. Marxist criticism did not reveal, in time and with the necessary depth, the essence and the roots of the wrong tenets, and it did not provide their complete and effective denial. The scientific theoretical activity remained largely in debt with the elaboration of the necessary creative answers. The effort to gather and to organize capable and well-

[16] *Népszabadság*, 8 June 1965.

prepared cadres was not adequately target-oriented and consistent. Our ideological work is not sufficiently courageous and it is not sufficiently quick in analysing and answering new questions raised by life and progress; and in the leadership of ideological work, the necessary *élan* and initiatives are missing. In ideological enlightening work and propaganda, in many areas one may still feel the old reflexes, the remnants of the attitude which—separating theory from practice—operates without the intensive analysis of concrete relations and tasks, with the mere repetition of familiar dogma.[17]

As if it were intended as an illustration for 'the old reflexes', for 'the mere repetition of familiar dogma', it is with threadbare platitudes that the ideological guidelines called upon the membership to fight and to argue. Nothing is more characteristic of the efficacy of the guidelines than an article in a provincial newspaper, published a few months after its appearance. To the question why party-members are on the defensive, why they do not dare to argue and to turn against the 'wrong views' of the non-communists, the writer answered with touching simplicity: 'There is not enough ammunition.'[18]

SOME CONCLUSIONS

On 23 October 1956 the Hungarian Communist Party—boasting of a membership of 1,000,000—disintegrated virtually within a few hours, to the extent that after a week, János Kádár had to announce the dissolution of the party officially as well. In the case of the new party, one could not expect such a spectacular collapse—this is so because of the bitter experiences of the Hungarian people ten years ago. The Hungarian Socialist Workers' Party is dissolving slowly, quietly, but with the same certainty as its predecessors, the Communist Party in Hungary and the Hungarian Workers' Party. The Stalinist Party received its mortal blow from the 20th Congress of the Soviet Union's Communist Party, but this same congress and its consequences—the revolutions in Warsaw and in Budapest, the 22nd Congress, the Soviet–Chinese conflict—are driving today's Hungarian communist party towards the graveyard. In connection with the Stalinist Party, it was demonstrated that what is built on naked force sooner or later collapses. In the case of

[17] *Társadalmi Szemle*, April 1965.
[18] *Kisalföld*, 18 September 1965.

the present party, this truth is complemented by another: the party, which chose terror, iron-clad discipline and intolerance of differing opinions as its central principles, is unable to undergo the process of liberalization consistently without endangering its own existence. From an organizational as well as from an ideological point of view, the new party is significantly weaker than the old one: it is less loud-mouthed, less terroristic, with reduced worshipping of the leaders, with shorter rhythmic applauses, and people are not as frightened by it as before. But as one may see from what has been said here, it is precisely this *thaw* that undermines the party's foundations and threatens it with collapse—the same thaw from which the party expected to be strengthened. The dilemma admits no hope for a solution: to return to the Stalinist methods is as impossible as further liberalization—both of them appear to be fatal.

This is not to say, of course, that the crucial 20th Congress was a mistake; the social progress in the European communist countries passed beyond the Leninist–Stalinist structure, stepped ahead of the Communist Party itself, and this is what produced the 20th Congress and the events that have taken place since then. One may still argue over the role of these parties in the past; and there is room for argument concerning the 'historical necessity' of their work. It can no longer be doubted, however, that today these parties hold back development and have come into conflict with the forces of social progress. In this conflict—which in Marxist terminology would be called 'irreconcilable opposition'—these parties will have to fall apart. When? Only fortune-tellers could give the exact date. How? Surely not easily, not without resistance and struggle. But perhaps it is worthwhile to quote a significant statement on the subject of perspectives, from an essay written by Sándor Gáspár, who is one of the leaders of the party, a member of the Political Committee and the First Secretary of the Budapest Party Committee: 'What presents the greatest difficulty in the life of the party-organizations is that they do not always see in the present conditions how they should perform their tasks.'[19] How could they see? 'In the present conditions', they have no real tasks, roles and functions— they are spokes in the wheels, they retard progress in the life of the country and the nation.

[19] *Társadalmi Szemle*, 'A Párt Vezető Szerepéről', October 1964.

FERENC A. VALI

The Regime and the Nation

RESISTANCE AND COEXISTENCE

THE Hungarian revolution of 1956 originated from demonstrations celebrating rebellious Poland and demanding reparation for Stalinist excesses coupled with the removal from office of their perpetrators. Shortsightedness and provocations on the part of the party leadership and, subsequently, the initial abortive Soviet intervention turned the originally peaceful demonstrations into a full-fledged national uprising. The goals of this spontaneous revolt by then had become clearly defined in the minds of the participants: national independence and popular democracy.

While the freedom fighters fought, the composition of the government and its political concepts were gradually brought into line with the revolutionary programme. In the last days of October, no fundamental difference appears to have existed between the consensus of popular opinion and the government which by then included four political parties. Thus, a state of 'national unity' was achieved, one comparable to the unity of the Hungarian nation during the first revolutionary months in the spring of 1848. Political life was to be renewed on the basis of free popular elections and a non-aligned status was to be sought for Hungary. While the Stalinist Communist Party was condemned as an agent of Moscow, a 'rejuvenated' Communist Party, freed from Soviet control and to operate under a democratic system, was not considered inconsistent with the demands of national unity. Such a party was devised by Imre Nagy and his supporters.

The second massive Soviet armed intervention was aimed at restoring Russian hegemony over an area which had slipped out from under Soviet control. The restoration of such control appeared, however, impossible without a return to integral communist rule; the pre-revolutionary *status quo* had to be re-established. This latter task was assigned to János Kádár and his group of communists. But the military campaign of the Soviets found the destruction of all national armed

137

resistance to be a quick operation compared to the task of restoring Communist Party control and overcoming the passive resistance of a frustrated, humiliated nation.

Kádár and his group sensed that first they had to destroy this front of national unity, formed during and by the revolution, before they would be able to restore communist power.[1] Presumably, they aspired to create *another* type of 'national unity', one which was no longer 'born on a reactionary platform', that is, one that would embrace communism and accept Soviet paramountcy. Such a plan already must have been in Kádár's mind at the time of his installation as a leader of Hungary by the Red Army. The new First Secretary and Prime Minister may have cherished hopes that it would be possible to restore order and peace without resorting to the terroristic and violent dictatorial methods practised earlier by Rákosi. But the extent of national resistance, encountered by the regime in the last months of 1956 and in the beginning of 1957, manifested the futility or, at least, the untimeliness of such an ambitious plan. Eventually, Kádár and his associates felt compelled to follow Soviet advice and resorted to methods of terror and oppression for the restoration of what they considered 'order' and 'peace'. The attempt to create broad national support for the regime was left as the undertaking for a later, more appropriate day.

When years later, Kádár reversed Rákosi's dictum and declared that all who were not against the regime were counted as being for it,[2] his hope and objective was to gain wider national sympathy in support of the government; co-operation and compliance with the government's programme was sought even if wholehearted approval was not.[3] It is therefore important and instructive to determine how far Kádár's claim

[1] Kádár subsequently admitted that: '. . . we had to make serious efforts to destroy the national unity . . . Why did we have to destroy this national unity? Because it was born on a reactionary platform . . . We do not want this kind of unity.' Speech delivered on 29 June 1957, at the party conference; Radio Free Europe, *Hungary 1957–61: Background and Current Situation*, Special Report (mimeographed), 16 May 1961, pp. 109–10; see also Francois Fejtő, 'Hungarian Communism', in William W. Griffith, *Communism in Europe*, Vol. I, Cambridge, Mass., 1964, p. 208.

[2] Kádár made this pronouncement in December 1961 before a meeting of the People's Patriotic Front. Rákosi had once stated: 'Who is not with us is against us.' Both have paraphrased from the New Testament ('He that is not with me is against me; and he that gathereth not with me scattereth.' Luke xi. 23).

[3] See further in Ferenc A. Váli, 'Hungary', in Adam Bromke, *The Communist States at the Crossroads Between Moscow and Peking*, New York, 1965, pp. 72, 78–9.

to have created a new *quasi-unity* of national support is consistent with reality and whether the evolution of national sentiment in Hungary during the last ten years has endorsed or rejected governmental attitudes, ideas and actions.

★ ★ ★

In times of life-and-death crises, national unity—a unity of purpose with regard to the fundamental aspirations of a national society—is the product of healthy and constructive national sentiment. Traditional nationalism, the concept of belonging to a nation, the attachment to one's country and its people, is nowadays often identified with ultra-nationalism, the extremist advocacy of national interests. Semantic confusion, for which Soviet-communist vocabulary is partly responsible, has contributed to the obfuscation of this term.[4]

For the present writer, nationalism is an emotional as well as a rational mental attitude, way of thinking (ideology in the wider sense) engendered by the very fact of belonging to a nation. Those who are ready to accept the concept of national societies (and who would not recognize their existence in this 'most nation-conscious of all epochs'),[5] cannot deny the justification for its conceptual product: nationalism, whichever name they wish to confer on it. Furthermore, it cannot be denied that nationalism meaningfully contributes to, and secures internal cohesion of, states and is therefore—at the present stage of international relations—indispensable for the stability of international order. Traditional, historically innate nationalism (national sentiment or feeling is the emanation of this phenomenon) should not be equated with extremist expressions of it, such as ultra- or narrow (selfish) nationalism, expansionism or imperialism. Abuse of an ideological attitude does not render harmful moderate and reasoned attitudes of similar nature and the acceptance of the latter as a politically meaningful concept. The love

[4] Authors often adopted their own terminology: John Plamenatz prefers the expression 'patriotism' while reserving the word 'nationalism' to its aggressive forms (*On Alien Rule and Self-Government*, London, 1960, p. 13); on the other hand, Leonard W. Doob defines 'patriotism' as the identification of one's welfare and interests with the group called nation, and 'nationalism' as the set of demands for action arising from patriotism (*Patriotism and Nationalism—Their Psychological Foundations*, New Haven, 1964, pp. 4–9). In Soviet terminology, patriotism is compatible with proletarian internationalism but nationalism (identified with chauvinism) is not.

[5] Edward Hallett Carr, *Nationalism and After*, London, 1945, p. 39.

of one's country and people does not necessarily (though it may) nurture a hatred against other countries and peoples.[6]

Totalitarian dictatorships, whether rightist of leftist, have undertaken to eliminate traditions of secular humanitarian individualism and also the universalist traditions of natural law. With such a levelling operation, a fertile ground was created for collectivist-nationalist attitudes of an extremist or Messianic type. The Soviet Union and communist China, both officially condemning what they call nationalism, have become the chief devotees of an imperialist nationalism, an attitude which they not only blame on Western so-called 'imperialists' but one which should be foreclosed to the smaller communist states. While the nationalism of the newly independent peoples of Asia and Africa is being encouraged by Moscow and Peking, in the East-central European area genuine national feeling is discouraged and condemned because it might (as it already has) turn against the leadership-role played by the communist super-powers and endanger the stability of communist rule.[7]

As a result of the disastrous outcome of the Second World War for Hungary, the public had become disenchanted with the nationalist-irrendentist tendencies of an earlier day and had become more receptive to ideas of European or Danubian co-operation and federation. However, Soviet designs to maintain strict control over individual East-central European countries prevented any confederative move. Moreover, any expression of innate, defensive national feeling (such as was aroused by the expulsion of Hungarians from Czechoslovakia) was to be checked, if not totally suppressed, by the local communist leadership. It was only natural then and in the manner in which nationalism reacts that this suppressed national feeling should be turned into vehement anti-Soviet antagonism. It should be recalled that the revolution of 1956 was directed against the Russian oppressor and it remained, despite allegations to the contrary, immune from irredentist aspirations.[8]

The impact of Soviet controlled communism on national sentiment in the East-central European area was, by and large, similar to that which

---

[6] The inevitability of having to deal with nationalism, as a political force, is well expressed by Crane Brinton: 'I shall conclude that what we call nationalism is for any reasonable period in our times a constant, not to be stamped out by conquest, nor even to be exorcised by professorial and editorial incantations.' *From Many One*, Cambridge, Mass., 1948, p. 17.

[7] About these trends see further Ferenc A. Vali, *Rift and Revolt in Hungary—Nationalism versus Communism*, Cambridge, Mass., 1961, pp. 501–8.

[8] Op. cit., p. 335.

had been given such a violent expression in Hungary though it was moulded into different reactions by the national temperament and historical reminiscences of the various nations involved. Experience incontrovertibly proves that the inculcation of the universalist communist secular religion, with its implied acceptance of Soviet overlordship, did not extinguish or even weaken nationalism. If nationalism in that area has changed at all it may have done so not for the better, but for the worse: traditional 'middle-class' nationalism may have been replaced in the minds of many by some 'economic-socialist national totalitarianism',[9] similarly to the process by which the Edmund Burke-type of *ancien régime* nationalism was transformed by the French revolution into a popular ultra-nationalism.

★ ★ ★

In Hungary, largely because of the frustration and disillusionment brought about by the abortive revolution, and also due to other individual factors, the evolution of national sentiment differed in some respects from developments in other countries of that area.

In the aftermath of the revolution the regime's primary task, as stated before, was to destroy the anti-communist and anti-Soviet national unity. To secure stability for the new government, those forces or centres of power which had been formed during the period of relaxation prior to the revolt, as well as those which had been created during the revolutionary days, had to be eliminated or put under party control. In other words, the entire social fabric had to be atomized in order to permit the operation of one single force, the party. Accordingly, revolutionary councils, workers' councils, the Writers' Association, the Churches and others had to be either dissolved, or subjected to the authority of the party.

The collapse of the revolution, the annihilation of every ideal for which the nation had striven, the restoration of a hated foreign-supported system and disenchantment because of the inactivity of the West, resulted, especially among the younger generation, in an alienation from society, in sharp contrast to the collectivistic exigencies of the communist system. Not only did writers choose 'internal emigration', but many other individuals, not only intellectuals, 'emigrated' into

---

[9] Such a development was foreseen by Edward Hallett Carr, op. cit., pp. 17–34.

themselves; while paying lip-service to the demand of the regime and participating in required activities physically, they lived for themselves and their closer family:

> ... Twice [in 1945 and 1956] we felt inspired, twice we were disappointed, in both cases so cruelly that it was not easy even for young elastic minds, to recover. For us it is now difficult to find enthusiasm: instead of ideals we rather seek force in ourselves ... .[10]

This disillusionment is also described by the peasant writer Péter Veres who discovered that its roots are to be found in the conflict before the Messianic promises of Marxism–Leninism and the unpleasant facts of life.[11] The pessimism of society is a current topic of Hungarian sociological-political articles and those writers, who try to be objective about it, refrain from proposing any remedy against it.[12]

Has this vacuum of ideals, indifference and individual egotism which characterize Hungarian society in the wake of the 1956 uprising to the present, extinguished or weakened attachment to the nation? Much evidence available demonstrates that the alienation from public affairs, from politics and the affairs of party and state, is the reaction against the concepts and ideology of the communist regime. It is not an indifference towards the interests and future of the nation, it is not an attitude devoid of national feeling. After the traumatic experiences of 1956, the average Hungarian became more pragmatic, realistic, developed a down-to-earth philosophy. He realized that there was nothing to be done to extricate the nation from the bondage of communism, that he has to live with it, for the time being, and make the best out of it. Indifference and egocentric attitudes did not efface national feeling, but toned it down into the inner recesses of the human mind where it continues to induce actions and govern the formation of opinions. Even in the background of complete nihilistic attitudes nationalism may even more prevail. Nor does devotion to communist doctrines always extinguish healthy national sentiment.

Nevertheless, it may appear that in communist countries the official

[10] From Ferenc Buda's article 'Confessions About Youth', *Uj Irás*, January 1965.

[11] 'A Letter on the Problems of Alienation', *Kortárs*, December 1964.

[12] János Kádár, in a speech delivered in the National Assembly on 15 February 1965, stressed the necessity for 'socialist optimism'. Thereafter, a number of articles dealt with this topic; see *Népszabadság*, 28 February ('Hurrah Pessimism', by János Komlós), 7 March and 9 March 1965.

ideology of the party competes with the ideology of traditional nationalism. A juxtaposition of these two concepts may serve to elucidate why nationalism proves to be an unconquerable rival to 'scientific' Marxism-Leninism:

(1) Traditional nationalism, while neither a biological phenomenon, nor a product of nature (as Hitlerites were ready to assume with regard to 'race'), does not originate from 'voluntarism' but is the result of historic development, of environmental influences and is enhanced by 'all the mystic chords of memory' (Abraham Lincoln), including community of language, love of native land and feeling of 'togetherness' with fellow-nationals. It need not be taught (though mostly it is) and still exists in the sentiment of individuals belonging to the same stock who together form the nation.

Marxism–Leninism or proletarian internationalism has to be taught, indoctrinated, while nationalism emerges spontaneously.

(2) Marxism–Leninism is, by virtue of its own teaching, a purely materialistic doctrine while nationalism is a blend of spiritual (idealistic) and materialistic concepts. We have been told, though this may sound exaggerated, that nationalism has a 'warmth and a pietistic character' which is certainly not to be found in communism.[13] In other words, nationalism is human, whereas communist doctrine must artificially be implanted into the human ego and, by its own terms, has to rely on 'dictatorship', class warfare, and other violent measures which are not the inevitable concomitant features of nationalism. The strength of national feeling is clearly demonstrated by the fact that communist states are organized upon the base of national societies, thus implicitly recognizing the forces of nationalism. There is little doubt that in all communist countries the great majority of the people had preserved their traditional national feeling.

(3) Nationalism, generally, inspires men to greater devotion and sacrifice than Messianic communism. Stalin, in the Second World War felt compelled to invoke Russian national sentiment together with its historic reminiscences, the love of Russia's sacred soil, instead of the love of Marx and Lenin, to inspire his soldiers to fight and die. Identification with one's nation strengthens self-confidence, self-esteem and induces man to noble actions (an idealist communist may also act in

---

[13] Carlton J. H. Hayes, *Nationalism: A Religion*, New York, 1960, p. 15.

such manner but does so less often, and less spontaneously).[14] A member of a nation may feel that he participates in the history of that nation, sharing in his self the nation's past and future. Comparing the social impact of nationalism and communism, C. J. H. Hayes reached the following conclusions:

> Nationalism, after all, now appears to be wider in scope than communism and more universally motivating. It is more capable of arousing a religious sense, both popular and impelling.[15]

With these general considerations in mind, and also in view of the more resilient and immanent character of nationalism it may already be assumed that apathy and frustration which has remained a dominant feature of the public psyche in Hungary since the downfall of the revolution nevertheless did not affect the basically nationalist-oriented disposition of the Hungarian public. This must also be deduced from the manifold official utterances warning against this 'danger to socialist progress' that under the armour of selfishness and indifference national sentiment is still or, perhaps even more than in the pre-revolutionary period, the major motivating element for most of the people in Hungary.

★　★　★

Doubtlessly, the suppression of the revolt of 1956 had imparted a shattering blow to national esteem and self-consciousness. Lethargy and despondency ruled supreme in the darkest months following the zenith of a short lived national renaissance. But it is in the nature of nationalism that oppression instead of softening, eventually strengthens its momentum. The fact that nowadays the liberalization of the regime is considered to be an achievement of the revolution provides evidence which demonstrates that reliance on national values is no longer diminished.

Concern by leading party members over the rising trend of national feeling has been voiced time and time again. Among the more recent and more explicit expressions of this anxiety, there should be mentioned the 'Ideological Offensive of Marxism'. This 'offensive' was opened in

---

[14] 'I think that to define nationalism as pooled self-esteem is to define it as something enduringly human. For though the forms and means by which people nourish their self-esteem change, though, to borrow again from the commonplace of psychology, self-esteem can be sublimated into very noble actions . . .' Crane Brinton, op. cit., p. 76.

[15] Carlton J. H. Hayes, op. cit., p. 18.

the second half of 1964 and aimed at dispelling apathy and indifference as well as at strengthening the communist ideological consciousness of the many. The campaign started with a nationwide ideological conference organized by the party between 24 and 26 September. Among the findings of this conference was the conclusion that:

> Nationalism is the *chief element and binding force* of the bourgeois and petty-bourgeois currents which are traversing and endangering the conquest of Marxism. The imperialists are hoping that with the help of nationalism, they would be able to disrupt the unity of the international communist movement and loosen the community of the socialist countries . . . In our country, too, *nationalism is the life-giving element* of many of the bourgeois ideology. . . .[16]

The report on the conference also stated that considerable attention was to be given to the struggle against nationalism. Complaints were expressed that 'some persons' (presumably the Rumanian or Chinese leaders) try

> . . . to superimpose the national form upon common socialist content, to set the national interests against the international interests of social progress and exaggerate the national characteristic of their own countries.

Presumably to defend themselves against reproaches, the leaders of the conference wished to emphasize that the Hungarian regime is, nevertheless, not unmindful of a 'national policy which serves the rise of the nation' but went on to declare:

> We do not fight against nationalism from the base of national nihilism. We cannot afford to abandon to reactionary nationalism the desires lying deep in the *national sentiments of the masses*. These desires are: the wish for national freedom and the emotion of national pride. In the socialist countries, all the preconditions exist for these feelings to develop into socialist patriotism united with internationalism.
>
> National nihilism is just as alien to the socialist ideology as is nationalism. Our socialist patriotism is based on the recognition that the construction of socialism in our country is′ the only possible national policy which serves the rise of the nation. However, this

[16] A report on the conference is published (unsigned) in *Társadalmi Szemle*, November 1964 (italics are added).

national policy can only be realized within the fraternal community of the socialist countries and by relying on the strength of united internationalist forces. Thus, for us, socialist patriotism and socialist internationalism are inseparable notions.[17]

Party Leader János Kádár in a speech delivered in the National Assembly on 11 February 1965, expounded his ideas about national feeling in Hungary in the following manner:

> Those who expect that awakening national consciousness will set the socialist countries against each other and against the Soviet Union . . . are in for a disappointment.
> Our national consciousness is growing to be a socialist awareness, an international awareness. National feeling, patriotism, is identical today with the love of the socialist fatherland and attachment to it. Socialist patriotism is, at the same time, a solidarity with all other socialist countries, brotherhood with all the peoples of the world. . . .[18]

The Central Committee of the party thereafter discussed and unanimously approved certain *Guidelines* for ideological activity. These precepts had been prepared by Politburo Member and ideological expert István Szirmai. The *Guidelines*, together with Szirmai's report were published in the April issue of *Társadalmi Szemle*, the party's ideological monthly.

Much in contradiction to Kádár's optimistic appraisal, the *Guidelines* declared that:

> In our country, nationalism is an ideology *which affects the broadest masses* and endangers socialist progress. . . .[19]

According to the *Guidelines*, 'nationalist ideology' is one of the principal ingredients and the 'binding substance' of petty-bourgeois and anti-Marxist thinking. It is also nationalism which, in the opinion of some people, supports the 'third-roader' attitude, rejecting class struggle and calling for non-alignment in the struggle between socialism and capitalism. Nationalism, in Szirmai's interpretation, is a remnant of the past which had survived in the minds of men. However, he takes care to emphasize that nationalism is not always reactionary as is shown by the

[17] A report on the conference is published (unsigned) in *Társadalmi Szemle*, November 1964 (italics are added).

[18] *Népszabadság*, 12 February 1965.

[19] Italics mine.

national sentiment of colonial peoples fighting for their freedom. But in Hungary—as clearly admitted by the *Guidelines*—nationalism is directed against communism and against a 'co-operation of socialist countries' and therefore unequivocally a 'reactionary, hostile ideology'.

The *Guidelines* themselves implicitly admit why Hungarian nationalism is hostile to the regime and the present international status of Hungary. This paper reiterates the well-known distinction between patriotism and nationalism, the former being inseparable from proletarian internationalism. We are further told by this document that the yardstick of proletarian internationalism is the measure of co-operation between members of the socialist world system, a co-operation where 'the relation with the Soviet Union remains to be a fundamental question'. At the same time, the Soviet Union is being described as the great power that is building communism, the pioneer of progress and chief protector of peace. It is also maintained that 'progress and anti-socialism are incompatible'. In conclusion of this train of ideas, the *Guidelines* makes the following momentous pronouncement:

> Who turns against the Soviet Union, becomes opposed to the interests of the whole humanity.

This sentence, implying a recognition of the Soviet leadership, dangerously resembles another declaration, made by the Bulgarian leader Vulko Chervenkov in 1948, which was considered as the formula of accepting Soviet control under Stalin:

> There cannot be true love for one's fatherland if the love is in one way or another opposed to the love of the Soviet Union.

Accordingly, in the interpretation of the Hungarian Communist Party, patriotism (the love of one's fatherland) cannot, by definition, come into conflict with the affection towards the Soviet Union; in other words, Hungarian patriotic feeling should include a similar attachment towards the Soviet fatherland. Such a thesis is, naturally, diametrically opposed to feelings of traditional (and spontaneous) nationalism which confer primary value on the attachment towards one's own country and, while not necessarily implying hostility towards other countries, cannot engender sympathy towards countries which endanger vital national interests or suppress the liberty of one's own fatherland.

Probably to forestall some unwelcome criticism against the *Guidelines'* Stalinist interpretation of Hungarian–Soviet relations, Szirmai's report submitted to the Central Committee on 11 March 1965, was published together with the *Guidelines*.[20] The clarification of the meaning of some principles laid down by the *Guidelines* seemed necessary because for those (and they are many) who remember the servility and toadyism practised by the Hungarian party and governmental leaders *vis-a-vis* the Soviet Union and its officials in Stalin's time, the renewed kowtowing before the Soviet state when defining Hungarian patriotism must have appeared not only ironic but overtly provocative.

Szirmai, in his article, was eager to explain that none of the relations with other socialist states, including those with the Soviet Union, would 'affect the independence and national sovereignty of our fatherland'. The relations, he was telling his readers, are based 'on equality, non-interference in internal affairs, and mutual assistance, and do not harm our country's independence, on the contrary, assure it'. One may, of course, imagine how unconvincing and hollow these explanations must sound to the average Hungarian, including party members as well.

The ideological expert of the party took pains to point out that:

> ... nationalism is an expressly bourgeois standpoint. ... In Hungary ... there is nationalism, not in the thinking of the political leadership but in the people's way of thinking.

His conclusion was that:

> Under socialist conditions, nationalism—by which we do not mean patriotism but national pride, the underestimation of other peoples, selfishness which is damaging to other free nations, as well as an *ideological trend opposing the fusion of socialist international forces*— exerts its influence in a direction opposed to the unity of the forces of socialism and is, therefore, a hostile attitude as the ideological weapon of the bourgeois and capitalist world.[21]

The constant hammering by party leaders on the dangers of nationalism, the repetitive insistence on the 'correct' interpetation of licit patriotism are clear evidence that, at least sceptisicm, if not outright disbelief, prevails with regard to the thesis of the party. Reports from Hungary confirm the admissions of party announcements—as reported above— that traditional nationalism is by far the strongest motivating force in

---

[20] The title of this article is: 'On some Timely Ideological Tasks of the Hungarian Socialist Workers' Party', *Társadalmi Szemle*, April 1965.

[21] Italics are added.

opposing the regime. The conviction that the country is dominated from without, that is, it is not really independent master of its own destinies, continues (despite the internal relaxation and material improvement) to engender what is known as 'counter-nationalism',[22] a violent antagonism against the nation's oppressor. This anti-Soviet 'counter-nationalism' is kept alive by the reminiscences of the suppressed revolution of 1956 which continues to rouse national consciousness and pride.

★ ★ ★

The touchstone for genuine national feeling in Hungary is still, and will remain for a long time to come, the attitude towards the revolution of 1956. In a way, the regime itself is responsible for such an approach: the meaning given to the events of 1956 had become the test of loyalty to the reconstituted Communist Party in 1957. The interpretation of these events is also the criterion of attitudes towards the Soviet Union. The dividing line between genuine supporters of the regime and its opponents is defined by the approval granted to the revolution or its condemnation as 'reactionary counter-revolution'.

Thus, in a January 1963 meeting of young poets in the city of Pécs, an attempt was made to create a new periodical which would reflect the ideas of their generation. Even then, the majority group refused to admit into their ranks poets who had contributed in 1958 to a collection of poems published under the title: *Fire Dance* which denounced the revolution and ended the self-imposed silence of Hungarian writers in the post-revolutionary era.[23]

Although ten years have passed since the revolution, the memory of the fateful events of 1956 is still very much alive in the minds of the Hungarian people. Both internal and external policies are still, consciously or unconsciously, influenced by these events. It is obvious that the year 1956 remained quite a touchy subject which, if handled at all, must be handled with care. And most touchy of all, is the personality and martyrdom of the revolutionary Prime Minister Imre Nagy. To justify his execution (ordered by the Russians) is risky and provocative; to rehabilitate him, would expose and compromise the regime. Thus

[22] Carlton J. H. Hayes, op. cit., p. 118.
[23] See 'The Conflict of Generations in Eastern Europe Today', Report of the Research Department of Radio Free Europe, 12 March 1965, p. 23.

Kádár and his associates have chosen to pass over in silence, as best they can, this tragic figure, sincerely hoping that the door covering this 'skeleton in a closet' will remain closed. Should it be opened (and it seems inevitable that, one day, it will), it might jeopardize the existence of the regime, just as the rehabilitation of Rajk (an unpopular figure, compared to Imre Nagy, in the public eye) in October 1956 contributed to the collapse of the communist system.

There is no doubt that the official explanation of the causes and suppression of the revolution is not accepted by the Hungarian people. This is just another proof of the national awareness of the masses. Whatever the success of Kádár's attempts to normalize the internal and external relations of his regime since 1956, the government's greatest political and psychological obstacle remains the stigma of the origin of the present regime.

★ ★ ★

Facts concerning the discrimination practised by the Rumanian government against the Hungarians in Transylvania and the attempts to Rumanize them are generally well known in Hungary where they are often discussed *in camera* within the party, and with much indignation by the man-in-the-street.[24] But, thus far, none of the Rumanian actions had been mentioned, let alone condemned, in the Hungarian press, nor has any official protest been launched by the Hungarian government. On the contrary, between 15–19 June 1965, a Hungarian party delegation, led by Politburo Member Gyula Kállai (who shortly thereafter became Prime Minister), visited Bucharest, 'to develop further the co-operation between the two parties', and was received in a 'comradely spirit'. While Kállai preached 'socialist patriotism' which should be free of nationalism, the Rumanian sister party undertook to oppress and ethnically absorb the Hungarian minority in the name of Rumanian nationalism.

It is hardly conceivable that, in the long run, aggressive nationalism should be practised in Rumania against Hungarians without provoking 'counter-nationalistic' reactions in Hungary. Complacency by the Hungarian party and government in such a matter would certainly expose them to renewed contempt in the eyes of the essentially national-

[24] This 'whispering campaign' is described by Ghita Ionescu, 'Communist Rumania and Nonalignment', *Slavic Review*, June 1965, p. 252.

minded public opinion. Overt discontent about this state of affairs has so far been silenced probably with the promise that most effective help to Transylvanian Hungarians could be extended by confidential party-to-party channels. It has also been hinted that intercession by the Soviet government and party may also be sought.

In view of Hungary's continued dependence on the Soviet Union, especially in matters of defence and foreign policy, communist Hungary could not stand up for the human rights of her co-nationals in Rumania if the green light is not given to her by Moscow. Whether such permission should be given or not, Hungarian national frustration and despair may reach dangerous proportions and the party-heralded 'socialist' patriotism may prove to be the traditional nationalism turned into a type of popular ultra-nationalism. Nationalism of widely popular masses is always more explosive and unpredictable than that of smaller circles.

Should Soviet–Rumanian relations develop into an open conflict, similar to the Sino-Soviet one, it is likely that Moscow itself would try to exploit Hungarian discontent and national exasperation for its own selfish purposes and use Hungary as its 'proxy' to threaten maverick Rumania. There is an ever-increasing danger of a violent nationalism developing in the East-central European area, one which would not only be directed against the common Soviet oppressor but one which would line up, once again, one small nation against the other. This development, which is the least desirable, could only be avoided if all the interested nations of the area would practise the necessary restraint in the pursuit of their national objectives. Of course, the communist regimes of the area are generally, by reason of their own unrepresentative character, unfit to lead their countries along moderate but, at the same time, nationally oriented political roads. The most dangerous aspects of feverish nationalism are those eruptions which spark an irrational *bellum omnium contra omnes*. Because communism had weakened humanism and individualism, without replacing it with an acceptable and healthy collectivist ideology, the ultimate heritage of a compromised communism might be ultra-nationalist ideology—unless wiser councils prevail.

★　★　★

Western observers, even if they are able to overcome obstacles of communication, find it difficult to extract clear statements from

Hungarian intellectuals, statements which would reflect their genuine attitude towards national sentiment in Hungary. Among a number of other reasons (such as general intellectual reticence, fear of misunderstanding, fear of indiscretions, etc.), many of them refrain from expressing opinion for reason of their genuine national feeling which forbids them to denounce even a contemptible government before slightly known foreigners. Nationalism works in many ways: one aspect of it is responsible for a certain reluctance to utter criticism, to commit an act which may be considered 'treacherous' or 'treasonable'. Thus nationalism itself may inhibit a person from exposing his innermost national sentiment.[25]

Opposition to communist regimes in Hungary and other people's democracies originates from various motivations. Desire for individual freedom, for a democratic form of government are certainly prime factors. However, in Hungary, as also in some other East-central European countries, nationalism—as admitted by the Hungarian regime—is the most persuasive motivating force which engenders antagonism towards the main facets of Soviet-communist rule. It is important to note that this national sentiment also brings into opposition to the regime those who are not, on principle, hostile to communism but dislike certain anti-national features of Hungarian political life, among them the overt or implicit recognition of Soviet overlordship.

It is, of course, nigh impossible to analyse fully the diverse motivations of masses, partly because the intensity of sympathy and antipathy, and their individual mental sources, vary from time to time and depend on concrete stimuli or provocations; partly also because nationalism may only be a single causative factor among others (e.g. supplementary to, but no less important than, libertarian aspirations)—all of which together, however, meaningfully and mutually strengthen one another's momentum.

As stated before, national feeling is the most difficult to identify because it is often unconscious and basically spontaneous. It is exactly this protean character of nationalism which makes it invincible to communist indoctrination and dictatorial intimidation.

[25] The inhibition is well explained by Mihajlo Mihajlov, the Yugoslav professor and writer who was purged because of having 'insulted' the Soviet Union; *The New Leader*, 30 August 1965, pp. 12-15.

MIKLOS MOLNAR

The Heritage of Imre Nagy

'What wood is this before us? The wood of Birnam.' WILLIAM SHAKESPEARE:
Macbeth.

THERE is an anecdote saying that when the 'Muscovite' communist
leaders returned to Hungary in 1945, their comrades at home assured
them that they had prepared everything for the reorganization of the
party, they had even found suitable headquarters: two nice bright rooms
sublet to them for that purpose.

The 'Muscovite' comrades smiled. And party headquarters, the headquarters of the proletarian communist party, moved not into two rooms
but into a Budapest palace that had housed, once, the German Embassy.
A little later it spread to the neighbouring house and subsequently
occupied all the building of the huge block. By the end of 1948 the men,
returned from Moscow, turned the entire country into a sub-tenancy.

For years their power appeared unshakeable. Their fortress, like
Macbeth's Dunsinane, unconquerable. '*Macbeth shall never vanquish'd
be until Great Birnam wood to high Dunsinane Hill shall come against
him.*' Can that ever happen? '*That will never be. Who can impress the
forest, bid the tree unfix his earth-bound root?*' Among the communist
leaders returned from Moscow there was but one who knew, who said,
and one year before the 1956 events put into writing, that the criminal
mistakes and acts of the leaders have pushed the apparently unvanquish-
able regime to the edge of catastrophe. That one man was Imre Nagy.
And when, ten years ago, Birnam wood again set out for Dunsinane, it
was this one man, Imre Nagy, who, after days of tormented delibera-
tion, took the side of 'Birnam wood' against 'Dunsinane'. Strangely
enough, only the Hungarian people, the 'man in the street' understood
Imre Nagy and followed him through a political labyrinth that mystifies
even today most political experts, especially in the West. This is why it is
not easy to speak about Imre Nagy to readers who know the Hungarian
events merely from Western political literature. The task has proved
even more difficult than I expected, not merely because of the unavail-

ability of documents, not just because I am addressing a reading public
in whose scale of values, in whose political and emotional world this
subject appears entirely different from the way it appears from the
author's own affectively coloured viewpoint. The principal difficulty lies
in the fact that now, after ten years, we have to disentangle the figure of
Imre Nagy, and everything connected with him, not merely from a
chaotic welter of occurrences and raw facts, but from a whole system of
stereotyped platitudes.

By this I mean not only the usual propaganda and counter-propaganda
which, guided by our own beliefs and attitudes, we reject, tolerate, or
even accept—though never as the full explanation of a complex historical event. Imre Nagy and the 'unknown insurgent of Budapest' were
traitors and counter-revolutionaries in the eyes of those who executed
them, martyrs and heroes in the eyes of the rebel nation, and heroes in
the Shakespearian and Cornelian sense of the word: 'The time is out
of joint . . .'

Moral or 'literary' judgements may move or annoy us but they will
deceive no one completely. Even the most enthusiastic participant in,
or admirer of, the Hungarian revolution will never ignore the fact that
an armed uprising, lasting for many days and mobilizing armed and
army-sized forces on both sides, is not just an adventure, a brave
gamble, not just a clash between Right and Wrong; more, it is a political
action, an historical event, in evaluating which we have to take into
account such criteria as its expediency, its scope and its consequence.
The causes and the circumstances of the fall of the Paris Commune
were more deeply and thoroughly analysed by the Communards and
their friends than by those who—literally or symbolically—stood on the
other side of the barricades. The same may be said about the Hungarian
revolution and Imre Nagy. The chroniclers of the 'Hungarian events',
at least the more conscientious ones, have neither glossed over the
failure of the Hungarian October, nor have they concealed the causes of
that failure, nor ignored Imre Nagy's vacillation, mistakes and weaknesses in those days that shook the Kremlin walls.[1] In other words,
although the moral and emotional partisanship of the authors was
obvious from every word in all their many books and articles, they did
not allow this to turn into an instrument of deception. The same cannot

---

[1] Tibor Méray, *Thirteen Days that Shook the Kremlin:* New York, 1959;
Tamás Aczél and Tibor Méray, *The Revolt of the Mind:* New York, 1959;
Ferenc A. Váli, *Rift and Revolt in Hungary:* Harvard University Press, 1961.

be said of that scientific—or rather pseudo-scientific—concept and method which raised the criterion of a certain kind of political effectiveness—in addition, effectiveness in a very limited sense—to a quasi-moral criterion.

★   ★   ★

All this can be summed up in a few sentences. What the Hungarian revolution attempted in 1956, was not less—even though indirectly and unconsciously—than a change in the whole international 'balance of power'. To be more exact: Hungary, the government of the 1956 revolution, the Hungarian press and the armed masses, formulated demands, the realization of which would have weakened the international power position of the Soviet Union to an incalculably serious degree.

The Soviet Union could not have conceded those demands and the West—i.e. the United States—could not have taken the equally incalculable risk inherent in the support of the Hungarian demands. Thus—so the argument runs—the demands were unrealistic and the responsibility for this lies, of course, not with the politically unschooled 'unknown insurgents' but with the leaders of the revolution, in the first place, Imre Nagy. What was so unrealistic about the demands? On this the authors do not always agree, but in most cases they refer to the demand for a multi-party system, withdrawal from the Warsaw Pact, and the declaration of Hungary's neutrality.

These 'excessive' demands rest—as everyone knows—both philosophically and historically on the great ideas conceived in the twentieth century. The American Declaration of Independence, the Universal Declaration of Human Rights, the revolutions and wars of independence of the nineteenth century, sanctioned the basic human rights on which the parliamentary multi-party system, and the right to national sovereignty—the national claims and demands of the Hungarian revolution—were founded. Ideologically and ethically, therefore, the Hungarian demands cannot be considered excessive at a time when progress towards the broadening of these rights is spreading throughout the world, in Asia, Latin America, Africa. There was, in fact no lack of sympathy of a moral, ethical, and, let us add, emotional nature. The 'Hungarian affair' moved the conscience of the entire democratic Western world very deeply; but soon a split developed between emotional reaction and practical 'political' assessment. Sympathy was all for the Hungarians; but the Western attitude to the Hungarian revolution and the revolutionary leaders, in the first place to Imre Nagy, became increasingly cool and formal. This attitude was somewhat softened but not basically altered, by the new emotional wave stirred up, in June 1958, when it was learned that the revolutionary Premier and his companions had been executed. Most writings present Imre Nagy to Western public opinion as a brave, decent, honest but impotent, mediocre rather than outstanding, politician. His martyrdom effaced his weaknesses not his greatest 'crime'—the fact that he failed.

So increasingly, success, 'effectiveness' has become the dominant criterion in the evaluation of Imre Nagy's political personality in the bulk of the Western press and political literature. In the course of a 'learned' debate the author of this article heard it asserted that Imre Nagy had, in effect, *spoiled things*, because his excessive demands *slowed down* the progress of Khrushchev's liberalization. Let us examine, to begin with, whether success, direct political effectiveness, is a sound historical or 'political-scientific' criterion, and whether it is indeed a political mistake for a small nation, in defence of its own interest, to throw down a challenge that conflicts with the rules of the existing balance of power.

In 1821, after the outbreak of the Greek uprising, the great European powers certainly thought so, and none of them went to the aid of the Greek freedom-fighters who had so daringly challenged the Turkish Empire. With the exception of a few hellenistically inclined intellectuals, Europe regarded the Greek cause a lost cause. Eight years later Greece achieved her national independence.

As all historical analogies, this one, too, limps a bit. In the 1820s, the Turkish Empire was on the threshold of its final decline. The triumph of the Greek cause was brought about by an element that is virtually negligible in our 'polarized' world: the struggle for supremacy within a European 'system' upheld by five pillars. We could go on *ad infinitum* citing arguments and counter-arguments. The Greek uprising challenged powers which—with the exception of Britain—were bound together against rebellion in that quarter by the ideological community of the Holy Alliance. As far as Britain was concerned, the dissolution of the Turkish Empire was far from being a British interest. Thus, the Greek 'challenge' was the boldest, and the most desperate imaginable, and its first phase ended in complete failure. Yet, in time, it led to success, and even if it had not done so, I wonder if a historian could be found who would regard the aims and demands of the *Heteria* as premature or 'excessive'.

We can cite other examples. The unsuccessful Polish uprisings of the nineteenth century, the Paris Commune or, not reaching back too far, the 1848–49 Hungarian war of independence have also given rise to innumerable contradictory arguments, evaluations and analyses. If, according to Marx, the Commune failed because it did not immediately turn its guns against Versailles (that is, it did not go *far enough*), others contend that the policies of the Commune were excessive, too radical. And who knows better than we, Hungarians, the contradictory evaluations of Kossuth's policies? Did not certain critics accuse Kossuth of not having relied with sufficient consistency on the Left-wing, plebeian forces of the revolution? And did not others declare that he had alienated the moderate elements who sympathized with the revolution, by his Debrecen speech dethroning the Habsburgs, and thereby annulling the possibility of military victory as well as the possibility of a negotiated peace? Yet, we repeat, it would be hard to find a serious historian who would 'strike off' either the premature Polish uprisings, or the defeated Paris Commune, or again the Hungarian war of independence from the list of significant historical events, regardless of their failure or the hesitations, mistakes or excesses of their leaders.

Success, we should like to add, does not always manifest itself immediately even in the case of outstanding statesmen. Bismarck was regarded as the greatest statesman of Europe, yet his 'regime' did not survive the 'Iron Chancellor'. Cavour died almost a decade before Rome became the capital of United Italy.

★ ★ ★

Let us, however, return to the Budapest of 1956. No political analysis with any claim to be considered scientific can rest content with simply sizing up the international power relations and possibilities. Decision-making derives from not one but several parallelograms of forces. The wrong conclusions will be reached by those who analyse the Hungarian events exclusively on the basis of Hungarian popular tradition and aspirations and conditions within the Soviet camp; but our chances of arriving at mistaken conclusions are just as great if we regard the Hungarian uprising merely as a trial of strength between two conflicting powers. Still, many commentators of the 1956 events—journalists, political experts, and lately even historians—start from the following premise: in the magic circle of the post-war 'polarized world outlook' *every* move is just one more battle in the global war between the 'socialist' and the 'capitalist' worlds. It is not surprising that from the euphoria of excessive hopes cherished in 1956, the champions of this outlook should soon have lapsed into disappointment.

The events of the decade since the Budapest uprising have shaken the 'bi-polar' world-outlook. Although it is still a naive dream to imagine that the 'third force' (be it Europe, China, or the countries of the *Tiers-Monde*) could oppose the military, political, or economic initiative of the two Super-Powers, the time is definitely over when all the trumps of the international game were held by the USA or the USSR. The 'bi-polar' system has become fluid and the change began about a decade ago. The Hungarian revolution was one of the first decisive moments of that change and it can be analysed and understood only in the context of this global development. Those who see in the Hungarian uprising only a conflict between communism (inflated to super-power status), and anti-communism, miss the historical lesson of the Budapest events and understand even less of the aims of the inner-party opposition and Imre Nagy which prepared the uprising.

In the *ideological* sense, the Hungarian uprising was the last, belated revolution of the nineteenth century. In the modern *political* sense it was the first attempt to alter the position of a small country not by exploding the framework of the existing balance of power but by taking advantage of the opportunities furnished by slow transformation precisely within that system.

This *post-facto* formulation is, of course, false in that it presupposes more conscious planning and sharpsightedness in the leaders of the revolution than there was. With the necessary corrections, however, this approach will bring us closer to an understanding of the true character of the 1956 events than any superficial comparison between Warsaw and Budapest, between Imre Nagy and Gomulka, that might indicate that instead of making excessive demands which doomed their struggle in advance, the Hungarians should have followed the Polish example and compromised.

It is self-evident that a country of ten million, left to itself, could achieve a *modus vivendi* with the second greatest nuclear power in the world only by *some sort of compromise*, never by force of arms. It is another question who *should have* (and who *could have*) followed whose example in 1956? Another question—albeit academic—is whether the Poles have indeed achieved more through Gomulka's 'political realism' than the Hungarians with their 'excesses and their heroic sacrifice'? Whatever the answer, it is an indisputable fact that, able to take advantage of international currents set in motion in 1956, Rumania, and tomorrow perhaps also Czechoslovakia will achieve greater political and economic independence than either Poland or Hungary. Both the Polish 'success' and the Hungarian 'failure' were the first steps in a long process of transformation, and both can be analysed only with an eye to the international parallelograms of forces and those within the Soviet bloc.

Only when seen in this perspective do the actions of Imre Nagy become understandable. But even that is not enough, another decisive factor is missing: knowledge of the internal forces of the Hungarian uprising. Imre Nagy undoubtedly had his own ideas, his own political plan, which he intended to realize within the possibilities limited by international power relations and the Soviet Union. But he had to count with a factor which plays no role in the present striving for independence of the East European People's Democracies, as it played no part in the case of Poland: the incalculable and uncontrollable force of an armed revolution.

The era of armed revolutions in Europe is past and the world of ideals that fed the revolutions of the nineteenth century has become part of history. And where these revolutions did not materialize, their ideals are appropriated by dictatorial forces in the service of their own political interests. Modern towns and modern weapons have—as Engels said—transformed the tactics of barricade warfare. Let us add that the modern world has transformed the whole concept of the armed revolution. Freedom, democracy, independence, human rights and national sovereignty—all these mean something entirely different to the modern revolutionary from what they meant to the *sans-culottes* of the French Revolution, the heroes of the July barricades, the idealists of 1848, the socialists of the Paris Commune or even the Russian revolutionaries. The Russian October was still a socialist and democratic revolution, still a nineteenth-century revolution in which—regardless of the role and tactics of the bolsheviks—the ideas of freedom and democracy were as important as motive forces as they were in the 'classical' revolutions. Nothing makes it more obvious that this era is past in Europe, that this once mighty historical driving force is no longer able to move the masses,

than the fact that since the revolutionary wave following in the wake of
the First World War, not a single revolution of any importance has
upset the doubtful calm of the European countries, either totalitarian or
democratic—until Budapest. In the thirties Spain was the scene of a
bloody civil war but the constitutionally elected republican government
was driven to defend itself against fascist oppression. All over Europe,
counter-revolution is the attacking, aggressive, active element, and
democracy the defensive.

It is not our task here to analyse the elements of the 1956 Hungarian
revolution. Yet, speaking of Imre Nagy, it has to be stated that the
revolutionary government consisted of the representatives of the democratic parties approved, after the war, by the chairman of the Allied
Control Commission, Marshal Voroshilov, and which, in coalition with
the Communist Party, brought into being and governed the Hungarian
Republic. These parties, revived in 1956, the masses supporting them,
the students and the workers' councils constituted the main force of the
revolution. It was on them that Imre Nagy's government relied. The
democratic parties, student organization and workers' councils, gave the
revolution its programme; a programme that included, but also
supplemented, Imre Nagy's earlier programme.

The different points and variants of this programme may be found in
the abundant literature devoted to the 1956 events. Freedom of the
press, freedom of conscience, national sovereignty, political democracy,
revision of the trials and legal procedure of the preceding autocratic era.
The revolutionary 'points'—as shown by several of the books on 1956—
were almost identical with the famous twelve points formulated by the
poet Sándor Petőfi representing Hungarian youth in 1848, preserving
even the noble, nineteenth century 'patina' of the formulation.

The real question, the question interesting the historian, is not
whether the programme concerned was 'revolutionary', or, as the official
Soviet–Hungarian version will have it, 'counter-revolutionary'. The
pertinent question is how such nineteenth-century demands came to be
voiced in the middle of South-eastern Europe as late as the second half
of the twentieth century?

It is well known that Stalinism had put the clock back as regards many
of the bourgeois democratic achievements; but the Hungarian revolution demanded more than what Stalin had done away with. It fought
for freedom and democracy, that is, for ideals and institutions that had
never yet been achieved in Eastern Europe in their entirety, and which in

Western Europe had *already* lost much of the attraction and meaning they had inherited from the era of liberalism.

Thus, responsibility for the ambivalent character of Western reaction to the Hungarian revolution lies not only with the 'bi-polar world'. The decline of democratic thought in the West also plays a part in the 'sensible', criticism, the constraint, mixed with the enthusiasm and glorification voiced in connection with the Budapest events. Often it sounds as if the critics of the Hungarian revolution and Imre Nagy were asking: 'Where do these people come from; from what hazy historical past; what anachronistic ideals inspire these men who speak of national sovereignty, political democracy, civic and human rights in the Europe of the fifties and sixties? . . .

Let us reply to these questions. They came from the University class-rooms, from the factories, from the offices and editorial desks of the communist system, from the officers' corps of the people's army and the ranks, that is, not from the past, nor from the world of dreams, but from the Hungarian everyday, and thus—unless we contend that politics can alter geography—from the same European ground which supports the Western student, the Western worker, the Western office worker, journalist, peasant, soldier or prime minister. And if demands for freely functioning democratic parties and institutions, civic rights, independence and the withdrawal of foreign troops appear anachronistic and excessive, it may well be that the fault lies with the distorted views of the observer. This distorted outlook lies at the root of the mistake made by both Moscow and Washington. Both regarded as an *anti-communist* uprising a mass movement which, though it was, immediately, the rebellion of a desperate people against a decade of Stalinist absolutism, essentially reached back for its inspiration to the liberal and socialist ideas of the nineteenth century.[2]

---

[2] Let us note that the liberal character, plus socialist and democratic elements, of the main stream of the revolution by no means excludes the existence and influence of various side currents of a radical nature. Every revolution propels to the surface vile instincts and representatives of vile ideas. A revolution is not an aesthetic phenomenon. In the street, the mob is egged on to violence, in the political arena demagogues and reactionaries from the pre-capitalist era are active. Intellectually, both are equally repulsive. Yet, neither the obsolete heritage of Metternich reaction, nor the still fresh heritage of Hitlerism was able to leave its mark on the Hungarian revolution, nor was it influenced by the anti-communist currents of 'Western imperialism'. Imre Nagy and his government can be criticized or accused of much but certainly not of having abused their power—if they had any power at all apart from the ideas they represented. And

Thus we can safely say that the last revolution of the nineteenth century took place in Budapest, in 1956. And what was witnessed here, could indeed be accomplished by 'the people' alone. It was a genuine revolution that no one could have organized, neither political parties, military juntas, rabble-rousers, nor professional revolutionaries, working-class leaders, capitalist agents, foreign agents, domestic demagogues, sober speculators or fanatical illuminators. No such revolution had been witnessed by Europe since the French Revolution and 1848. Perhaps the Paris Commune and Kronstadt (1) are the two revolutions whose heritage was, by some inscrutable historical osmosis, revived in Budapest. The Russian October, though, as I mentioned above was still an authentic, a 'classical' revolution as far as the role of ideas was concerned, no longer sprang from the same source of spontaneity as those before it. The bolsheviks brought something entirely new to history: the technique of the revolution. It is to this that the Russian October owes its success. But it is also responsible for the fact that ever since the role of the political dreamers, thinkers and tribunes has been taken over by the political technicians and organizers.

The Hungarian uprising had no technicians, no organizers. Once more, for a historical moment, perhaps for the last time, poets, dreamers and thinkers prepared the social and national uprising of a people. In addition to 'untimeliness' also anachronism is an inseparable part of 1956 Budapest and of Imre Nagy himself.

★ ★ ★

Imre Nagy's ideas were not identical with the liberal and in some respects socialist programme of the revolution, but they coincided with it on many points. Three years before the revolution as president of the first East European 'reform-government' of the post-Stalin era, Imre Nagy had wanted to realize many of the demands voiced in October 1956. The reader, interested in details, can find the entire political history of this epoch in the abundant literature dealing with the Hungarian events;[3] here it is enough to point out briefly the principal

---

yet, not even the joint censorship of Stalin and Hitler could have banished chauvinistic anti-semitic and anti-communist manifestations as successfully as did the 'censorship' of the Hungarian revolution exercised by public behaviour and by nothing else.

[3] In addition to the above mentioned works: Miklós Molnár and László Nagy, *Imre Nagy: Réformateur ou Révolutionnaire?*, Geneva, 1959.

characteristics of Imre Nagy's programme. When he was appointed Prime Minister, in June 1953, Imre Nagy, Professor of Agriculture, honoured veteran of the Communist Party who had repeatedly been censored for his liberal 'deviations', hoped to realize the dream of his youth: a dictatorship for the proletariat on democratic principles, a socialist economy in which the craftsman and peasant could breathe freely; party rule without police terror, unconditional submission to Moscow without giving up Hungarian interests or the Hungarian national character. During the 'reform-era' of the Nagy government which lasted less than a year and a half, the peasants could indeed breathe more freely, police-terror abated, national feelings had more outlet and numerous new economic and administrative directives were carried out. In the eyes of the worker and peasant millions as well as of the intelligentsia the Prime Minister became identified with the promise of a better future.

Moscow gave its blessing to the programme; it had even helped to formulate it; for everything Imre Nagy envisaged seemed to remain within the framework of Khrushchev's projected reforms. Ideologically, the programme contained nothing new: every point can be justified in one or another of the Marxist classics. What Imre Nagy added to it was —apart from a few economic details—his personal prestige, his obviously sincere faith in his undertaking, and—perhaps most important of all—his determination to carry out his programme over the head of the recalcitrant party-apparatus, relying on the people and on the intelligentsia. This, however, was enough to prove his undoing at the first change of political climate—the preparation of the Warsaw Pact—to jettison the reform programme and to compel all the parties to draw their own conclusions. Moscow put the 'old Stalinist guard', that is to say, Rákosi, back in the saddle and a spirit of revolt began to mature in the disappointed masses. And, in spite of constant worry and growing peril, Imre Nagy began to work on the voluminous 'memorandum' which was published, after 1956, in many languages.(2) This book is the key to Imre Nagy's policies when, in the stormy days of the revolution, he again assumed command. This was the first time that Nagy introduced something ideologically new: it is in this memorandum that he laid the foundations of the crucial political steps of November 1956, withdrawal from the Warsaw Pact, declaration of neutrality and socialist political democracy.(3) If the formulation is somewhat cautious and sometimes hesitant, this is due to the political climate of the months when it was written (end of 1955, beginning of 1956) and the fact that the memorandum was addressed to the *party*. And if a year later, when the time came to put those ideas into practice, he wavered, that can be explained by the ingrained 'party loyalty' of a veteran communist and certain reservations concerning the revolution. Recognizing the truth and putting it into practice are two different things. Though it is a fact that in November 1956, the revolutionary masses expected Imre Nagy to carry out not a new, alien programme, but his very own, he could no longer identify himself with it; the uprising had changed the context, just as earlier Nagy himself had changed the 'tone' of the 1953 reform programme. In spite of his sympathy for the revolution and agreement with its principles, Imre Nagy failed for a long time to recognize its liberal-democratic 'nineteenth century' character. To him, as to Moscow, and in another sense also to Washington, the forest had started marching: Birnam wood was coming to Dunsinane. Nevertheless, the encounter between Hungarian national aspirations and Imre Nagy's conceptions and their brief realization constitute the end of an historical era and the beginning of a new one, even if that 'new historical era' was, for the time being, only a three-day wonder. For three days there existed the socialist democracy with a free press and free institutions dreamed of by the idealists of the nineteenth century. Revived, for a moment, were the local and workers' councils, organs of a people's power based on self-government. And for three days there existed on the map of Europe a socialist country which had declared its neutrality, had placed itself outside the Great Power system and requested the guarantee of the United Nations to safeguard its neutral status.

We have referred to the widespread view that this was precisely, the mistake, the exaggeration, the last drop that made the glass overflow, the act that led to the second Soviet intervention on 4 November. We disagree;(4) but whatever the short-term truth is, in historical terms it was through, or perhaps at the price of, these steps, that the Hungarian uprising became the harbinger of a new European order.

Let us, however, return to the genesis of Imre Nagy's policy. As we said before, Imre Nagy had put nothing ideologically new into his reform programme of 1953. It was after his fall, in the loneliness of his 'exile', that he composed the above-mentioned Memorandum, including the chapters on political democracy and national neutrality. Though he may have hesitated when, in 1956, the words became deeds and the ideas facts, it is undeniable that *ideologically* Imre Nagy accomplished in his Memorandum what, as a *politician*, he accomplished only under the pressure of events. The programme contained in the Memorandum, even though it was addressed to the party, draws the most important conclusion from the failure of the 1953 reform programme, namely, that the democratic, humanistic and national ideas it contained, are realizable only through a fundamental transformation of Soviet-Hungarian relations and Hungary's domestic affairs. Imre Nagy understood—although he may not have drawn all the conclusions—that in 1953 he had undertaken the impossible. Police terror and party dictatorship can be relaxed—as Khrushchev proved—the limits of political and intellectual freedom can be extended—again as Khrushchev proved—the drawbacks of Soviet-Hungarian relations can be improved, but within the given international and domestic political framework there can be no question of freedom or independence.

★　★　★

In other words, Imre Nagy 'overstepped' his own reform programme and thereby, though probably unaware and against his own convictions, he overstepped the limits of Khrushchev's policy of reform. Since then, and especially in the last few years, this reform policy has brought about eminently important changes both in the physiognomy of Eastern Europe and in international relations and holds further, incalculable, promises. Not without cause has world public opinion concentrated its attention for the last ten years on the internal affairs of the Soviet bloc, on the Sino-Soviet conflict, on the growth of polycentric tendencies, on the internal reforms of the Soviet system, on Polish, Rumanian and Czech political moves, and last but not least, on the aspirations of the Hungarian Kádár-regime. We are witnessing one of the most important political phenomena on a world scale of our time: the ever more sweeping transformation of the Soviet world. At the time of Imre Nagy's first reform attempts, in 1953, this process was just starting; and in 1956, on the eve of the Hungarian revolution, it was regressing rather than progressing. It can be assumed—it is too soon to draw final conclusions—that it was precisely the upheaval caused by the Hungarian revolution that gave a fresh impetus to Khrushchev's reform policy that, in turn, led to important consequences, and helped it to 'overstep' its own limits. What Imre Nagy had in mind first of all was the 'Hungarian version' of the communist reform policy. That is, it was a reform policy initiated from above, planned behind the bastions of power, and placed under the control of the party apparatus. The party issues the directives—the 'people', the workers, experts, peasants, carry out the directives, as usual; the only difference is that they obey more willingly because, contrary to Stalinist policy, their interests are also being served. This is the substance of the idea; this is what happened in 1953, and this, essentially, is what is happening today with the important modification that as the initiative is gradually taken into the hands of the experts, the entire mechanism of power is being transformed.

All this has already been analysed in greater depth by the experts of 'Sovietology', so we need not go into detail. It has to be said, however, that Imre Nagy lacked the necessary prerequisites and experience, nor did he have either the means or the time to develop reform policies in the Hungarian sector of the Soviet empire to the point subsequently reached. In 1953–54 he had no control over the party apparatus and even less so during the revolution when the party collapsed like a house of cards. This was his misfortune. It was also his fortune. Had the party apparatus—the only effective means of the *first phase* of Khrushchev's reform policies—sided with Imre Nagy, the way of the Soviet party apparatus sided, though hesitantly, with Khrushchev and Gomulka, the 1953 experiment would have turned out differently and there would probably never have been a revolution.

But the party apparatus did not side with Nagy. Only the narrow circle of his friends and champions was familiar with his new and bold ideas. History went its own way, or rather, it advanced along two roads at once. In Hungary the revolutionary fuel smouldered till it blew up in 1956 but Khrushchev's reform policy continued to ripen and with it ripened the developments which we were to witness only a few years later and which we shall witness in the future.

In October 1956, these two trends, these two waves, met; the wave of Hungarian revolutionary, democratic liberalism, and the wave of Soviet liberalization. One sprang from the past of the West, the other was a harbinger of the East's future. If the storm had not swept him away, Imre Nagy could have been the bridge between the two.

The tragic misunderstanding—of Shakespearian dimensions but in a Camusian sense of the word—began on the day of the revolution: 23 October 1956. Everyone misunderstands, misinterprets everyone else. Authority provokes the peaceful demonstrators, fires at those with whom it could come to terms. The insurgents interpret the political success of the uprising as a military victory. Imre Nagy mistrusts the masses and puts himself in the hands of those who mistrust him. The communist leaders, suspicious of Imre Nagy, misunderstand the entire situation, or, rather, fail to understand that only Imre Nagy can save what is still to be saved. The masses misunderstand, or rather, fail to understand Imre Nagy's situation. The Soviet leaders, betting on two horses, lose on both. The Soviet soldiers shoot blindly, understanding nothing. The West understands even less, it is busy fighting at Suez; it has an entirely wrong picture of Imre Nagy, and misunderstands the successes and failures, as well as the possibilities and limitations of the revolution.

Imre Nagy was the only one who, after his initial hesitations, recognized the real nature of events and attempted to reconcile, co-ordinate the two programmes, the two trends. On the Soviet side—as far as it can be judged from the available, incomplete data—Mikoyan was nearest to understanding Imre Nagy. Nagy, of course, did not stand alone: we know his advisers and followers, the former communist intellectuals and bourgeois democratic politicians, who stood by him in those crucial days. Perhaps Mikoyan was not the only Soviet leader who would have preferred an honest compromise to a dishonest 'victory', if only for the sake of the future. In the abundant literature dealing with Nikita Khrushchev's famous slips of the tongue we can find certain indications that the Soviet leaders were by no means united in their attitude to the Hungarian revolution. Mikoyan—and perhaps also Khrushchev—had different ideas on what had to be done from the 'toughs', the Stalinist diehards who, possibly at Peking's behest, obtained the decision for armed intervention in Hungary.

Whatever happened, the Soviet intervention dispelled the last illusions concerning Soviet foreign policy and ideology, and identified Imre Nagy once and for all with the epoch-making events of the Hungarian revolution. It is possible that—as many people contend—Imre Nagy was only a mediocre Gomulka. But how pitiful the Polish leader appears if we compare him to Imre Nagy! Gomulka remained what he was: a party functionary, raised in Comintern schools and their palace revolts, who took advantage of the crisis following Stalin's death and cleverly won the Polish party leadership over to his side and achieved the maximum possible in those days. But that was all there was to 'Gomulkaism'. The rest—minor reforms, innovations in foreign trade, cultural artifices, required only party clerks and specialists, no matter whether we call them Kádár, Maurer or Novotny. The great mechanism revolves, the rest is up to the 'worthy pioneer', the Shakespearian 'old mole', working in the ground.

That also is how Imre Nagy started out in the beginning: reforms initiated from above which would have borne fruit in ten or fifteen years, like the inner transformation we are witnessing in Poland, Rumania, and now even Czechoslovakia. Imre Nagy had also gone to the party school, the Comintern, the Kremlin, and the Budapest Party HQ palace revolts and intrigues, which killed off in all party leaders the ideals that had once driven them to the Communist Party. Nagy is one of the rare, very rare, exceptions. Party work was unable to kill the human being in him, party policies did not make him forget the 'idea', thirty years of being a 'professional revolutionary' had not blotted out the revolutionary. This is why Nagy's spirit could transcend the narrow circle of the so-called 'inner-party opposition': this is why in Hungary a revolutionary movement could spring from a meeting of 'liberalization from above' with popular aspirations from 'below' from historical tradition and an unfinished bourgeois revolution.

★   ★   ★

Western readers know a great deal about the period that came after Imre Nagy from the reports of journalists visiting Budapest. Hungary has remained an interesting subject. From the reports of journalists and tourists a picture has emerged that has remained unchanged for years: although the Hungarians bemoan their defeated revolution and mourn their martyrs, they are not as discontented as we might think . . . The shops have more goods, the cinemas show more Western films, the women of Budapest are pretty and well dressed, the intellectuals travel and buy motor-cars, the political police is less active in harnessing the population. Of course everything is not as should be yet, there are difficulties in agriculture, in industry, the buildings are not being restored . . . Most of the reports could just as well be written in London, in Paris or in New York. It is a waste of money sending people to Budapest. On the whole, the same is true of the political commentaries. What the many hundreds of articles published in the Western press since 1956 have to say about the Kádár regime boils down to this—*it could be worse.*

True: it could be worse. Had Kádár followed Khrushchev into oblivion, as the servants of the ancient Hungarian lords followed their masters into the grave, things *would* probably be worse in Hungary today. However, as far as basic changes and the trend of development are concerned, it could have been neither much worse or much better. Nor can fundamental changes be expected on the day when János Kádár or Gyula Kállay go into well-deserved retirement. In Hungary, as in the Soviet Union, the political atmosphere is motionless and colourless. It is the rule of relatively well-intentioned mediocrity with all the virtues of mediocrity. Only rarely are people imprisoned for their political opinions and even more infrequently executed. And if it does happen . . . everyone is deeply sorry. Writers and journalists are left in relative peace because it has been ascertained that the publication of a few ambivalent sentences causes less trouble than party intervention. They let the specialists do the job of the specialists; the peasants do the work of peasants; teachers do the work of teachers.

Is that all that remains of 1956? Is that the end product of the sacrifices and Imre Nagy's ideas? Even if it were all, it wouldn't be negligible. The fruit trees bear fruit, the teachers teach a new generation, the sculpture and paintings, novels and poems of this freer era will survive. Ten years ago, compared to the Rákosi regime, this very relative freedom, prosperity and security would have been regarded as a gigantic change. What is more important, however, the relinquishing of the priority of politics for the sake of 'better business', is gradually transforming not only the mechanism of the economy and of public administration but also the structure of society and, in the last analysis, the structure of power. Examining this process, political sociologists have come to numerous interesting conclusions,(5) but let us confine ourselves here to saying that this structural transformation observed in Hungary and the other countries of the Soviet bloc is but the result and continuation of the reform policy begun in 1953. In Hungary, the beneficial achievements of the Kádár regime spring from the reform policy linked with the name of Imre Nagy, many of whose ideas have been appropriate and developed.(6)

But this is not all that came after Imre Nagy. The ill-famed Soviet intervention of 4 November 1956, was first followed by long weeks of rear-guard fighting (of which the Western reader knows much less than he does about the more dramatic days of the revolution), then by hopeless lethargy which was only gradually dispelled by the realization that though the revolution had been defeated, the fighting and the sacrifice had not been in vain.

This writer remained in Budapest for several months after 4 November and watched developments. His last image of Hungary is not the tragic experience of a defeated revolution but the historical moment when, after the ecstasy of the revolution and the despair at its defeat, life went on—towards the everyday. The revolution was still there in people's mood, in their consciousness, but already the new system was there as well. The armed force of the revolution was broken, Imre Nagy's government was in the hands of the Soviets, the West washed its hands . . . There was nothing to prevent the 'victors' from turning 'sinful Budapest'(7) into a slaughterhouse. The number of victims was large, but there was no massacre. Kádár considered a policy of promises, procrastination and negotiation more expedient than a day of reckoning. He was inspired not merely by personal considerations but also by the great domestic and international prestige of the revolution. The Central Workers' Council, the Revolutionary Council of the Intellectuals and other bodies carried on negotiations with Kádár for several weeks; Nehru's personal representative tried to mediate; the overwhelming majority of factories, offices and editorial offices were on strike, using passive resistance to put a pressure on Kádár.

In these days of transition the captive Imre Nagy was not only a symbol but a political factor in the eyes of the nation. Nobody believed that without Nagy there was a way out. Kádár did not believe it either. In his speeches he promised that the revolutionary programme would be implemented and in the course of the negotiations there were endless variations on the theme of Imre Nagy's possible participation.

But time was on Kádár's side. As resistance crumbled, as it became more and more obvious that apart from gift parcels Hungary could count on no help from abroad, not even effective political and diplomatic support, the tone of Kádár's speeches changed.(8)

The dissolution of the Central, and subsequently, of the local workers' councils mopped up the last ineffective remnants of the revolutionary 'dual power' in Hungary. When, on 16 June 1958, the Kádár government delivered Imre Nagy into the hands of the executioner, the Prime Minister of the reform era and the revolution had long ceased to be a political opponent. He was but a symbol, the symbol of a hope and of an ideal. All that Kádár adopted from Imre Nagy's heritage was the reform policy; he destroyed Imre Nagy's greatest achievement, the *unification* of his reform policy with the revolutionary democratic popular movement, just as he destroyed Imre Nagy himself. However, neither the liquidation of what was left of the revolutionary institutions nor this insane political murder could remove the influence of Imre Nagy's ideas from history and from living reality.

★　★　★

We do not say this to comfort ourselves with the thought that 'ideals live for ever'. Ideals lose their appeal, change meaning, become obsolete. If we examine the *surface* of political and intellectual life in Hungary today, we find no cause for optimism. Who, today, dreams of the dissolution of the Warsaw Pact, of Hungarian neutrality, of constitutional guarantees of institutions of political democracy? The question is academic. It is obvious that the crucial points of Imre Nagy's revolutionary programme have been dropped from the agenda for a long time to come. Nor is the political climate any more promising. The former opposition, the so-called 'Imre Nagy circle', no longer exists. Those of its former members who remained in Hungary, have retired as far as possible from the political arena. Imre Nagy's so-called 'revisionism' cannot recruit a political movement under the present circumstances. This 'revisionism'—whether we think of Tito, Imre Nagy, Gomulka or Khrushchev himself—fulfilled its historical role when it wrote the obituary of Stalinism. It was a great task, a giant historical role, but also a limit. Beyond this limit Tito remains what he was, a far sighted politician who gave his poor little country international weight and importance; and Khrushchev remains the statesman responsible for one of the greatest changes in the history of international relations. However, what has Khrushchev's revisionism produced that was *ideologically* new after the 20th Congress? He produced a pragmatic and chaotic economic programme from which changes of major importance may still arise, but the ideological value of that programme compared with Leninism is less than the value of the latter compared with Marxism. Modern revisionism, if there is such a thing, can grow into a genuine ideology only through a complete re-appraisal of Marxism-Leninism. This historical role will not be played by Tito nor by Khrushchev, even less by the latter's half-hearted successors. Nor will it be played by Imre Nagy. Still, both as regards his ideology and his foreign policy Imre Nagy far surpassed the limits of present-day revisionism. Imre Nagy, as Prime Minister of the Revolution, was the first—and so far the only one—to push revisionist reform policies beyond their own limit.

Perhaps this was his doom. Historically, however, this was his greatest and most durable deed.

As we said above, Budapest was the scene of the last European revolution in the nineteenth century sense of the term. It may well be, however, that this was also the first twentieth-century revolution, the first real meeting of the national and democratic ideals of freedom with a new social and economic system.

Imre Nagy's historical role and his life, have come to an end. His ideological work, as we said, was too pragmatic, his career too short and fractured, his concepts too humane and schoolmasterishly intellectual, for his spiritual heritage to serve a new epoch as a point of departure under new conditions. But this heritage has its place in history.

It may be, however—let us express this doubt—that we have judged this ideological heritage from the wrong perspective. It is possible that the world of men has reached the end of all ideologies, the point where only the words of specialists, traders and organizers carry weight. It is also possible that in twenty years time the world will be much more worried about the catastrophic problem of birth control than about the principle of national sovereignty or freedom of the press. If this is so, it will be in the Soviet world also the task of cautious reformers and specialists—not of thinkers—to carry the 'revolution'—the revolution of things, not of people—through to victory. What we have written here, the way we have evaluated the past and guessed at the future, may be informed, like the Hungarian revolution by the scale of values of an obsolete world. But as long as this scale of values means something to man, Budapest and Imre Nagy's heritage will point like a signpost to the truth that man does not live by bread alone.

NOTES

(1) The revolutionary attempts organized by the Comintern 'technicians' cannot be included among the great revolutionary movements, even less the putsches of the fascist or military juntas. Nor can we analyse on the basis of European criteria the Latin-American, Asian, and more recently, African actions. In spite of the geographical distance and the lapse of time as well as the difference in circumstances, the 1921 Kronstadt uprising shows

the largest number of common features with the 'Hungarian October' apart from the Berlin and Posnan uprisings that took place immediately before the Hungarian revolution. Neither the common features, nor the historical data rendering this analogy arguable can be analysed in the framework of this study. Whatever the differences, *ideologically*, the sailors of Kronstadt, the workers of Berlin and Posnan and the Hungarian revolutionaries were, just as the anti-fascists, the participants of the same, great, historical anti-totalitarian struggle.

(2) Imre Nagy, *On Communism*, Praeger, New York.

(3) In this respect Yugoslavia played the pioneer; still, there can be no doubt concerning the originality of Imre Nagy's ideas. Belgrade's political concept was the 'non-engagement' of Yugoslavia; the neutrality envisaged by Nagy would have Hungary the same 'status', determined by Hungarian and international law, that Austria and Switzerland enjoy. His ideas on political democracy require no explanation.

(4) In the No. 4, 1962, issue of the quarterly *Review* published in Brussels we analysed in detail the factors inducing Imre Nagy to take this step, namely, the demands formulated by the people. A politician is never uninfluenced in his decision, in every system governments have to take into account the wishes of various political forces, allies, oppositions, 'pressure groups'. This is even more valid in a revolution where the power is frequently 'dual power', that is, divided between the government and the masses (in this case the armed insurgents, the workers' councils and various revolutionary councils). We have pointed out that the return of the withdrawn Soviet troops created a situation in which the declaration of neutrality was not an aggressive, anti-Soviet step but, on the contrary, a defensive step to avert an intervention that was already in full swing. We referred also to the conferences with Suslov and Mikoyan which had Imre Nagy, the responsible politician and communist, of Moscow's approval.

(5) See, among others, László Nagy's work soon to be published on the structure and evolution of the 'elite' in the communist countries.

(6) See among others, this author's article in the No. 1, 1962, issue of the quarterly *Review*.

(7) Words of Admiral Horthy, later Regent of Hungary, in 1919, at

the time of the 'white terror' that followed the short-lived Hungarian Soviet Republic.

(8) Eighteen years after the defeat of the 1848–49 Hungarian War of Independence, in 1867, Hungary came to terms with the Vienna government, regained part of her constitutional rights, and achieved increasing independence and influence in the dualist system. According to various Western historians, from the 1870s Hungarian influence—exercised in the first place through Andrássy—played a decisive role in the foreign policies of the Austro-Hungarian monarchy.

VINCENT SAVARIUS

The Ethics of Survival and the Survival of Ethics

PUBLIC MORES: INDIVIDUAL MORALITY

IT CANNOT be denied that the social and political influence of intellectuals in the countries under communist rule far exceeds their influence in the Western democracies. This is true especially for the writers and poets. It even happens that poets, as for instance Yevtushenko, give poetry readings in football stadiums filled to bursting point. Some of the Western observers are inclined to explain this phenomenon by saying that the Soviet Union and the people's democracies are to an extent *undeveloped*, '*not yet adult*', countries that honour their intellectuals as charismatic prophets and expect guidance from them as from spiritual *adults*, though, by Western standards even they are backward.

It appears more likely, however, that this phenomenon is not a symptom of *backwardness*, and even less the result of a mystical admiration of literature and literate men, but simply the product of a series of dictatorships. Everywhere and at all times dictatorships strive to prevent non-conformist social and political thought from expressing itself in *direct* social or political activity. Therefore, it had to find *indirect* ways. As László Cs. Szabó, Hungarian writer in exile, formulated it: 'The people developed the habit to live, with the better part of its soul, outside its real fatherland: in a fatherland built by literature from wishdreams, with heroic ambition, in an irresistible language.'[1]

For the last century and a half—with short breaks—Hungary has lived under more or less severe totalitarian regimes. The reading public looked to literature to express its political attitudes, even if camouflaged. They would even construe political implications into something written completely without such purpose. The result of this attitude was not merely that the public always ascribed political purpose to literature but also that the non-political scale of values inherent in literature penetrated deeply into the people's political thinking.

[1] László Cs. Szabó, *Ország és Irodalom* ('Country & Literature'), Brussels, 1963.

This is why, long before the 1956 uprising, Hungarian public opinion followed with such interest the discussion between a part of the Hungarian communist writers and the Communist Party although, at the time, the subjects discussed did not concern the population as a whole. But the rebellion of the communist writers grew into a nation-wide affair, and later into a national uprising also because even the communist leaders themselves were unable to exclude non-political standards from their political thinking.

They allowed themselves to become involved in ethical arguments with the writers, though their intention was to discuss aesthetical differences of opinion, and therefore the political battle was *a priori* lost. Their defeat was all the more unavoidable as, after the details of the Hungarian sham-trials had become public and after Khrushchev's revelations, in the secret session of the Soviet Communist Party in February 1956, concerning Stalin's atrocities, pragmatic political arguments became ineffective in the face of the writer's moral indignation. Pragmatism and moral indignation can have no common denominator. The comfortable theory that the tasks of art and the moral maxims must at all times be determined by the interests of the party, turned against itself, for the very fact of the indignation proved that in its ultimate result the machiavellian theory and practice did not serve the interests of the communists.

Thus, on the moral plane, the fight of the party leaders against the intellectuals was just as hopeless as, on the military plane, the fight of the insurgents against the Soviet tanks.

The period following the defeat of the revolution was characterized by the disillusionment of both parties: writers and government. The communist leaders lost their faith in the undefeatability of their systems and the illusion that they could count on the blind solidarity of their intellectuals, a solidarity that would always serve the momentary interests of the party without criticism or reservation. The communist intellectuals, on the other hand, lost the illusion that by a—temporary—relinquishing of their intellectual independence they could serve the advancement of their people and perhaps the political and intellectual freedom of future generations.

As time passed most of the destroyed and damaged houses were rebuilt, but, though ten years have gone by, neither party was able to restore its destroyed illusions. This emerges clearly from the cultural policies of the Communist Party, but it is evident also in the attitude of the former communist, and non-communist, intellectuals, whether they resisted or compromised with the regime. In such conditions the maximum anyone could hope to achieve was a *modus vivendi* based on mutual mistrust. For in this domain co-existence was not a political choice but a thing physically imposed.

★ ★ ★

During the period immediately following the uprising the moral indignation of the rebellious writers compelled them to stubborn resistance. Intellectuals could no longer be classified according to whether or not they had been members of the Communist Party, whether they had served it as fellow-travellers, or, hostile to it, had been silenced for many years. In those days the Hungarians said that there were four kinds of writers in the country: those who dared write; those who dared not write; those who dared not—not write; and those who dared—not to write.

Early in 1957, the writers opposing the party dared *not to write* and the ultra-conformist Muscovite group dared not yet *write*, but even the party feared that it would harm its cultural policy should it give voice exclusively to this ultra-conformist and from a literary point of view mediocre group. Still, there were also former non-party writers who did not have the courage not to write and there was also an enthusiastic horde of cub-journalists whose literary and publicistic attempts had never before appeared in print because they did not satisfy even the most modest people's democratic standards.

At the same time, centralized cultural policy made only insignificant changes in the plans of the publishing houses prepared before the revolution, at the time of the 'thaw'. The preparation and printing of a book in Hungary takes approximately one year. Therefore, had the government compelled the publishing houses to drop their plans and prepare new ones, no book would have been published in Hungary for months. However, as the party considered it necessary to create *an appearance* of movement and vitality in literary life, many authors banned during the Rákosi era and prepared for publication before the revolution (among foreign authors, Joyce, Maugham, Hemingway, etc.), were now published. By this the government wished also to show its liberalism. For the same purpose they allowed the theatres to perform plays by foreign authors and revive pre-war Hungarian hits that a few years ago were still branded 'petty-bourgeois'. During this period, characterized *politically* by a ferocious police terror intended to extirpate the 'remnants of the counter-revolution', only Russian classics were published, the theatres did not perform plays by Soviet playwrights, and very few Soviet films were shown.

At first the party attempted to win over the writers by fair means, it did not demand unconditional support but accepted their neutrality and was content if they were not hostile. The party was not strong enough yet to launch an offensive and it took some time before the cultural administrative apparatus was again functioning. What is more, Kádár's partisans and the old Stalinists were still fighting for the party's cultural-political leadership. József Révai, Hungarian representative of the Zhdanovist cultural policy, returned to Budapest from Moscow where he had taken refuge at the time of the revolution.

In the spring of 1957, however, the party felt strong enough to start a counter-offensive. Tibor Déry, Gyula Háy, Zoltán Zelk, Tibor Tardos, and other writers who had played important roles in the revolution were arrested and the Writers' Association dissolved. The majority of writers, among them the most outstanding, still dared *not to write*, but by now the members of the ultra-conformist guard *dared to write*.

To replace the Writers' Association the party appointed a Council of Literature in which the Muscovite party scribes obtained a majority. At the same time, however, negotiations were carried on with members of the Writers' Association's praesidium who were not under arrest and rumours were started in Hungary and abroad—presumably at the party's initiative—that Déry and his companions were going to be condemned to death. In the course of the negotiations one of the writers' demands was that Déry and his companions be spared, and the party's principal demand that the writers pronounce themselves in favour of the government. This is the background of the protest signed by the Hungarian writers against the 'intervention' of the UNO committee investigating the Hungarian affair.[2] Each word of the carefully formulated protest was preceded by a struggle but finally the party obtained that, accepting the Soviet attitude, the writers qualified the Hungarian uprising and the intervention of the Red Army as an 'internal affair'. It failed, however, in its attempts to get the writers to condemn their imprisoned colleagues and Imre Nagy. As it was emphasized in the official party organ *Népszabadság*, on 27 September 1957, it would have

[2] *Népszabadság*, 5 September 1957.

been a mistake to presume that signing the statement indicated a change of attitude on the part of the writers. The article confirmed Hungarian public opinion in its belief that the writers have not given in, merely compromised. But as a result, they began to publish without, however, dropping their reservations: they published exclusively non-political works.

After the imprisonment of the former communist writers, Déry and his companions, the party launched a 'socialist cultural offensive' in the beginning of 1958. The target of the offensive were mainly the populist writers. On 27 January, 1958, Kádár declared that: 'We regard the group of so-called populist writers not representatives of a literary trend but a political grouping that in one way or other resists progress.' By 'progress' one is, naturally, to understand 'party direction'. This emerges also from the speech delivered by Gyula Kállai, then cultural political chief, who declared that the aim of the 'large-scale cultural and ideological offensive' was to create the most severe party control on cultural and scientific life, in order that 'the press should not take different stands on one and the same question' but should publicize 'the opinion of the party and Marxist criticism'.

By breaking their silence for rational and understandable reasons the writers became more vulnerable. Now they were no longer classified according to who dared write or keep silent and who didn't, but according to *what* they wrote. However, the cultural offensive was not very successful in determining who should write what. The regime had to acknowledge that it could not achieve results with the administrative means applied in the Stalin and Rákosi era.

* * *

In the days immediately following the crushing of the revolution the regime began to rebuild its administrative apparatus under the protection of the Soviet army. By 1958, Khrushchev's practical thinking had gained ground in the Soviet Union, economic and political centralization began to diminish. The Hungarian communist leaders followed Khrushchev's economic policies, experts played an increasingly important part in industry, science, foreign trade. People were beginning to be awarded posts for their capabilities, not for their party loyalty. This meant that individual initiative and a certain pluralism of thought began to prevail in production. It would have been difficult to reconcile this trend with the application of Stalin's drastic methods in intellectual life and with the implementation, at any price, of Kállai's directive that 'the press should not take different stands on one and the same question'.

The system was also trying to change its 'image' in the eyes of the West, all the more so as Hungarian economy badly needed exports to the West. This was an added incentive moving the government to 'normalize' its relations with the intellectuals. It released the political prisoners and Kádár declared: hitherto our slogan was 'He who is not with us is against us', henceforth it will be, 'He who is not against us is with us'. The Hungarian Writers' Association was re-formed, the Hungarian branch of the PEN was restored. The government issued more and more passports valid for the West and allowed the writers, imprisoned after the revolution and released before their term was up, to travel.

As a result of the new economic policies a new middle stratum was developing in Hungary. The composition of this layer was more heterogeneous than Milovan Djilas's 'New Class' consisting of party functionaries. Side by side with the party officials, this new stratum in Hungary embraced also members of the 'meritocracy': scientists and specialists, export experts, and even outstanding artists and writers. This new middle stratum was in many respects amazingly similar to the middle class which, between the two world wars, supported Admiral Horthy's semi-feudal system. More than one member of the new middle stratum, factory directors, financial experts, etc., had filled important posts in the Horthy regime. Nor does the present regime prevent their children from making a career: a working-class or peasant origin is no longer a *sine qua non* of admittance to the university. Thus, the children of former middle-class parents will also have their place in the new middle stratum of the future.

This, we can safely say, structural change of society manifests itself also in the ideological field. The national ideological conference held in Budapest in the autumn of 1964 to discuss the philosophical and ideological developments of recent years, was the manifestation of a general trend, because what emerged most clearly at this conference was the characteristic feature of the Khrushchev era: practicism, that his successors show no inclination to drop. Briefly, it turned out, that ideology is really secondary because '*the facet which comes more and more to the fore*' is that it should serve the increase of production. This is how the ideological periodical of the Hungarian Communist Party words it: '. . . *the important and ever more prominent feature of the connection between the work of economic construction and ideological work is the active role played by the mental, moral and political factors in the solution of economic tasks.*'[3] Stripped of its frills this seems to mean that in their 'ideological' work party-members should strive to put the '*moral and political factors*' as well in the service of the solution of economic aims.

Orthodox Marxism would have rejected the reference to 'moral factors' as unscientific rubbish. Yet, ethics was already rehabilitated by the 23rd Congress of the Soviet Communist Party. Marx himself denied the existence of immanent moral norms. He proclaimed that each social class creates its own moral maxims, that is, that there is no general morality, only class morality. Still, in the programme of the Soviet Communist Party we read: 'Communist morality includes the principal general human moral maxims evolved by the masses in thousands of years in the struggle against social oppression and immorality'. Thus, we have here 'general moral maxims', a thousand years old, that is, immanent morality. Enumerating the basic moral principles, the programme voices a demand for 'human relationships and mutual appreciation', and 'honesty and righteousness'. In this it conflicts with Lenin's norm: that what is useful to the party is moral, and it virtually sanctions the moral indignation which, before the revolution, turned the Hungarian intellectuals against the Communist Party. Thus, in the last ten years, the question of morality has run full circle.

* * *

The now sanctioned interest in ethics has allowed articles, and debates concerning moral problems to appear in the Hungarian periodicals. One of the most popular debates began on 23 October 1965, and ended on 27 February 1966, in *Élet és Irodalom* ('Life and Literature'), organ of the Writers' Association. These short, and often colloquially informal articles show much more clearly than many abstract expositions and cautious theoretical essays carefully concealing their message in the liturgical language of Marxism, what the Hungarian intellectuals

[3] *Társadalmi Szemle*, November 1964, p.9.

think ten years after the revolution of themselves and of the society in which they live.

In its debate-opening article the weekly states that 'public opinion shows an increasing interest in the problems of morality, or, to be more exact, socialist morality. This interest is fed by many sources, not only the experiences of each individual but also the news published in the press. Among these, many are, unfortunately, negative: indifference towards other people's affairs and public affairs, irresponsibility towards old people, desertion, bullying, sexual libertinism, uninhibited material greed, corruption, desertion of the fatherland, etc., etc.'

It can safely be assumed that these objections were raised and are still raised today in any country called 'capitalist', and that most are condemned not only by 'socialist' morality but by Christian morality. This is what also Lásló Garai believes when he states that revolutionary morality seems to run the same course as bourgeois morality: men lose faith in it, its norms are rejected. '*The only important difference is*—he writes—*that the medium in which revolutionary morality loses its validity is consolidation: the revolutionary class turns itself into the ruling class, then, achieving a compromise with the overthrown class it relinquishes the "excesses" of its original aim, that is, the ambition to lay the foundations of the validity of its system of moral norms.*' A few lines later the author explains clearly and in practical terms what he sees in Hungary. '*There are symptoms*—he writes—*that seem to justify Peking's accusations and the wishes of the West. We witness the evolution of a new blend of habit and morality in which one can easily discern the "optimal" ingredient-proportions of the old proletarian morality and the old bourgeois morality: the gauge is the already hodge-podge morality of the petty-bourgeois which ensures an optimal adjustment to the existing social conditions if those are not absolutely intolerable.*'[4]

The former Prime Minister of the Rákosi regime, András Hegedüs, who works at present as a sociologist, also participated in the debate. It is noteworthy that the Prime Minister of one of the most ruthless dictatorships of Hungarian history approves of *adjustment* but condemns *conformism* without which it was difficult to survive and even more difficult to avoid imprisonment in Rákosi's days. Hegedüs differentiates between *conformity* and *conformism*. He considers *conformity* 'a necessary ability in every living being' enabling it to 'adjust to the demands of the environment in order to survive'. Conformism, according to him, is

[4] *Élet és Irodalom*, 8 January 1966.

conformity carried to excess, '*a conscious subordination of the self to real or imagined social norms which kill man's individuality, that is, all that is human in him*'. He regards development of conformity to conformism a danger threatening first of all American society though he does not deny that it threatens Hungarian society as well. There are, of course, people, who have lost '*even the minimum capacity for adjustment and this permeates their entire world, even their nervous system. A more frequent type, however, is the bureaucrat in whom not a spark of individuality is left. He has but one worry: to guess, find out or figure out to what and to whom to adjust in different, often rapidly changing situations.*' '*On the face of it* [conformism] *ensures the smooth functioning of the office, but in reality there is no more noxious poison for it kills precisely that which we need most for social progress: the creative initiative of the individual.*'[5] One could ask whether the former Premier bases his conclusions on his own experience or on the works of Mills, Fromm, Whyte and Reisman, to whom, by the way, he refers in his article.

What emerges from the two articles is that the moral indignation once felt by the Hungarian intellectuals has been replaced by an 'adjustment' of the middle stratum which even the regime itself finds suspicious. This is what is expressed in Gyula Csák's article entitled, 'How to live?' '*I know men*—he writes—*contemporaries of mine, with greying hair and incipient paunches, who lean back in their chairs, stretch out their legs under the table, and declare with cheerful irresponsibility: "My shift, friend, is over, let others open their big mouths, let others risk their skins, those who aren't fed up with it yet, those who haven't risked anything so far.*' About himself, Gyula Csák says the following: '*I must frankly admit that I have even tried to imagine myself in the place of those who have absconded abroad but I soon realized that this was no solution. Apart from my more serious objection to such a course, also because I am somewhat lazy but at the same time proud, and nowhere are conditions more favourable to these traits than at home.*' But, though he resigns himself to his situation, Csák by no means approves of everything, nor does he observe his environment with the sort of conformism condemned by Hegedüs. '*It has become obvious*—he writes—*that life is not idyllic even under socialism. We are exposed to good and bad. We must live our lives in a way to be able to stand our ground even in the face of the unexpected.*'[6] Whether by the 'unexpected' Csák means a situation in which the

---

[5] *Élet és Irodalom*, 13 November 1965.
[6] *Élet és Irodalom*, 11 December 1965.

regime attempts to re-introduce the old methods, he does not say. Nor does he say whether the 'lazy and proud', as he describes himself, would act as lazy men or proud men should the 1956 events repeat themselves in 1966?

It is probable that they would be led by a disillusioned laziness rather than by heroic quixotism. For, as the introductory article of the debate stated, people are, in general, indifferent to public affairs, they prefer to tend their little gardens.

'*Selfishness and self-centredness have grown to impressive proportions in our days,*' writes Lajos Kónya. '*More and more people have no other aim than to create a comfortable little existence for themselves, if possible, with a car. To achieve this, they forego having children (although that is no sacrifice to them) and, if there is no other way, would renounce their fatherland.*'[7] It is unlikely that Kónya's last remark should refer to the fugitives of the revolution who crossed the border to escape from the threat to their life and liberty. He probably means those members of the new middle stratum who, taking advantage of the opportunity offered by the regime to travel, failed to return because their skills ensured them a higher standard of living abroad.[8]

It seems, however, that the young generation does not consider the utilitarian aspects only, on the contrary, they oppose their indolent, comfort-loving fathers. 'It would never have occurred to the enlightened, thinking, thirty-year-olds of the 1930s to call Horthy's Hungary to account for the moral norms proclaimed by it and by the Catholic Church, but we are called to account even for those proclaimed then, and today, by the Catholic Church.' The twenty-year-olds of today feel that 'not only the obsolete moral norms of the past are tottering but also those they are supposed to follow today'. The author ascribes this to 'dual education'. '*This generation was prepared in the schools to become citizens of a society in which merit and the work done are decisive, and not "pull". At home, however, their neighbours and their families taught them that it wasn't so at all, that one made one's living the best one could, no matter how . . .*' This is the notorious "*dual education*" against which we have so often protested.' Still, the neighbours and families appear not to be totally wrong, for a few lines later, the author admits: '*The twenty-five-year-olds of today indeed often run their heads into the wall of a*

[7] *Élet és Irodalom*, 15 January 1966.

[8] According to reports that are difficult to check, 17,000 Hungarian visitors to the West failed to return home in the course of 1965.

hierarchy built of accepted authority, come up against professional jealousy ready to commit any villainy, against social inequalities, all due to the fact that in many places it is not merit that counts but pull."[9]

On 26 February 1966, the weekly *Élet és Irodalom* closed the debate, probably on order from 'above', for the editors admitted in their self-criticism, that they had *'failed to formulate with sufficient precision what the exact aim of the debate was'*, and that *'it had remained rather far removed from practical life'*. This statement is all the more significant as the authors of the articles—as it emerges from the quotations—drew, in general, practical conclusions from practical premises, although perhaps these conclusions were not of much practical use to the Communist Party. The editors reproach themselves and their contributors because *'with its scientific cumbrousness and the over-emphasizing of objective circumstances, our debate may have strengthened in many readers the already existing view that the individual is essentially helpless, that he is at the mercy of unswayable historical and social factors . . .'* In addition: *'Views of this sort provide a favourable ground for open or concealed existentialist intellectual activity.'*

In other words, the debate was stopped short not because it revealed a number of disagreeable facts but because it provided a favourable ground for existentialist intellectual activity and the existentialist philosophy conflicts with the Marxist ideology. Therefore, as Marxism is the only scientific ideology, existentialist tenets are unscientific, thus, untrue.

This attitude strikes one as the schizophrenic symptom of a false consciousness, the 'invalidation of (known) events (facts)', the 'invalidacion de lo accedido' as Honorio Delgado, outstanding South American psychiatrist, defines similar phenomena observed in mental patients.

A noteworthy example of the 'invalidation of known facts' took place at the 24–25 November 1965, plenary session of the Hungarian Writers' Association. One of the speakers was Ferenc Sánta, author of one of the most daring books of the last decade (*Húsz óra* ('Twenty Hours'), Magvető, Budapest, 1964). In his book Sánta takes his readers to a small Hungarian village where he makes both friends and enemies of the system and relates with merciless objectivity how the inhabitants of the village experienced the events of the revolution. The organ of the Writers' Association reported the author's speech as follows: ' *Ferenc Sánta confronted the principle of the writer's committedness with the*

[9] *Élet és Irodalom*, 4 December 1965.

idea of uncommitted humanism. In his view the world is carried forward by level-headed objectivity, the uncommitted passion for truth, and not committedness which may turn into a source of fanaticism.' Thus, Sánta expounded also in the Writers' Association the principles that guided him when writing his book. After several speakers had attacked Sánta, *'Imre Dobozy came back to this subject in his closing speech. Sánta has formulated here the* ars poetica *of uncommittedness*—he said—*but his works bear witness to his committedness as a writer.'*[10]

Perhaps the secretary of the Writers' Association was only trying to prevent the threatening scandal, but as a functionary he would hardly have applied the method of the 'invalidation of known facts' if this were not the accepted party practice.

A similar phenomenon was observed in the West when Roger Garaudy's theory of "non-partisan realism' showed up Picasso or Kafka as realists. Marxist aesthetics cannot afford the luxury to exclude world-famous artists from its protocol of evaluation only because they are not realists. Therefore, it prefers to invalidate the known facts and extends the category of realism to the non-realist artists. In this way, however, the category loses not only its style-historical meaning but also its later-day, somewhat obscure, ideological significance, and turns into a value judgement category that can be broadened at pleasure. The more it is broadened, the more meaningless it becomes.

The Communist Party, however, sticks rigidly to its old ideological liturgy. In its theoretical manifestations it continues to preach socialist realism, the committedness of the writer. In the practice it cannot avoid admitting existing facts but, faking consciousness, it consistently invalidates them in its theory. It accepts the idea of co-existence, for instance, only in the political and economic sense, in the domain of ideology it rejects it as a non-Marxist thought. In real life, Marxism *de facto* co-exists with other systems, though perhaps more fearfully than peacefully.

The works of Western scientists are published in Hungary in impressive editions. They are particularly keen on works on cybernetics. Thus, for instance, the volume entitled *The Classics of Cybernetics*, contains essays by Norbert Weiner, Johann von Neumann, A. M. Turing, and others. Heisenberg's book, *The Contemporary World Concept of Physics*, for instance, was a tremendous success even among the lay readers. To mention only a few more examples, they published in

[10] *Élet és Irodalom*, 4 December 1965.

Hungarian the works of André Vallon, Ronald Meck, Max von Lau, David Bohm, Hunter Schwarze and Hans von Sellye. Scientific works praised in the West are usually soon translated into Hungarian even if they contain dangerous implications, that is, implications conflicting with Marxism.

In theory, however, the party will not allow a plurality of thought even in the field of science but insists that Marxism is the only infallible scientific theory. The cause of this seemingly false consciousness lies in the fact that the system wishes to safeguard for itself the possibility to resort once more to the means of oppression should the—economically and scientifically necessary—pluralism of thought endanger its power position. For the 'most acute inner contradiction' not only of the Hungarian, but of all communist parties, to use the Marxist term, lies in the circumstance that, in the interest of economic advancement, of production, it has to grant the individual a certain amount of freedom and independence, a certain pluralism of thought, but should pluralism spread to public life it would shake the foundations of the system.

'*Marxism has lost its power to immunize*' wrote György Lukács in the Vienna monthly *Forum*. Let us add to this that the old, Soviet type Marxism, had the power to immunize only when it was supported by the secret police and the appropriate administrative apparatus. Thus, the regime maintains the fictions of Marxist ideology ten years after the revolution in order to be able—should it become necessary—to apply the 'immunizing effect of Marxism' with the help of practical administrative instruments.

In such an atmosphere one cannot rightly say that the regime which crushed the revolution has—subsequently—fulfilled a large proportion of the demands made by the revolution and that, therefore, the 1956 uprising was 'victorious in its defeat', as Claude Bourdet words it.[11] This is true only in that, as a strange paradox of history, usually the defeated revolutions are morally victorious. Only the ideals of defeated revolutions survive the heroic days of the armed uprising and the moral purity of the first days. In general, the revolutions called triumphant suffer moral defeat because the stabilization following the heroic days demand practical measures which compel the leaders to drop a large proportion of their original aims, so much so, that often posterity will even deny them the rank of revolutionaries.

The atmosphere of moral victory and practical defeat is present also

[11] *Les Temps Modernes*, March 1964. Paris.

in contemporary Hungarian literature. The young generation admires poets near to surrealism, and not the party-scribes. Professor William Juhász of Columbia University, New York, defines the characteristics of Hungarian literature as follows: 'Hungarian literature in the communist era is a literature of solitude. This is true too in Poland, where irony and satire had been more extensively developed than in Hungary. Solitude is poison, antidote, narcotic and medicine at the same time. It is a cure for totalitarian interference, a buffer against a power that strangles the soul and mind, and insurance against servility. Although the forces that precipitate this mass retreat into solitude are far less powerful than after 1956 or during the Rákosi era, the literary output of solitude increases daily . . .'[12]

This observation has not lost its validity in three years and it will obviously remain valid as long as the solitude of the poets remains the only connecting link, or rather, the only dividing line between the ever more decaying public mores and an individual morality attempting to preserve its norms. According to the Hungarian writers who have visited the West, the need for this dividing line is made evident by the differentiation the writers themselves created in defence of their moral bases: the order of merit which raises the writers above the party's scale of values and places them—or, rather, replaces them—into a real system of values. This *official* and this *secret* orders of merit are perhaps the most interesting traits of the people's democratic system in the domain of literature and the arts, because they clearly show the chasm between public mores and individual morality. It is possible to belong to both orders of merit simultaneously, for the regime cannot afford to exclude outstanding Hungarian writers known also abroad from its protocol; but the *secret* protocol expresses two factors in correlation: the artistic standard and the moral attitude. Thus, the *secret* order of merit excludes the mediocre enemy of the regime but it excludes also a gifted artist serving the system. This indivisible unity of artistic standard and moral attitude is the gold reserve of the Hungarian arts and literature and, at the same time, the guarantee of their future.

It can be said that among the Hungarian intellectuals the 1956 revolution was survived by its ideals and moral attitude. The writers, artists, intellectuals, no longer take unrealistic risks. But no matter what compromise they have to make between their ideals and everyday reality, they fulfil the first duty of all intellectuals: the duty to doubt.

[12] *East Europe*, December 1963.

Not to keep faith with some solemn pledge, but only because, after the historical and intellectual experiences of the last ten years, this is the only way in which they can live. And, because their attitude springs from the same morality, the same recognition of truth, which guided the writers and intellectuals of 1956, their future is not devoid of hope.

TAMAS ACZEL

The Mythology of Full Consciousness

IDEOLOGY AND TACTICS

Tempora mutantur? Observing the stages and forms of Hungarian ideological thinking and political tactics during the last ten years, one could clearly witness the classic process of disintegration of closed ideological systems or, at any rate, a period of conflict which, still in the framework of an autocracy, led from active political offensive to more or less passive ideological defensive; from the armed terror of 1957 to the badly composed and sometimes even openly apologetic 'ideological guidelines' of the mid-sixties. Seen from the ringside, the emergence of 'rational utilitarianism' replacing slowly the 'eschatological fanaticism', or what remained of it, could even be interpreted as a kind of 'progress' from the absolute towards the relative, from the merciless 'historical vengeance' of 1957–58 to the shaky *Treuga Dei* of 1966. Has Hungary changed, then, in the course of these years? The answer is, no doubt, in the affirmative. Yet the question remains as intriguing as ever for, without determining the context of the change, that is, the political content of the eschatological fanaticism of 1957 and the ideological content of the rational utilitarianism of the mid-sixties—always provided that we are willing to accept the term for characterizing the tactical-political line of the party—we shall be left with a map on which east and west, south and north have completely lost their meaning and the traveller will find himself unable to get his bearings. The question is, then, to what extent could the nadir of 1957 be exemplified as 'absolute' and, similarly, to what extent could the present 'peaceful co-existence' between the party and the nation, be deemed as 'relative'. *Et nos mutamur in illis?*

I hasten to add that those who interpret the period as a kind of 'evolutionary process' leading from worse to better, are, in a certain sense, right—but only if they separate ideological phenomena from political events; the strategy aimed at safeguarding the fundamental dogmatic tenets, from the tactics directed at a compromise. When and if this differentiation is accepted, the discrepancy within the process itself becomes at once clearly visible and the conflict between tactical aims and strategical goals reveals itself as one of the most characteristic, if not the most characteristic, feature of the period. Thus the proper balance between progress and stagnation, between the 'positive' and 'negative' aspects of the policy of the party, which have their roots in precisely this conflict, is re-established.

At the same time, however, concealed in this conflict, we find the two sides of a recognition. The leaders of the party realized, as early as 1957, that without political compromise power cannot be consolidated; and yet without maintaining or even strengthening ideological autocracy, it cannot be extended in full depth. The impasse is shown by the fact that while they have succeeded in consolidating their power, they have failed to extend the range of ideology; on the contrary, they have been forced, by their very policy, to take up defensive positions in the battle-field of ideology, and have had to tolerate, willy-nilly, the spread of 'class-alien' concepts which, after a time, inevitably made their effects felt in life, and in the creative activities of literature and art in particular.

★ ★ ★

I need not stress here that the revolution of 1956 meant, for the Hungarian communists, not simply the beginning of a new and, admittedly, different era, but the commencement, as it were, of history itself; a kind of geological cataclysm, in the surge of which past, present and future changed their form and substance, often beyond recognition. From November 1956, the world—that shining reflection of historical necessity—could be viewed, explained and understood, if at all, only in the light of this shadowy explosion of 'unhistorical' and, consequently, unintelligible, coincidence. For it soon became evident that the party, armed to the teeth with the objective laws of society, proved totally incapable of comprehending, let alone interpreting, the events with its own methods. The inheritor of Cartesian logic, the incarnation of rational, and what is more, dialectical thought, turned for help to the powers of darkness. From behind the barricades of various 'leftist' and 'rightist' deviations, sectarian monsters and revisionist devils would crane their necks, jeering. Instead of a scientific analysis, a demonology was born, according to which 'our external and internal enemies, preparing for *revanche*, were lying in wait and, exploiting the division within the leadership of the party, the embittered mood of the masses (mainly that of the youth) have provoked a demonstration which was immediately followed by an armed *putsch* against the people's democracy'.[1] And if someone had asked—as indeed many did—how it was possible that after years of uninhibited terror, the enemy was still lurking in practically every bush, he was told that 'under the cover of criticism directed towards the errors and illegal acts of the former leadership of the MDP—the Hungarian Worker's Party—and chiefly against those of Mátyás Rákosi and Ernő Gerő, the counter-attack of the enemy, *weakened but not annihilated*, was prepared'.[2] (My italics.) In other words, the greatest error of Rákosi and Gerő was not that they violated 'socialist legality', not that they used terror which was, anyhow, theoretically justified, but simply that they did not use enough terror to annihilate the enemy which was preparing its vengeance. Thus, the practical failure of the previous leadership to kill the *daimon* emerged as the theoretical basis of the new leadership, to justify its own fight against it. To be more exact, the strengthening of the terror was made theoretically possible by precisely those practical errors that had been solemnly condemned. The Devil to the rescue? It seemed, that with the political demonology firmly established, the time had come to work out the ideological mythology which was supposed to furnish it with the necessary foundations. For this, the country did not have to wait too long. It was, in fact, a device as old as Leninism itself.

One of the basic characteristics of Leninism is that it views 'spontaneity' and 'consciousness' as opposing categories which preclude each other. According to Rousseau, 'left to themselves, the people always desire the good, but, left to themselves, they do not always know where that good lies. The general will is always right, but the judgement guiding it is not always well informed.'[3] Rousseau, then, postulated a certain unalienable correlation between the spontaneity of the general will, which was always right, and the consciousness which was supposed to express its rightness.

The party, however, is 'the vanguard, the ideology of which is capable of formulating the basic interests of the masses with scientific exactitude and is, consequently, able to see further than the masses,

---

[1] *Társadalmi Szemle*, June 1957.
[2] Ibid.
[3] Rousseau, *Le Contrat Social*, quoted by J. L. Talmon, *The Origins of Totalitarian Democracy*, Mercury Books, No. 6, London, pp. 47–8.

and, thereby, to supervise critically the *spontaneous endeavours and aims* of the working class, and of the toiling masses in general'.[4] (Italics added.) Therefore the party is not simply the manifestation of a general will which is always right, but the 'critical supervisor' of the often erroneous—because *spontaneous*—will of the masses, the representative of 'scientific exactitude', as opposed to 'irrational spontaneity'. By counterposing categorically consciousness with spontaneity, however, the party has inevitably cut itself off from the umbilical cord of reality—whatever this may be—and thus, instead of basing its actions on scientific exactitude, has thrust itself into the stormy ocean of 'irrational spontaneity'.

As a result, an almost comic situation arose: the party interpreted the spontaneous eruption of the revolution as a consequence of the conscious preparation of the class enemy, whereas it attributed its own spontaneous reactions to the conscious efforts of the working class and its theory for the restoration and stabilization of power. Thus, 'the counter-revolutionary attack, although it erupted, in the view of many people, with surprising unexpectedness, foretold well before October what was to come with a number of statements and events'. Simultaneously however, 'the party supported by the masses loyal to the cause of socialism, and with the unselfish help of the Soviet army, was prepared to annihilate the counter-revolution and succeeded in consolidating the political and economical situation of the country'.[5] The fact that, in trying to square the circle, the ideologists concocted a mixture consisting of the mythological elements of theory and the practical elements of power revealed not only the Marxist–Leninist 'erudition' of the ruling hierarchy, but also its psychological make-up; the interplay between waning eschatological fanaticism and rising rational utilitarianism was to yield interesting results.

From the artificial antagonism of spontaneity and consciousness, there sprang, first, the 'absolute schematism' of the analysis of the situation, luckily, perhaps, the sole absolute category of the period. As the 'mystery' of the revolution could not be solved but with prefabricated schemes, the age of prefabricated schemes marched in, ceremoniously, together with, or rather preceded by, the furious vengeance of the hierarchy helped back to power by the Soviet army; fortunately however, far from unchanged.

[4] *Társadalmi Szemle,* June 1957.
[5] Ibid.

For, if this hierarchy was incapable of perceiving that the 'spontaneity' of the revolution was, essentially, the realization of the classical Leninist postulate of revolutionary situations in general, namely, the historical moment when the ruling classes are unable to govern and the oppressed classes are unwilling to live 'in the old way', yet it was capable of perceiving, in connection with the given situation, that to govern the old way was impermissible, because to live in the old way proved impossible. In that respect, it is clear that, apart from the absolute schematization of ideological analyses, even this period of 'historical vengeance' could not be considered or interpreted as absolute; it is absolute only to the extent that the *Treuga Dei* of 1966 is relative, and it is precisely in this relativeness that the most characteristic features of the period could be found both in the political and cultural spheres of the country. It is, in fact, its hope and its hopelessness at one and the same time. Accordingly, by 1966, it was evident that the political content of eschatological fanaticism was power politics, and the ideological content of rational utilitarianism was mythology.

All this, of course, did not mean that, together with an early realization of the necessity of a series of compromises, the frightful vengeance of the ruling hierarchy did not assert itself against those whom they thought, rightly or wrongly, had threatened their basic existence a few months before. In November 1956, history repeated itself almost word for word; the voices of freedom were silenced, exactly as 117 years ago, by Russian weapons, and again the same deadly silence fell upon the country. The temperature sank below zero, and this icy world was suddenly populated by demons waiting to assert their supernatural powers over the party, representing the natural powers of society. 'Our task in strengthening revolutionary vigilance and the power of the proletariat is commandingly prescribed by the fact that, although we have defeated the counter-revolution, we have yet to annihilate the remnants of the beaten ruling classes which went underground, in order to incite and influence great numbers of hooligan and *lumpen* elements and even those honest people who were deceived by counter-revolutionary demagogy . . . They are supported by Western imperialists who . . . send agents and saboteurs to our country, organize military columns from the masses that left the country, and are in touch with illegal counter-revolutionary centres in Hungary. They spread confusion by distributing leaflets and committing economic crimes. This is the reason why we have to strengthen the proletariat by increasing its severity'.[6]

The fact that this open threat did not remain merely verbal, is well known. The vengeance was cheap, cowardly and cynical; its road was lined with gallows, writers in prison, organizations banned and dissolved —the Writers' Association, for instance—millions silenced and intimidated, and lastly, there lay the corpses of Imre Nagy and his friends. However, simultaneously with this vengeance, the pendulum of 'progress' had already been set in motion by a series of compromises which led, years after, to a certain improvement of the general state of the country and its intellectual atmosphere; they led, inevitably to another conflict.

What was it all about? Primarily, that while the last years of the Rákosi era were characterized by a certain kind of political solipsism, the essence of the tactical-political conglomerate of the party, now led by Kádár was, right from the beginning, a definite attempt to escape the trap of political solipsism. This tactical line had two reasons that contradicted each other; one was the tremendous influence of the revolution itself on the life of the post-revolutionary period and atmosphere; the second, the intention of the leadership to maintain and even to strengthen its ideological autocracy, if only to curb the influence of the revolution, to minimize its effects on the developments of ideology. It soon became clear that the post-revolutionary party could not follow its predecessor on the path of political solipsism, that is, on the path of an absolute disregard of individual and social realities, for this kind of extreme 'subjectivism' was made apparently impossible both by the essentially different historical situation and by the human experiences of the leadership. Nevertheless, the party was determined to follow its predecessor in making ideological autocracy absolute, for it seemed the best way to maintain and widen its power. While then, the direct effect of historical reality had thrust the pendulum towards political compromise, the ideas and notions of the leadership on this very reality retarded its swing. In other words, the strength and effects of reality influenced the developments towards a greater political flexibility, whereas the forces of ideas operated in the direction of ideological intransigency. Political solipsism was replaced, or rather substituted, by what one might be tempted to call emotional solipsism. From these conflicting trends the main characteristic of the situation emerged.

[6] *Társadalmi Szemle*, July 1957.

Political flexibility became increasingly offensive, while ideological intransigence took up a defensive position. This is the point where it becomes clear why tactical compromises could have been born, but the emergence of a national synthesis within the framework of the system, proved—and will prove—to be impossible; in short, we are at the source of ideological disintegration.

As a result of growing political flexibility aimed at tactical compromise, literary and cultural life was beginning to show signs of change. The inflow of modern Western literature, forbidden under Rákosi for so many years, soon made its effect felt, and intellectual life in general and literature in particular, was on its way to catch up, true to its tradition, with Western trends of ideas, forms and experiments. The unthinkable of 1957 became the commonplace of 1966. The discussions of today, to take one example, are not concerned whether Beckett's *Godot* should be performed on the Hungarian stage at all,[7] but whether *Godot* represents the 'most bitter, most disillusioned bourgeois *Weltanschaung*' or whether 'the basis of its philosophical problem is erroneous' or again, whether Beckett's aim 'was to shake up the viewer with cruel, bitter and unrelenting means, to get man to recognize himself.'[8] Naturally, Beckett's name is mentioned here only to indicate a trend and a phenomenon. Instead, I could have used almost any of the well-known names of contemporary Western literature, from Kafka through Robbe-Grillet, Sarrault and Salinger, Osborne and Bellow to Dürrenmatt, Genet, and Peter Weiss. Thus, the most 'problematic works of modernism' were beginning to penetrate, almost regardless of their 'alien ideological concepts', the hunting ground of socialist realism, carefully mined not so long ago, and the battlefield was soon littered with the corpses of yesterday's heroes. The fact that these works could only have been published with suitable comments and explanations had, essentially, no bearing on the situation; the reader or viewer felt free to make his own judgement, without the help of 'ideological crutches'. It could hardly be disputed that the political flexibility aimed at tactical compromise, and based on the realization of certain historical and psychological factors, led first slowly, but later with increasing speed, to the upswing of the intellectual and literary life. Consequences followed.

[7] It may be remembered, that in the summer of 1955, a great debate was raging whether Hemingway's *Old Man* could be published at all, and its publication was, eventually, forbidden by the party.

[8] *Nagyvilág*, February 1966.

For, simultaneously with the development of literature, the basic ideological point at issue remained as rigid and inflexible as it was in 1957 or, what went with it, refusing all forms of spontaneity as being the manifestation of bourgeois ideological systems and stressing the importance of 'full consciousness' as the sole, and what is more, scientific method of creative activity, of cognition of 'reality', or 'life'.

It is, then, no coincidence that the party's demand for full consciousness, as the foundation of a new theory of knowledge, runs right through the ideological discussions of the last ten years. For this is the very last bastion which is destined to defend the ideological supremacy of the party as a whole; it is the *coincidentia oppositorum* that unites in itself a whole complex and co-ordinated set of operations to secure its ideological autocracy. Once this bastion is besieged, and the time may be nearer than we think, the fortress of ideological autocracy will collapse, leaving behind a smoky trail of frustrated functionaries who prove to be incapable of achieving their own ideological salvation. At the same time, it is the problem where the conflict between political efficiency and ideological autocracy burst forth. For, while for the party it is of vital importance to defend to the end the positions of 'full consciousness', it is also of vital importance for the writers and intellectuals to attack it, trying to gain ground for 'spontaneity' for 'subjectivity', for the notions and phenomena that lie outside the terrain of full consciousness, thus securing their individual freedom and with it, the free unhindered development of literature and art.

In 1957, that is, in the period of historical vengeance, the party's attack was straight and unambiguous. The original sin of György Lukács was that 'he placed bourgeois spontaneity over socialist consciousness', while abstract and surrealist painters have been taken to task for having 'locked themselves up in the formations of inorganic nature or in the primordial world of microscopical creatures', for 'having surrounded themselves with the hazy mist of instinct and half-consciousness' and though 'Marxism understands these trends from their class and historical roots', and what is more, 'it understands them better than the abstract and surrealist painters do themselves—who in line with the current boom—refer sometimes to the development of science and technology, and sometimes to the instincts and demons in man, in order to justify their own artistic endeavours.' Nevertheless, 'to understand everything . . . never meant for a Marxist to forgive everything. We unveil all the historical and class roots of the phenomena not because we intend to excuse their deep anti-humanism ... but because we intend to fight against them.'[9] The battle-cry of full consciousness which identified spontaneity with anti-humanism—instinct with counter-revolution—lost some of its initial impetus in the years that followed, but never its basic importance. While the process of political consolidation was on its way in 1958–60, and with it, as an inevitable result of tactical compromises, the freer development of literary ideas and forms, the attack against all manifestations of spontaneity continued with unusual vehemence, identifying now openly full consciousness with socialism, built in as an inseparable constituent of the teleological process of historical necessity: 'It is evident that from the point of view of the laws of society, asserting themselves in history, it cannot be considered indifferent to what extent people are capable of applying their activities consciously in line with the basic objective necessities. Their consciousness is functional to the economic structure of society. As long as antagonistic interest should atomize society, the organized and united action of society as such remains objectively impossible. It remains also impossible that society as a whole should recognize these laws in its own interest and use them for the development of society ... Under these circumstances these laws manifest themselves spontaneously. With the elimination of private property, however, circumstances are bound to change. The atomization of society ceases to exist and instead of antagonistic interests, there emerges society's more and more conscious and concerted actions. The laws of society act no longer as blind forces, it becomes possible to use the objective laws purposefully and consciously in the interest of society as a whole ... *Spontaneity gives way to full consciousness.*'[10] (Italics in original.)[11]

[9] *Társadalmi Szemle*, July-August 1958.

[10] *Társadalmi Szemle*, November 1960.

[11] It is interesting to note that a young generation of Marxists, to whose presence and activities in Poland and in Hungary Professor Polanyi has drawn attention in his essay *On Modern Mind*, Encounter, May 1965, see this problem in a different light. One of their representatives even goes as far as to deny the teleological process of historical necessity: 'Is history a purposeful, objectively teleological process? To this question we must answer with an unambiguous *no*. The alternatives of history are always real, but decisions other than those already decided can be taken. The development of society should not necessarily assume the one definite form as it had assumed, only it could develop in this direction as well as in other different directions.' Let us add that the above denial of teleological necessity which is in direct contradiction to the official view, was published in a *Hungarian language monthly in Yugoslavia*. Agnes Heller, Value and history, *Hid, Novi Sad*, No. 9, 1965.

No wonder that in the alpine air of a fully conscious society—all extra-conscious, half-conscious, sub-conscious motifs of the individual could only pollute the atmosphere. They could only hinder the leadership from using 'the objective laws purposefully and consciously', and the writers and intellectuals from establishing a direct relationship with reality; they become superfluous and, what is more, inimical to the interest of revolutionary progress, for 'it is proved by the tremendous achievements of science and technology, together with the growth of revolutionary movements, that man is capable of recognizing and making use of the laws of nature and society which previously asserted themselves as "blind and mysterious" forces' and, consequently, all phenomena that bear witness to the survival of these 'blind and mysterious' forces are declared illegal.

Not without impunity. For while the conflict between political flexibility and ideological intransigence was developing ever more rapidly, it became abundantly clear that the artificial antagonism between spontaneity and consciousness could not be solved either by party-semantics or by equating 'progress' with the developments of science and technology and the growth of revolutionary movements. The 'cold equations' did not work, simply because they left out of the reckoning the intricacies of human nature and its relationship to creative activities. As a result of political compromise, the 'forms of spontaneity'—to mention only a few among many: existentialism, surrealism, pessimism, biological realism, abstract art, in short, and again in party-parlance, 'the distortions of reality'—multiplied; poems, short stories and even novels were published in which the pathetic idyll of full consciousness was replaced by the story visions of an underworld, teeming with the *daimons* of the reality of the sub-conscious. For, paradoxically indeed, the development of literature and art in this particular period can be seen also as a *conscious* effort of poets and writers to reach down to the *subconscious*; to free themselves from the strangling effect of full consciousness; to create, as in the poetry of Ferenc Juhász, László Nagy, János Pilinszky, Sándor Weöres, Ágnes Nemes Nagy and others, a kind of Schoenbergian atonality or, perhaps, of a Bartokian depth of primeval unity which, by linking together ancient and modern, rational and irrational and showing, simultaneously, the indivisible structure hierarchy of spontaneity and consciousness, would later emerge and spread in a diversity which is life itself. The electrifying shock of being suddenly 'in touch' with an underworld of spontaneity, of instinct, of macrocosmic and microcosmic reality, of *universality*—with a world which was far superior to the super-world of full consciousness where, strangely enough, 'objective reality' existed only on a plane of emotional solipsism—had the effect of a revelation. So much so that, after a time, even the most party-minded young believers have begun experimenting in abstract poetry and soon we heard the slogans of the May Day celebrations proclaimed with the voice of Apollinaire and Tzara.[12] Although the *Styx* of this underworld was closely guarded by party-secretaries, the poets and writers crossed its currents without the compulsory *obolus* of obedience. One is, sometimes, tempted to think that it was not that Apollinaire of Kafka—let us use their names here again only as symbols—had a shattering impact on the writers, but rather that the writers had a shattering impact on them; for, in a world where value-judgements are mass-produced on the production-line of the party, the dead are often more sensitive than the living.

Accordingly then, while the poets were well on their way to liberate the energies of instinct, subconsciousness, extra-consciousness, thereby introducing or, rather, re-introducing a new element of individual morality and truth—as distinct from the collective immorality of power —into their own work and into the intellectual atmosphere of the country, the party, with teeth clenched, set out to launch yet another attack against the manifestations of spontaneity in general, and against the ethics of a newly-born poetry in particular. It accused the poets of having fallen into the bourgeois trap of 'subjective morality', and the moral philosophers of over-emphasizing those 'retrograde, negative moral trends' which 'by letting the evolution of new socialist morality assert itself through the forces of spontaneity' lead, inevitably, 'to confusion and pessimism', when it is more than obvious that 'from the political point of view, as well as from the ethical one, it cannot be considered indifferent whether we act in the spirit of *spontaneity* or in that of *consciousness*.'[13] (Italics in original.) This time, however, the party was on the defensive. It recognized that 'some of our writers and artists create works which move away from the ideas of socialism', and there were some 'who cannot perceive the real movement of society and the role of artistic creation in it and, seeing the mistakes and deficiencies

[12] By the fiftieth anniversary of the *Dada*—and the thirtieth anniversary of socialist realism—dadaism was, if not officially accepted, at least half-heartedly tolerated and explained away, for want of a better explanation, as a "progressive" —if bourgeois—tradition of the working-class movement.

[13] *Társadalmi Szemle*, April 1965.

of our life, fall easily into despair and come under the influence of bourgeois and petty-bourgeois ideas' and, moreover, 'there is a growing number of works which confront morality with power, individuals with society, literature with politics'. This vital recognition was, however, not followed by the battle cry of 1957. On the contrary, the party was now compelled to justify and defend its very existence, pointing out rather apologetically that 'the fashionable view, according to which we live in an "ideological vacuum" is completely untrue', and the charge that 'the policy of the party lacks foundation, and Marxism has failed to answer the great questions of our time' is nothing but the manifestation of the 'enemy' who 'sometimes even through men of good-will, succeeds in imposing on us the subjects we do not intend to discuss' and 'in such instances we are, willy-nilly, forced on to the defensive, at least temporarily'.[14] Here, the conflict between political compromise and ideological intransigency unfolds before our eyes in its entirety. As a consequence of this compromise, we have now reached a point where, on the stage Vladimir and Estragon are *Waiting for Godot*, that is, precisely those characters who incarnate that 'irrational, senseless, and grotesque world which has been deprived of all its values'[15] but, at the same time, the representatives of the official ideology continue their attack, however different in tone, against irrationalism, existentialism, modernism pessimism and spontaneity; against a world 'which flashes its pictures from the irrational zones of the human soul and thus is opposed, essentially, to the socialist world-outlook whose basic characteristic is the belief in full human consciousness'[16]; against the 'one-sided, dark, superfluous depicting of reality', the 'political content of which is distortion and objectivism, causing cynicism and pessimism, and thus trying consciously to instil its message: you see, even socialism is unable to solve our problems'.[17] *Spontaneity* which is *consciously* distorting: we find ourselves here in the *cul de sac* of emotional solipsism from which the party cannot free itself, because it would mean giving up its basic tenets and, together with them, its fundamental *raison d'être*. In this totally confused world of 'objective subjectivity' we are now made to witness, as a result of the conflict between political compromise and

---

[14] *Társadalmi Szemle*, April 1965.
[15] *Nagyvilág*, February 1966.
[16] *Kortárs*, April 1959.
[17] *Társadalmi Szemle*, April 1955.

ideological intransigence, the emergence of what one might safely call 'Marxist irrationalism' or, in other words, the mythology of full consciousness.

★ ★ ★

In April 1955, the official theoretical monthly of the party, *Social Review*, carried an article by its leading theoretician, István Szirmai, in which the Secretary of the Central Committee endeavoured to analyse the social and individual—the objective and subjective—causes of pessimism, as one of the most significant manifestations of spontaneity. According to this analysis, 'pessimism is the ideology of the disillusioned, insecure, panic-stricken man, stumbling along the blind alley of life. Its causes could be found relatively easily in societies where exploitation still exists. There, in the final analysis, pessimism is the concomitant of private ownership which, in effect, isolates man from his fellow-men and feeds the feeling of solitude. In capitalist societies where insecurity is the basic social phenomenon, the classes are affected by pessimism, practically without exception. There is only one class capable of conquering pessimism and thus showing a path for mankind as a whole, and this is the class of the proletariat.' But, then, what are the 'social and individual causes of pessimism' in a country where the proletariat is in power, private ownership is abolished and, consequently, man is no longer isolated from his fellow-men? First, it is 'the spectre of war which affects not only the masses of capitalist countries, but also certain sections of the population in socialist countries'; second, 'the great shocks of our historical development, such as, for instance, the cult of personality and the counter-revolution of 1956'; thirdly, 'our real economic and ideological problems'; and fourthly, 'naturally [*sic*] the problems experienced in individual lives, among them, above all, the housing problem'.[18] We should not attach too much importance to the phraseology; nevertheless, here the bureaucracy, which proudly views itself as the sole inheritor of rational 'mind' and 'scientific consciousness', exposes its ultimate and pathetic failure with an almost self-tormenting candour.

'As modern physics started with the Newtonian revolution,' wrote Arthur Koestler, 'so modern philosophy starts with what one might call the Cartesian Catastrophe. The catastrophe consisted in the splitting

[18] *Társadalmi Szemle*, April 1955.

up of the world into the realms of matter and mind *and* the identification of "mind" with conscious thinking.'[19] One of the extreme consequences of this 'Cartesian Catastrophe'—bordering on the comic—is, the ideological 'development' of the Hungarian Communist Party. However, the sight of the writers escaping in an ever-increasing number from the straitjacket of full consciousness is, at any rate, more than consoling. It raises our hope that the *finale* of this ear-piercing tragi-comedy might, perhaps, be nearer than we dare think.

[19] Arthur Koestler, *The Act of Creation*, The Macmillan Company, New York, p. 148.

ARTHUR KOESTLER

The Ubiquitous Presence

MY LAST visit to Hungary dates back to 1935. My memories of it have faded like old photographs and at the same time acquired the maudlin colouring which nostalgia lends to the past. But I found a record of that visit in a passage I wrote some years later in an autobiographical book.

'Within a few days I had met nearly every Hungarian writer and his retinue; for the more prominent were always followed to their cafes by a suite of wives, ex-wives, mistresses, and the wives' and mistresses' boy friends. The latter were a tribe of extremely correct, nice and well-behaved young men who felt deeply honoured by being admitted to the society of celebrated writers.

'It was a strange society, and quite different in atmosphere from literary cliques in Paris, London or Berlin. Post-war Hungary was a dwarf-state, with a population of seven million of whom the majority were semi-literate peasants. Like Austria, it lived in a permanent economic depression, punctuated by acute crises. But unlike Austria and other small countries, it had no ties, through a shared language, with the cultures of larger neighbours; the Magyars are an isolated, ethnic enclave in Europe, and their only relatives are the distant Finns. Hungarian writers could only secure a larger audience by emigrating, and learning to write in the language of their adopted country. But to abandon his native language and traditions means in most cases death to the writer, and his transformation into a nondescript, cosmopolitan journalist or literary hack. Hungary's main export since the First World War had been reporters, script-writers, film producers, magazine editors, commercial artists, actresses, and manufacturers of topical best-sellers—the international demi-monde of the arts and letters. They were strewn all over the world by that centrifugal force which is generated when an exceptional amount of talent is cooped up without means of expression in a small country.'[1]

[1] *The Invisible Writing*, Collins with Hamish Hamilton, London, 1954

This, I now realize, though partly true, was nevertheless grossly unfair. No doubt, that demi-monde exists and keeps spawning in the cafes and goulash bistros from Vienna to New York and Tokio; but this is only the conspicuous, sleazy part of the Hungarian export. Its less conspicuous, incomparably more valuable portion was absorbed in the physics, mathematics and biology departments of universities; in orchestras and string quartets, in hospitals, research laboratories and government agencies. I have before me a list of 300 names, ranging from art historians to zoologists, and from the prominent to the world-famous. I do not think there has been a migration of scholars and artists on a similar scale since the fall of Byzantium.

Part of the explanation of the phenomenon is, as I have just said, the ethnic isolation, the pronounced minority mentality of the Hungarian enclave in its Germanic and Slavonic surroundings. But there is an additional factor to be considered: a large proportion of the list before me consists of Hungarian Jews. This is only to be expected in view of the fact that one third of the pre-war population of Budapest was Jewish, and provided the bulk of the intelligentsia in that predominantly rural, semi-feudal country. *Qua* Jews, they were conscious of their precarious minority status in a small country intensively conscious of its minority status. They were a minority within a minority—a minority of the second order, so to speak. If Toynbee's theory of 'challenge and response' has any truth in it—as I believe it has—then the pressure of such an intense challenge could not fail to provoke an explosive response.

I shall not attempt to explain how the Jews in Hungary (and Austria) came to occupy this numerically disproportionate position in the intellectual and professional life of their countries: the explanation can be found in any serious book on their social history. But the causes were social, not racial. The Jews of Germany and Eastern Europe are an extremely mixed race; a substantial proportion of them is supposed to be not of semitic, but of Caucasian (Khasar) origin; and the Jews of Hungary, Poland, Russia are not only in appearance but also in the relative distribution of blood groups, more closely related to their respective host nations than to each other. A gene transmitted from ancient Canaan must by now have become a rarity.

If one compares the Hungarian emigration with others—such as the Russian emigration after the revolution, or the German anti-nazi emigration of 1933–39, one finds an important difference in motivation and structure. The 'white' Russians and the anti-nazis (again mostly

Jews) emigrated under duress during a relatively short critical period. They were pushed out of their countries by a repellent force. The Hungarian talent export on the other hand has been going on steadily for about two generations, and (except for the short burst after the defeat of the 1956 revolution) embraced a politically heterogeneous group of all persuasions who emigrated on their own initiative, without immediate duress—not so much repelled, as attracted by the larger possibilities of intellectual or material fulfilment offered by the world outside. The Russian or German emigration was a flight for survival; the Hungarian was more of a brain-drain—as England is experiencing ing it now—on a proportionately larger and intenser scale.

We can only conclude—as George Mikes would put it—that if there are intelligent beings on Mars, they almost certainly will greet each other with *kezét csókolom*; and that the mysterious red spot on the planet, discovered by Russian astronomers, is a large paprika mine.

APPENDIXES

ABBREVIATIONS

MDP:	Magyar Dolgozók Pártja (Hungarian Workers' Party)
MSzMP:	Magyar Szocialista Munkáspárt (Hungarian Socialist Workers' Party)
CC:	Central Committee of Party
CPSU:	Communist Party of the Soviet Union
KISz:	Kommunista Ifjusági Szövetség (Communist Youth League)

Bibliography of the Hungarian Revolution

COMPILED BY STEPHEN BARLAY

TEN years after the Hungarian revolution, the list of works on the subject appears to be tremendously long, even though we have not attempted to list the articles and essays published by the daily press and periodicals.

This bibliography contains 373 entries, all of which are books, pamphlets, leaflets, separate reprints and special editions of journals and magazines.

We excluded straight translations (some works were published in more than twenty languages) but included translations and later editions of a few books which were brought up to date or changed considerably in length or structure or both. From the various translations and publications of the same title, we chose the one which could be regarded as the original one. Of the bibliographies on the subject, we included only the specialized ones.

Since every single political or historical book published since 1956 deals, of course, at varying length with the Hungarian revolution, we included only those general works which were written with the purpose of exploring the background or effects of the revolution and some others which bear an obvious relevance on the subject.

S. B.

ACZEL, TAMAS and MERAY, TIBOR. *The Revolt of the Mind.* New York: Frederick A. Praeger, 1959: pp. 449.

ADLER, HANS. *Zwischen Kairo und Budapest: die Geschichte einer Verschwörnug.* Berlin: Kongress-Verlag, 1957: pp. 124.

ALBA, VICTOR. *Hungria 1956. ¿Quien vencera a Moscu?* Mexico City: B. Costa-Amic., 1957: pp. 382.

——*Las lecciones de un mes tragico. Hungria y el Cercano Oriente.* Mexico: Ediciones del Centro de Estudos Sociales, 1956: pp. 32.

Anatomy of Revolution. A Condensation of the United Nations Report on the Hungarian Uprising. Washington, DC: Public Affairs Press: 1957. Illustrated: pp. 65.

ANDERSON, ANDY. *Hungary 56.* London: A Solidarity Book, 1964. Illustrated: pp. 48.

ANNABRING, MATTHIAS. *Der Freiheitskampf in Ungarn. Ursachen, Verlauf und Auswirkungen.* Stuttgart: Verlag Unsere Post, 1957: pp. 68 (map, photographs).

APTHEKER, H. *The Truth About Hungary.* New York: Mainstream, 1957: pp. 256.

ARDREY, ROBERT. *Shadow of Heroes* (Play). London: Collins, 1958: pp. 127.

ARENDT, HANNAH. *Die ungarische Revolution und der totalitäre Imperialismus.* München: R. Piper Verlag, 1958: pp. 69.

ARNET, EDWIN, ed. *Aufstand der Freiheit: Dokumente zur Erhebung des ungarischen Volkes.* Zürich: Artemis Verlag, 1957: pp. 120 (Illustrated).

BAEHRENDTZ, NILS ERIK, ed. *Vi sag det hända; en bok om den ungerska folkresningen.* Stockholm: Raben & Sjörgen, 1957: pp. 158 (Map, illustrated).

BAIN, LESLIE B. *The Reluctant Satellites. An Eyewitness Report on East Europe and the Hungarian Revolution.* New York: Macmillan Co., 1960: pp. 233.

BAK, ISTVAN, ed. *A magyar mezögazdaság az ellenforradalom után* (Hungarian agriculture after the counter-revolution). Budapest: Kossuth, 1959: pp. 267.

BALINT, IMRE. *Hungría no muere.* Florida: Editada por Soc. San Pablo, 1956: pp. 222.

BARBER, NOEL. *A Handful of Ashes. A personal testament of the battle of Budapest.* London: A. Wingate, 1957: pp. 130.

BARATH, TIBOR. *Le cri de la Hongrie.* Montréal: Le Monde Hongrois, 1957.

BARLAY, S. and SASDY, P. *Four Black Cars.* London: Putnam, 1958: pp. 260.

BAUDY, N. *Jeunesse d'octobre. Témoins et combattants de la révolution hongroise.* Paris: La Table Ronde, 1957: pp. 447.

BECK, MARCEL. *Frei lebt wer sterben kann . . . Eine Ansprache.* Winterthur: 1957: pp. 34.

BEKE, LASZLO. *A Student's Diary, Budapest, October 16–November 1, 1956*. London: Hutchinson, 1957: pp. 125.

BELOKON, A. and TOLSTIKOV, V. *The Truth about Hungary; facts and eyewitness accounts*. Moscow: Foreign Languages Publishing House (also USSR Legation, Canada), 1957: pp. 205 (Illustrated).

BENEDEK, EUGEN. *Einige juristische Aspecte der 'Ungarischen Frage'*. Budapest: Ungarischer Juristenverband, 1957: pp. 31.

BERKESI, ANDRAS. *Októberi Vihar* (October Storm). Budapest: Zrinyi, 1958: pp. 426.

—— *Vihar után* (After the Storm). Budapest: 1959.

BIBLIOGRAPHIES

BAKO, ELEMER. 'Selected References on the Hungarian Revolution of 1956.' In Society for the Investigation of Human Ecology, Inc. New York. 'The Hungarian Revolution of October 1956' Second Seminar, 6 June, 1958, Columbia University Men's Faculty Club. New York, 1958. Bibliography pp. 90–100.

Bibliography of the Hungarian Revolution. New York: Free Europe Press, 1957: pp. 32.

Ellenforradalom Magyarországon, 1956. Budapest: Hadtröténelmi Közlemények, H 1/2 1958: pp. 299–305 (Counter-revolution in Hungary).

GOSZTONYI, VON PETER. *Die ungarische Revolution von 1956*. Frankfurt am Main: Bernard & Graefe Verlag; Sonderdruck aus Jahresbibliographie Bibliothek für Zeitgeschichte, Weltkriegsbücherei, Stuttgart: Jahrgang 35, 1963: pp. 604–633. (Books and articles; 320 entries, including translations of same titles.)

HALASZ DE BEKY, I. L. *A Bibliography of the Hungarian Revolution, 1956*. University of Toronto Press, 1963: pp. 179. (2,136 entries—428 books and pamphlets including translations of same titles, 12 motion pictures, 88 monitored broadcasts and 1,608 articles—covering the October 1956–December 1960 period. Index).

SZTARAY, ZOLTAN. *Books on the Hungarian Revolution. A Bibliography*. Brussels: Imre Nagy Institute for Political Research, 1960: pp. 14 (218 entries, including translations of same titles, and twenty bibliographies).

BIBO, ISTVAN. *A harmadik út*. London: Magyar Könyves Céh, 1960: pp. 380.

BISZKU, BELA. *A proletárdiktatura időszerü kérdései hazánkban* (The

Current Problems of the Dictatorship of the Proletariat in Hungary) Budapest: Kossuth, 1957: pp. 39.

BOLDIREV, Z. *Sturm über Europas Vormauer. Die ungarische Erhebung vom Oktober 1956 und ihr Schicksal.* Köln: 1956: pp. 55.

BOSQUET, ALAIN, ed. *Homages des poetes francais aux poetes hongrois.* Paris: Seghers, 1957 (Illustrated).

BOZSIK, V. *A nógrádi kommunisták harca az ellenforradalmárok ellen* (The Nográd Communists' struggle against the counter-revolutionaries). Budapest: Kossuth, 1957: pp. 141.

Brottet mot Undern. Stockholm: Natur och Kultur, 1956: pp. 79 (Illustrated).

BURSTEN, MARTIN A. *Escape from Fear.* Siracuse University Press, 1958: pp. 224.

Captive Hungary. An Unsolved problem of Soviet aggression. New York: Hungarian Freedom Fighters Federation, 1960: pp. 69.

Case (The) of Hungary; a Canadian viewpoint of the tragedy of that country, of the United Nations' failure and the West's responsibility as set out in editorials of the *Globe* and *Mail,* Toronto, October to December. Toronto: 1957: pp. 23 (Illustrated).

Ce qu'il faut savoir sur la Hongrie. Budapest: Revue Hongrois, 1958: pp. 66 (Illustrated).

Ce qui s'est passé en Hongrie. Comité directeur national provisoire de l'Union révolutionnaire de la jeunesse ouvrière hongroise. Budapest: Athenaeum, 1957: pp. 125.

CERVO, ROBERTO. *Canto di libertà. I poeti italiani per la martoriata Ungheria.* Antologia. Bergamo: La Nuova Italia Letterari, 1957 (Numero Speciale).

CHIESURA, G. *Non scrivete mio nome.* Torino: Editione G. Einaudi, 1957: pp. 270.

CINGOLANI, MARIO. *Per l'Ungheria libera, per una Europa unita.* Roma: Tip. La Sfera, 1956: pp. 8.

Comité des naciones en lucha contra el communismo: Hungría martir; primer aniversario de una insurreccion contra la tirania, 1956—23 octubre—1957. Montevidéo: 1957: pp. 38.

Communist Party of Great Britain: Facts on Hungary. London: 1956: pp. 7 (Illustrated).

Contribution de la révolution hongroise a la pensée socialiste. Bruxelles: Institut Imre Nagy de Sciences Politiques, 1960: pp. 160.

COSIC, D. *Sedam dana u Budimpesti.* Beograd: 1957: pp. 75.

COTTE, JEAN LOUIS. *Le sang des taureaux.* Paris: A. Michel, 1960: pp. 258.

COUR ETUDIANTE DE JUSTICE INTERNATIONALE. *L'affaire de Hongrie.* Aix-en-Provence: La Pensee Universitaire, 1957: pp. 64.

CREMER, FRITZ. *Ungarische vision 1956.* Berlin: Verlag d. Nation, 1958: Leaflet.

Crimen (El) de Hungría y los intelectuales libres. Mexico City: Asociacion Mexicana por la Libertad de la Cultura, 1956: pp. 81.

Criminal Justice in Hungary after the Revolt. In Memory of the Martyrdom of Prime Minister Imre Nagy and his Fellow-Fighters. New York: Hungarian Freedom Fighters Federation, Inc., 1959: pp. 56.

Cry Hungary. A Tribute to a Tortured People by the World's Reporters and Photographers in Aid of the Refugees. London: 1956: pp. 99 (Illustrated).

Cuba condena este crimen. Habana: 1956: One leaf.

Cuori contro cannoni. La lotta ungherese per la liberta. Roma: Tip. La Sfera: pp. 100.

CSABA, ISTVAN. *Az elsüllyesztett háború; történelem-politikai dolgozat a magyar október összefüggéseiről* (The buried war; a historico-political essay on the correlations of the Hungarian October). Salzburg: 1957: pp. 150.

CSEREI, PAL and VARGA, TIBOR. *Ködös napok* (Foggy days). Békéscsaba: Békés Megyei Lapkiadó Vállalat, 1958: pp. 98.

CSICSERY-RONAY, ISTVAN. *Költők forradalma, Antológia 1953–1956* (Poets' Revolution; an anthology 1953–1956). Washington: Occidental Press, 1957: pp. 103.

CSIZMADIA, Z. *La rivoluzione ungherese del 1956.* Roma: 1962: pp. 245.

DANER, LAJOS. *Rot-weiss-grün. Drama von der ungarischen Revolution in 3 akten.* 1957: pp. 105.

DARNOY, PAUL. *Ungarn nach dem Volksaufstand.* Köln: Berlin, 1960: pp. 196.

DAVIDSON, BASIL. *What Really Happened in Hungary.* London: U.D.C. Publication, 1957: pp. 24.

DELANEY, ROBERT FINLEY, ed. *This is Communist Hungary.* Chicago: Henry Regnery Co., 1958: pp. 260.

Democrazia (La) Cristiana, la crisi del communismo e l'insurrezione d'Ungheria. Roma: Ed. Cinque Lune, 1957: pp. 21.

DEWAR, HUGO and NORMAN, D. *Revolution and Counter-Revolution in Hungary.* London: Socialist Union of Central-Eastern Europe, 1957: pp. 96.

Documents on Hungary: speeches at UNO with appendix. London: Soviet News, 1956: pp. 71.

DOLMATOVSKIY, E. A. *V Vengrii vesnoi 1957. Goda; iz dnevnika.* Moskva: Sovetskii pisatei, 1957: pp. 97.

DONNA D'OLDENICO, GIOVANNI. *La missione di soccorso ai profughi ungheresi dalla delegazione piemontese del S.M.O.G. di Malta.* Torino: Cirie, 1956: pp. 32.

Drama de Hungría. La Revolucion Hungara. Emisiones Radiales en Hungría en orden cronologico desde el 23 de octubre hasta el 4 de noviembre. Buenos Aires: Diario Hungaro de Buenos-Aires, 1957: pp. 44 (Illustrated).

Ellenforradalmi erők a magyar októberi eseményekben (Counter-revolutionary forces in the October events in Hungary). Bratislava: Szlovák Politikai Kiadó, 1956: pp. 31.

Ellenforradalmi események a gyulai járásban (Counter-revolutionary events in the Gyula district). Gyula (Hungary): Az MSzMP Városi és Járási Végrehajtó Bizottsága, 1958: pp. 102.

Ellenforradalmi események Békés megyében (Counter-revolutionary events in Co. Békés). Gyula (Hungary): A Békés Megyei Tanács Végrehajtó Bizottsága, 1957: pp. 24.

Ellenforradalmi események Tolna megyében (Counter-revolutionary events in Co. Tolna). Budapest: Tolna Megyei Tanács, 1957: pp. 55.

Ellenforradalom (Az) a marxizmus-leninizmus fényében (The counter-revolution in the light of Marxism-Leninism). (Speeches and articles by J. Kádár and others.) Budapest: Kossuth, 1957–58: pp. 215.

Ellenforradalom a siklósi járásban (Counter-revolution in the Siklós district). Pécs (Hungary): 1957: pp. 39 (Illustrated).

Ellenforradalom (Az) Baranyában (The counter-revolution in Baranya). Pécs (Hungary): Az MSzMP Baranya Megyei Bizottságának Agit. Prop. Osztálya, 1957: pp. 95.

Ellenforradalom (Az) és tanulságai a pécsi járásban (The counter-revolution and its lessons in the Pécs district). Pécs (Hungary): MSzMP Pécsi Járási VB, 1957: pp. 23.

Ellenforradalom (Az) Komárom megyei eseményeiből (The counter-revolutionary events in Co. Komárom). Tatabánya: 1957: pp. 30.

Ellenforradalom Magyarországon, 1956 (Counter-revolution in Hungary, 1956). Budapest: Kossuth Kiadó, 1958: 2 vols.

Ellenforradalom Somogyban (Counter-revolution in Somogy). Kaposvár (Hungary): MSzMP Somogy Megyei Bizottsága, 1957: pp. 127.

Ellenforradalom (Az) Szabolcs-Szatmárban. Megyei Fehér Könyv (The counter-revolution in Szabocs-Szatmár. County White Book). Nyíregyháza (Hungary): Megyei Tanács, 1957: pp. 76 (Illustrated).

Ellenforradalom (Az) támadása a néphatalom ellen Pest megyében (The counter-revolutionary attack against the people's power in Co. Pest). Budapest: 1957: pp. 55.

Ellenforradalom (Az) támadása Győr megyében (The counter-revolutionary attack in Co. Győr). Budapest: MSzMP Győr-Sopron Megyei Párt V.B., 1958: pp. 107.

Ellenforradalom (Az) tényei Hajdu-Biharban (The facts about the counter-revolution in Co. Hajdu-Bihar). Debrecen: 1957: pp. 91.

Ellenforradalom (Az) tevékenysége Heves megyében (The activities of the counter-revolution in Co. Heves). Eger: 1957: pp. 35.

Ellenforradalom (Az) tevékenysége Zala megyében (The activities of the counter-revolution in Co. Zala). Zalaegerszeg: 1957: pp. 32.

Ellenforradalom (Az) Veszprém megyei ténykedéséről. Fehér Könyv (About the counter-revolutionary activities in Co. Veszprém White Book). Veszprém (Hungary): MSzMP Veszprém Megyei Bizottsága, 1957: pp. 47 (Illustrated).

EROSS, FERENC. *Magyar 'Munkásvezérek' Nyugaton* (Hungarian 'Labour Leaders' in the West). Budapest: Pannonia, 1961: pp. 98.

Ez történt Borsodban (This happened in Borsod). Miskolc (Hungary): 1957: pp. 175 (Illustrated).

Ez történt Vas megyében (This happened in Co. Vas). Ed. by KLARI FARKAS. Budapest: 1957: pp. 94.

Exodus (The) From Hungary. Reprint from the United Nations Review, January 1957. New York: United Nations, 1957: pp. 18.

Fakty i dokumenty: o sobytijah v Vengrii. Moskva: Gosudarstvenno Izdatelstvo Politicesko Literatury, 1957: pp. 304.

FALUDY, GYORGY, TATAR, MARIA, PALOCZI-HORVATH, GYORGY. *Tragödie eines Volkes; Ungarns Freiheitskampf durch die Jahrhunderte.* Wien: Europa-Verlag, 1957: pp. 166 (Maps, illustrated).

FARKAS, JOZSEF, ed. *Die ungarische Revolution 1956.* Rundfunk-Dokumente unter besonderer Berücksichtigung der studentischen Bewegung. Köln: Amerikanisch-Ungarischer Verlag, 1957: pp. 28 (Illustrated).

Fasti (I) del communismo. Il martirio dell'Ungheria. A cura del Comitato Civico. Napoli: Tip. G. D'Agostino, 1957: pp. 32.

Fatti (Sui) d'Ungheria. Testo del Rapporto del comitato speciale del

ONU. Roma: A cura della Presidenza del Consiglio dei Ministri, Servizio dell'Informazione, Centro di Documentazione, 1957: pp. 504.

FEJTO, FRANCOIS. *La Tragédie Hongroise, ou une Révolution socialiste anti-soviétique*. Paris: Pierre Horay, 1956: pp. 315 (Map).

FEKETE, ATTILA: *El asesinato de Hungaría*. México: Editorial Jus, 1957: pp. 174.

Felszabadult (A) Budapest 15 éve. 1945–1959 (The 15 years of liberated Budapest). Budapest: Közgazdasági és Jogi Kiadó, 1959: pp. 160 (Illustrated).

FIALA, F., *Ungarn in Ketten. Die Hintergründe der Ungarischen tragödie*. Göppingen: Württ., 1957: pp. 31.

FIORE, ILARIO. *Ultimo treno per Budapest*. Milano-Verona: Mondadori, 1957: pp. 308.

FLORIDI, U. A. *I lavoratori contro lo sfruttamento comunista nell'Europa orientale e nell'URSS*. Roma: La ciltà cattolica, 1957: pp. 87.

FLORIS, GEORGE. *Hungary Behind the Headlines*. Calcutta: New Horizon, 1959: pp. 152.

FLOYD, D. *L'Etat d'esprit en Europe orientale depuis la révolte hongroise*. Paris: Articles et Documents, No. 0434, 2 novembre 1956.

Fontosabb adatok az 1956 október-december időszakról (Selected data about the October-December quarter of 1956). Budapest: Országos Statisztikai Hivatal, 1957: pp. 81.

FOSSATI, LUIGI. *Qui Budapest!* Torino: Einaudi, 1957: pp. 158.

FREE EUROPE COMMITTEE. *Inquiry into political and social attitudes in Hungary of the Free Europe Press*. New York: Free Europe Committee, 1957: pp. 157 (Illustrated).

FREY, OSKAR. *Budapest und wir*. Schaffhausen: Verlag der Schaffhausener Nachrichten, 1957: pp. 76 (Illustrated).

Frihedskampen i Ungarn. En dokumentarisk rapport. Saernummer af Perspektiv—December 1956. Overs: fra engelsk af Merete og Per Moller. Hans Reitzel, 1956: pp. 94.

FRYER, PETER. *The Hungarian Tragedy*. London: Dennis Dobson, 1956: pp. 96.

——*Hungary and the Communist Party*. An appeal against expulsion. London: P. Fryer, 1957: pp. 48.

FULOP, GABOR. *Gondolatok az Irodalmi Ujságról* (Some thoughts about the Literary Gazette). Budapest: Zrinyi Honvéd Kiadó, 1957: pp. 96.

GELLERT, G. and Zs. *Az igéretek földje* (The Land of Promises). Budapest: Kossuth, 1958: pp. 147.

GEOFFRE, FRANCOIS DE. *Hongrie terre déchirée; je reviens de Budapest.* Paris: Editions Fleuve Noir, 1956: pp. 219 (Map, illustrated).

GEZA, DR (pseud.) (As told to Godfrey Dias). *Doctor in Revolt.* London: Muller, 1958: pp. 214.

GIOVANNINI, ALBERTO. *La Tragedia dell'Ungheria.* A cura del Centro Italiano Studi Informazioni Sociali. Roma: Ed. ITE, 1957: pp. 64.

GLEITMAN, HENRY. *Youth in Revolt.* The Failure of Communist Indoctrination in Hungary. New York: Free Europe Press, 1957: pp. 46.

GONZALEZ ABERDI, PAULINO. *Hungría, la batalla que perdio la reacción; mi visita a Budapest, tras los sucesos de octubre 1956.* Buenos Aires: Editorial Anteo, 1957: pp. 108.

GRANERI, LINO. *Rapsodia ungherese.* Roma: Edizioni Finzia, 1957.

GREAT BRITAIN, FOREIGN OFFICE. *The Hungarian Uprising;* an abridgement of the Report of the United Nations Special Committee on the Problem of Hungary. London: H.M. Stationery Office, 1957: pp. 32.

GRUNINGER, WUNIBALD. *Der Junge mit dem Siegerlorbeer.* Würzburg, Arena-Verlag, 1958: pp. 123 (Illustrated).

Guide pratique à l'usage des réfugiés hongroise et de leur famille. Paris: Impr. nationale, 1956: pp. 38.

HALASZ, PETER. *Tatárok a Széna-téren* (Tatars in Széna Square —Novel). Niagara Falls, Ontario, Canada: Rodostó Kiadó, no date: pp. 256.

HAMORI, LASZLO. *De gevaalrijke reis.* Amsterdam: Arbeiderpres, 1958: pp. 183 (Illustrated).

——*Flukten til Norge.* Oslo: Tiden, 1957: pp. 120.

Hangarii wa shinazu. Tokyo: Nippon Hangarii Kyuyenkai-Shinskeikisha, 1957: pp. 287.

Hangari. Tokyo: 1957: pp. 47.

HAVASI, T., HERCZEG, J. and KEREK, G. *A Rádió ostroma, 1956. október 23* (The siege of Broadcasting House). Budapest: 1957: pp. 95.

HAYWARD, MAX. *The ideological consequences of October 1956.* Oxford: St Anthony's College, 1957: 20 leaves.

Hazatértek tanusitják (Repatriates prove it). Budapest: Magyarok Világszövetsége, pp. 63 (Illustrated).

HELLER, ANDOR. *No more Comrades.* New York: Regnery, 1957: pp. 256.

HELMREICH, ERNST CHRISTIAN, ed. *Hungary.* New York: Praeger, 1957: pp. 466 (Illustrated).

HENRIKSEN, OLE BERNT. *Beretninger fra Ungarns frihedskamp.* Kobenhavn, Frihed og folkestyre; i kommission, Schönberg: 1956: pp. 39 (Illustrated).

HILFSKOMITEE FUR DIE OPFER DES KOMMUNISMUS. *Ungarns Jugend klagt on.* Bern: 1958: pp. 30 (Illustrated).

HINKLE, LAWRENCE E., JR., MD. *Health, Human Ecology and the Hungarian Revolution.* New York: National Association of Science Writers and the American Medical Association, 1958: pp. 9.

——*Hungarian Refugees*: Life experiences and features influencing participation in the revolution and subsequent flight. New York: 1958: pp. 8.

Hivatalos közlemények, magyar menekültek számára (Official announcements, for Hungarian refugees). Graz: 1956: pp. 5.

HOFER, W. *Die Weltpolitische Bedeutung des ungarischen Freiheitskampfes.* Zurich: St Gallen, 1958: pp. 24.

Hongrie après la contre-révolution. Budapest: Impr. universitaire, 1958: pp. 16.

Hongrie un an après la drame. Paris: Démocratic Nouvelle, 1957: pp. 63 (Illustrated).

HONTI, FRANCOIS. *Le Drame Hongrois.* Paris: Edition du Triolet, 1959: pp. 320.

HORVATH, JANOS. *Revolution for the Privilege to Tell the Truth.* Reprinted from the Comment (Manila) v.7. 3rd quarter 1958. New York: The Kossuth Foundation, Inc., 1960.

Hungarian Refugee Students and United States colleges and Universities; a progress report on the emergency programme to aid Hungarian University Students in the US October 1956–February 1957. New York: Committee on Educational Interchange Policy, 1957: pp. 13.

——New York: 1957–1958: 2 vols.

Hungarian (The) Revolution of October 1956. Second seminar of the Society for Investigation of Human Ecology, 6 June 1958. Forest Hills, NY: Columbia Univ. Men's Faculty Club, 1958: pp. 100.

Hungarian Workers' Revolution. London: Direct Action, 1956: pp. 18.

HUNGARICUS. The complete text of the 'Hungaricus' pamphlet written and disseminated secretly in Hungary in December 1956. Documents I, Brussels, Imre Nagy Institute for Political Research, 1959: Part I pp. 33—Part II pp. 21.

Hungary and Poland. Canadian Department of National Defence. Ottawa: Queen's Printer, 1956: pp. 4.

Hungary and the World. Speeches from a meeting in commemoration of the third anniversary of the Hungarian revolution. London: Hungarian Writers' Association Abroad and the Hungarian Freedom Fighters Federation, 1959: pp. 28.

Hungary's Fight for Freedom. A special report in pictures. New York: Time-Life, 1956: pp. 94.

Hungary Under Soviet Rule. A survey of developments since the Report of the United Nations Special Committee. New York: The American Friends of Captive Nations, 1957: 2 parts. pp. 60 (Map).

Hungría. Informe de la Comisión Especial de las Naciones Unidas. Collección Hombres y Problemas. Buenos Aires: Editorial Agora, 1957: pp. 493 (Maps).

Hungaría no se rinde. Buenos Aires: Diario Húngaro de Argentina, 1956: pp. 40.

Hun nieuw leven. Hongaren te Leuven. Leuven: ons Leven, 1956: pp. 15 (Illustrated).

IGAZY, JANOS (pseud.). *Aan de Rode Donau.* Bussum: Morissault, 1957: pp. 200.

ILLIK, MARTIN. *La Hongrie et sa révolution.* Bruxelles: Paix et Liberté, 1957: pp. 80 (Illustrated).

Imre Nagy. Zur politischen und rechtlichen Bedeutung seiner Ermordung. Bern: Schweizerischen Ost-Instituts, 1959: pp. 69.

Indian Attitudes Toward Egypt and Hungary. New Delhi: The Indian Institute of Public Opinion, 1957: pp. 24.

Insurrection (L') Hongroise. Question aux militants du P.C.F. L'insurrection hongroise. Paris: Socialisme ou Barbarie, 1956: pp. 48.

International Commission of Jurists. The Hague: The Hungarian Situation and the Rule of Law. *The Hague,* 1957: pp. 144 (Bibliography).

INTERNATIONAL CONFEDERATION OF FREE TRADE UNIONS (ICFTU). *Four Days of Freedom; the uprising in Hungary and the free unions of the world.* Brussels: 1957: pp. 216 (Illustrated).

——*Report on Hungary.* Brussels: 1957: pp. 24.

INTERNATIONAL RESCUE COMMITTEE. *The Sorrow and Triumph of Hungary;* Report of the Donovan Commission of the IRC to study the Hungarian refugee situation in Hungary. By William J. van den Heuvel. New York: 1957: pp. 15.

INTERNATIONAL RESEARCH ASSOCIATES. *Hungary and the 1956 Uprising;* 1,000 refugees interviewed in Austria. New York: 1957: pp. 95 (Illustrated).

INTERNATIONAL UNION OF SOCIALIST YOUTH. *Why?* The History of a Mass Revolt in Search for Freedom. Vienna: 1957: pp. 16.

JACOMETTA, GIUSEPPE. *Rose di magiari. Manibus date lilia plenis.* Sampierdarena: Gazzo, 1957: pp. 7.

JAGGI, A. *Die Erhebung der Ungarn im Spätherbst 1956 und die ungarischen Flüchtlinge in der Schweiz.* Bern: pp. 20.

JEUNESSE LIBRE. Bulletin Mensuel du Conseil de la Jeunesse Libre de l'Europe Centrale et Orientale. Numéro spécial, No. 17-18, Octobre–Novembre 1956.

JUHASZ, WILLIAM. *The Hungarian Revolution: The People's Demands.* New York: Free Europe Press, 1957: pp. 60.

——and ROTHBERG, ABRAHAM (editors). *Flashes in the Night.* A collection of stories from contemporary Hungary. New York: Random House, 1958: pp. 87.

KADAR, JANOS. *Szilárd népi hatalom: független Magyarország* (Firm popular power: independent Hungary). Budapest: Kossuth, 1959: pp. 429.

KALLAI, GYULA. *A magyarországi ellenforradalom a marxizmus-leninizmus fényében.* (The Hungarian counter-revolution in the light of Marxism-Leninism). Budapest: Kossuth, 1957: pp. 38.

KAMPIS, GYORGY, ed. *Az 1956 évi október hó 23. napját követően jogellenesen külföldre távozott személyek vagyonjogi helyzetének rendezése* (The settlement concerning the property rights of persons who left the country illegally after 23 October, 1956). Budapest: Közgazdasági és Jogi Kiadó, 1957: pp. 75.

KARDELJ, EDVARD. *La ragioni della crisi ungherese.* Firenze: Quaderni di 'Nuova Republica' Nr. 8., Tip. Tipocalcografia Classica, 1957: pp. 27.

KAROW, D. *Ungarn in Flammen.* Munich: 1957: pp. 22.

KECSKEMETI, P. *The Unexpected Revolution.* (Social Forces in the Hungarian Uprising.) Stanford, California: Stanford University Press, 1961: pp. 181.

KERSTEN, HEINZ. *Aufstand der Intellektuellen.* Wandlungen in der kommunistischen Welt; ein dokumentarischer Bericht. Stuttgart: H. Seewald, 1957: pp. 158.

Kinder der Kommunismus. Opfer der Kommunismus. Ein Teilnehmer über die ungarische Revolution. Bern: Schweizerischen Ost-Institut, pp. 57.

KIRALY, B. and KOVACS, A. F. *The Hungarian revolution of 1956.* New York: Hungarian Freedom Fighters Federation, Inc., 1960: pp. 31.

KIRALY, E. *Die Arbeitsverwaltung in Ungarn.* Aufstieg und Niedergang 1956 bis 1958. Ein Dokumentarbericht. München: 1961: pp. 111.

KIRKPATRICK, EVRON M., ed. *Years of Crisis, Communist Propaganda Activities in 1956.* New York: Macmillan: pp. 414.

KISHI, TETSUO, ed. *Shi no jussannichikan; sukui o motomeru Hangarii hoso no kiroku.* Tokio Mainichi Shimbunsha, 1957: pp. 202 (Illustrated).

KISJOKAI, ERZSEBET. *Hongarie. Land van martelaren.* Bruxelles: Magyar Ház, 1957: pp. 48.

KOLOZSVARY, GYULA. *L'acteur hongrois, héros de la Révolution d'octobre.* Impr. Monce, pp. 23.

Kommunisták a viharban (Communists in the storm). Budapest: Kossuth, 1957: pp. 158.

KOMMUNISTISCHE PARTEI OSTERREICHS. *Ungarn; Tatsachen, die zu Denken geben.* Wien: 1957: pp. 31 (Illustrated).

KONKOLY, KALMAN and ABRANYI, AUREL. *Ein Land in Flammen. Der Opfergang Ungarns.* München: Isar Verlag, 1956: pp. 159.

KOVACS, IMRE, ed. *Facts about Hungary.* New York: Hungarian Committee, 1959: pp. 315 (Tables, bibliography).

KOVACS, KAROLY. *Den ungarske tragedie.* Udsent som saernumber af tidsskriftet Centrum og Horisont. Arhus: 1957: pp. 32 (Illustrated).

KOVACS, TIBOR. *Het drama Hongarije.* Utrecht-Antwerpen: Prisma boeken—Spectrum Uitgeverij, 1957: pp. 202.

KOVRIG, B. *National Communism in Hungary.* Milwaukee, Wis.: Marquette Univ. Press, 1958: pp. 185.

——*The Rebellion of '56 Phase of Hungary's 20th-century Revolution.* Based on refugee interviews, and questionnaires, and Hungarian source materials. Milwaukee, Wis.: Market Univ., 1963.

KOVAGO, JOZSEF. *You Are All Alone.* New York: Frederick A. Praeger, 1959: pp. 295.

KRUSINSKIJ, S., MAEVSKIJ, V. and EFIMOV, M. *Cto proisoslo v Vengrii?* Reportaz. Moskva: Pravda, 1956: pp. 157.

KUZNETSOV, V. V. *Documents on Hungary.* Speeches by V. V. Kuznetsov, Deputy Foreign Minister and head of the Soviet delegation to UNO at plenary meetings of the General Assembly. London: Soviet News Booklet No. 26, December 1956: pp. 31.

La lotta eroica dell'Ungheria resta indimenticabile. Documenti e realta sulla occupazione russa in Ungheria e sulla rivolta popolare dell' autunno del 1956. Roma: Ed. Comitato Civio, 1957: pp. 64.

LASKY, Melvin J., ed. *The Hungarian Revolution*. The Story of the October Uprising as Recorded in Documents, Dispatches, Eyewitness Accounts and Worldwide Reactions. New York: F. A. Praeger, 1957: pp. 318 (Illustrated).

LEONOV, V. *The Events in Hungary*. Moscow: Foreign Languages Publishing House, 1957: pp. 49.

LETTIS, R. and MORRIS, W. E., ed. *The Hungarian Revolt, October 23–November 4, 1956*. New York: Scribner, 1961: pp. 219 (Illustrated).

LIQUE, RODOLFO N. *Menos goberno y mas libertad*. Buenos Aires: Ediciones Gure, 1957: pp. 157.

LORENZO, GIUSEPPE DE. *La saga degli Ungheri*. Napoli: Libreria Scientifica Editrice, 1957.

LOUVAIN-BUDAPEST. Publié par 'L'Ergot', organe de la Fédération wallonne des étudiants de Louvain. Louvain: Les Presses 'Arta', 1956: pp. 2.

LOVAS, MARTON, *Mi történt Budapesten Október 23.-tól November 4.ig* (What happened in Budapest between October 23 and November 4). Budapest: 1957: pp. 155 (Illustrated).

MACARTNEY, C. A. *Hungary, A Short History*. Chicago: Aldine Publishing Co., 1962: pp. 262.

MAGYAR (A) FORRADALMI MUNKAS-PARASZT KORMANY közérdekű rendeletei és nyilatkozatai. Budapest: 1956: 2 parts. (Decrees and statements by the Hungarian Revolutionary Workers-Peasants' Government.)

——*nyilatkozata a legfontosabb feladatokról, 1957. január 6* (The Government's declaration on the most important tasks). Budapest: A Magyar Népköztársaság Minisztertanácsának Tájékoztató Hivatala, 1957: pp. 9.

MAGYAR (A) NEPKOZTARSASAG MINISZTERTANACSANAK TAJEKOZTATO HIVATALA. *Ellenforradalmi erők a magyar októberi eseményekben. Fehér Könyv* (The Information Bureau of the Hungarian People's Republic's Government: Counter-revolutionary forces in the October events in Hungary. A White Book). Budapest; 1957–58. Vol. I, pp. 62—Vol. II, pp. 157—Vol. III, pp. 140—Vol. IV, pp. 136 —and

——Vol. V: *Nagy Imre és bűntársai ellenforradalmi összeesküvése* (Counter-revolutionary conspiration of Imre Nagy and his accomplices). Budapest: 1958: pp. 159.

MAGYAR (A) SZOCIALISTA MUNKASPART *Ideiglenes Központi Bizottságá-*

nak határozata (The decision of the Provisional Central Committee of the Hungarian Socialist Workers' Party). Budapest: 1956: pp. 11.

——*A párt vezető szerepének megerősitéséért; az 1957. február 26.-i ülés határozatai* (For the strengthening of the party's leading role). Budapest: Kossuth, 1957: pp. 23.

MAKAI, GYORGY. *'Itt a Szabad Európa Rádió* (This is Radio Free Europe). Budapest: Kossuth, 1957: pp. 47 (Illustrated).

MALFATTO, FRANCO MARIA. *La crisi del comunismo e la rivolta in Ungheria.* Roma: Ed. Cinque Lune, 1956: pp. 227.

MANUEL, F. *La Révolution hongroise des conseils ouvriers.* Paris: 'Pour la vérité', 1956: pp. 68.

MAROSAN, GYORGY. *A párt és a tömegek kapcsolatának néhány kérdése* (A few questions of the party's relationship with the masses). Budapest: Kossuth, 1957: pp. 47.

MAZOV, V., PULJACH, A. and SIMAKIN, M. *O sobytijach v Vengrii.* Moskva: 1957: pp. 102.

MECKERS, MICHAEL. *Húngria in sangre.* Buenos Aires.

MECSERI, N. *A dunántúli laktanyából az ungvári börtönbe. Egy szabad fëldre szökött magyar katona a szovjet deportációkról* (From the Transdanubian barracks to the jail at Ungvár. A Hungarian refugee soldier about the Soviet deportations). München: Amerikai Magyar Kiadó, 1958: pp. 49.

MERAY, TIBOR. *Thirteen Days That Shook the Kremlin.* New York: F. A. Praeger, 1959: pp. 290.

MESZAROS, ISTVAN. *La rivolta degli intellettuali in Ungheria.* Torino: Einaudi, 1958: pp. 213.

MICHENER, JAMES ALBERT. *The Bridge at Andau.* New York: Random House, 1957: pp. 270.

MIKES, GEORGE. *The Hungarian Revolution.* London: A. Deutsch, 1957: pp. 192 (Illustrated).

——*A Study in Infamy.* London: A. Deutsch, 1959: pp. 175.

MILLOK, EVA. *A névtelen tiszt* (The anonymous officer). Budapest: Móra Ferenc Kiadó, 1958: pp. 59 (Illustrated).

Mindenkinek . . .! Harc a munkáshatalomért—1956 november–1957 május (To everybody . . .! Struggle for the power of the workers). (On events in the Kisalföld.) Győr (Hungary): MSzMP Győr-Sopron Megyei Intéző Bizottság, 1957: pp. 80.

MINDSZENTY, JOSEPH, Cardinal. *'. . . The world's most orphaned nation'*

(Excerpts from his speeches, letters and private writings.) New York: The Book Mailer, Inc., 1962: pp. 111.

——*Mindszenty breviarium*. Detroit: Amerikai Magyar Kiadó, 1958: pp. 30.

MISHRA, ANAND. *Eastern European Crisis of Stalinism*. Calcutta: 1957.

MOLNAR, E. G. *Tagebuch in der Aktentasche*. Wien: Ars Hungarica, 1958: pp. 182.

MOLNAR, MIKLOS and NAGY, LASZLO. *Imre Nagy, Réformateur ou Révolutionnaire?* Genève: Publications de Hautes Etudes Internationales, No. 33, 1959: pp. 256.

MONDADORI, ALBERTO. *Canto d'ira e d'amore per l'Ungheria*. Verona: Ed. di Camaiore, 1959: pp. 114.

Murder (The) of an Idea. The execution of Imre Nagy. New York: Intercontinental Press Service, 1958: pp. 10.

MUNNICH, FERENC. *A magyar nép a Nagy Októberi Szocialista Forradalom utján* (The Hungarian people on the road of the Great October Socialist Revolution). Budapest: Kossuth, 1957: pp. 39.

NADANYI, P. *The Revolt that Rocked the Kremlin*. Washington: Hungarian Reformed Federation of America, 1963.

NAGY, B. *Journal d'un insurgé hongrois*. Paris: Edition de la Pensée Moderne, 1956: pp. 221.

NAGY, BELA. *Watashi mo ju o totta*. Tokio: Heibon-sha, 1957: pp. 254.

NAGY, IMRE. *On Communism*. New York: F. A. Praeger, 1957: pp. 306.

NEMES, JOSEPH. *Signs in the Storm*. London: Hodder & Stoughton, 1956: pp. 189.

Non, nous ne nous tairons pas. Bern: Comité d'Aide suisse aux victimes du communisme, 1958: pp. 112 (Illustrated).

Nueva Victima de la Bestia Roja. Mexico: Ediciones de la Union Civica Internacional, 1957: pp. 126.

Origini e sviluppi dei moti d'Ungheria. Caraterre popolare della rivolta e suoi fini sociali e democratici nella documentazione ufficiale. Cronologia della rivoluzione. Roma: Solidarietà del PCI con le repressioni, 1957: pp. 131.

OTTA, I. *Miért tartózkodnak szovjet csapatok Magyarországon* (Why there are Soviet troops stationed in Hungary). Budapest: Kossuth, 1958: pp. 77.

OVSYANNIKOVA, M. *Glazami starogo druga. Vengerskie zapiski*. Moskva: 1957: pp. 92.

PAAL, G. *Hungarian Revolution and the Hungarian People's Army*. New York: Free Europe Press, 1957: pp. 40.

Pakistan and Hungary. Calcutta: Bulletin of the Pakistan Committee for Cultural Freedom, 1957: pp. 40.

PALOCZI-HORVATH, GYORGY. *The Undefeated*. Boston: Atlantic-Little, Brown, 1959: pp. 305.

——ed.: *One Sentence on Tyranny*. Hungarian Literary Gazette. Anthology. London: Waverley Press, 1957: pp. 110.

——*Elveszett nemzedék* (Lost generation). London: Big Ben, 1958: pp. 165.

PARTI COMMUNISTE FRANCAIS. *Vérités sur la Hongrie*. Paris: 1956.

Partis (Les) communistes occidentaux et les événements de Hongrie. Paris: Articles et Documents No. 0431, 13 Novembre 1956.

PATAKI, LASZLO and DERI, ERNO. *Az ellenforradalom Miskolcon* (The counter-revolution in Miskolc). Budapest: 1957: pp. 69.

PEDERSEN, POUL. *Trier. Ungarns frihedskamp; med et kort rids of Ungarns historie ved Poul Holt*. Kobenhavn: Samlelrens forlag, 1956: pp. 155 (Illustrated).

Peuple (Le) hongrois contre communisme. Paris: Est et Ouest, Numéro spécial, 16–31 Octobre 1957: pp. 144.

PFEIFFER, E. *Child of Communism*. London: Weidenfeld and Nicolson, 1958: pp. 239.

PHILIP, F. X. *So berichtete ADN Berlin über Ungarn*. Dokumentation. Köln: Greven & Brechthold, 1956: pp. 98.

PISTOLESE, F. *Ungheria 1956–1958*. Roma: Editori Riuniti, 1958: pp. 208.

PLATTHY, JENO. *Hungary Never Dies* (In Japanese). Tokyo: 1957: pp. 285.

POGANY, GEZA and MOLDEN, F. *Ungarns Freiheitskampf*. Wien: L.V.W., 1957: pp. 127.

POLGAR, D. *A szuezi háború és Magyarország* (The Suez War and Hungary). Budapest: Kossuth, 1957: pp. 31.

PONGRACZ-JACOBI. *Piger i Ungarn*. Kobenhavn: Frederick E. Pedersen, 1957: pp. 78.

Pourquoi et comment se bat la Hongrie ouvrière. Des faits, des documents, des chiffres. Paris: Union des Syndicalistes, 1957: pp. 32.

PRIESTER, E. *Was war in Ungarn wirklich los?* Berlin: Dietz Verlag, 1957: pp. 124.

Problem (The) of Hungary. New Delhi: A Praja Socialist Publication, 1957: pp. 68.

Problem (The) of Hungary, conclusions from the report of the Special Committee. Canadian Department of External Affairs, Ottawa: Queen's Printer, 1957: pp. 5.

Protestation yougoslave auprès du gouvernement hongrois au sujet de la disparition de Nagy. Paris: Articles et Documents, No. 0437, 27 novembre 1956.

PUCHINGER, G. *Hongarije's opstand en Nederlandse Universiteit*. Utrecht: H. de Vroede, 1957: pp. 12.

RAMON, CUE ROMANO S. J. *Sangre de Hungría*. La Coruña: Santiago de Comportela, 1957: pp. 60.

Rapport sur la Hongrie par la délégation de la Fédération Syndicale Mondiale. London: W.F.T.U. Publications Ltd., N.D.: pp. 56.

Rapport sur la visite fait en Hongrie par une délégation de mineurs écossais. Budapest: Fédération de mineurs de Hongrie, Athenaeum, 1957: pp. 31.

RED CROSS INTERNATIONAL COMMITTEE. *Report on the relief action in Hungary, October 1956 to June 1957*. Geneva: 1957: pp. 58 (Illustrated).

Refusal of a Compromise. Document Concerning the Indian Attempts to Mediate in Hungary, December 1956. Bern: Schweizerischen Ost-Institut: pp. 12.

REINHARD, MARGUERITE. *Die Ungarnhilfe des Roten Kreuzes*. Zürich: 1958: pp. 87 (Illustrated).

RENYI, P. *'Szabad Földről' üzenik* ... (Messages from the 'Free World'). Budapest: 1957: pp. 156.

Report of the Lord Mayor of London's National Hungarian and Central European Relief Fund, November 1956–September 1958. London: 1959: pp. 83 (Illustrated).

REVESZ, GY. ISTVAN. *Idegen pénz, magyar vér* (Foreign money, Hungarian blood). Budapest: Kossuth, 1957: pp. 47.

Revolt (The) in Hungary: a documentary chronology of events based exclusively on internal broadcasts by central and provincial radios, 23 October–4 November 1956. New York: Free Europe Committee, 1956: pp. 112 (Illustrated).

Révolte (La) du peuple hongrois. Lausanne: Edition de l'Aide suisse aux victimes du communisme, 1957: pp. 120.

Révolte (La) de la Hongrie. Paris: Les Temps Modernes, Numéro spécial, 129–130–131, novembre décembre 1956, janvier 1957.

Revolución (La) Popular Hungara. Hechos y documentos. Buenos Aires: Editorial Reconstruir, Collección Radar, 1957: pp. 95.

Révolution (La) hongroise vue par les partis communistes de l'Europe de l'Est. Présentation quotidienne par les organes officiels (23 octobre–15 novembre 1956). Paris: Centre d'études avancées du Collège de l'Europe libre, 1957: pp. 317.

RITGEN, HERMANN. *Einsatz Budapest.* Tagebuch-Blätter aus dem November 1956 vom Einsatz des DRK-Hilfszuges in Ungarn. Bonn: Deutschen Roten Kreuzes, 1956: pp. 44 (Illustrated).

ROCSKAR, JANOS, ed. *Tótkomlósi ellenforradalom* (Counter-revolution in Tótkomlós). Békéscsaba (Hungary): Az MSzMP Tótkomlósi Bizottsága és a Tótkomlósi Községi Tanács, 1957: pp. 24.

Rodt er blodet i Pest's gader; seks digte. Kobenhavn: Komitéen for frisindet kulturkamp, 1956: pp. 22.

ROMAN, ERIC. *The Best Shall Die.* Englewood Cliffs, NJ: Prentice Hall, 1961: pp. 251.

ROSSOVA, A. *Vid'eli jsma kontarrevoluci v. Mad'arsku.* Prague: 1956: pp. 45 (Illustrated).

ROSTBOLL, E. *Ungarske Vidnes byrd. Rejse til Budapest November 1956.* Oslo: Gyldendal, 1957: pp. 109.

RUBINOS, JOSE. *Seleccion de cien artículos y ensayos cortos.* La Habana: Impr. Ucar, Garcia, 1957: pp. 300.

RUFF, LUDWIG. *La Machine à Laver Les Cervaux.* Paris: Fasquelle Editeurs, 1958: pp. 174.

SAGER, PETER, ed. *Ungarns Freiheitskampf. Betrachtungen aus der Distanz eines Jahres.* Bern: 1957: pp. 32.

SANDERSON, JAMES DEAN. *Boy with a gun.* New York: Henry Holt & Co., 1958: pp. 277.

SAVELIN, Z. *Zagovory—oruzhie reaktsii.* Moskva: Gos. izd-vo polit. lit-ry, 1956: pp. 39.

SCARLETT, DORA. *Window onto Hungary.* Bradford: Broadacre Books Ltd., 1958: pp. 336.

SCHNEIDER-HENN, DIETRICH. *Griff nach der Freiheit.* Frankfurt-am-Main: Europäische Verlagsanstalt, 1956: pp. 83.

SCHRAMM, W. L., ed. *One day in the world's press.* Stanford, California: Stanford Univ. Press, 1959: pp. 138 (Illustrated).

SCHUSTER, G. N. *In Silence I Speak.* New York: Farrar, Straus & Cudahy, 1956: pp. 296.

SCHWEIZERISCHES OST-INSTITUT. *Imre Nagy. Zur politischen und rechtlichen Bedeutung seiner Ermordung.* Bern: 1959: pp. 69.

SEBESTYEN, GYORGY. *The Doors Are Closing*. London: Angus & Robertson, 1958: pp. 254.

SEDOUY, ALAIN DE. *Indomptable Hongrie*. Paris: Edition les Quatre Fils Aymon, 1956: pp. 182.

SETON-WATSON, HUGH. *The East European Revolution*. London: Methuen, 1956: pp. 435.

SETTERLIND, BO. *Mot valdet. Svenska dikter publicerade med andledning av Ungern-revolten 1956*. I urval av B. Setterlind, Stockholm: 1956: pp. 37.

SEYMOUR, ALTA HALVERSON. *Toward Morning*. Chicago: Follet Publ. Co., 1961: pp. 144.

SIEGLER, HEINRICH VON. *Die Ereignisse in Polen und Ungarn*. Bonn: Siegler, 1957: pp. 93 (Illustrated).

SINOR, DENNIS. *History of Hungary*. London: George Allen & Unwin, 1959: pp. 310.

SOLYOM, J. *Széna téri banditák* (Széna Square Bandits). Budapest: Kossuth, 1958: pp. 94.

——and ZELE, F. *Harcban az ellenforradalommal* (Fighting against the counter-revolution). Budapest: Móra Ferenc kiadó, 1957: pp. 161.

Sonderpostmarke zugunsten der Hilfsaktion der österreichischen Bundesregierung für ungarische Flüchtlinge. Wien: Osterreichische Staatsdruckerei, 1956 (Leaflet).

STIBI, GEORG. *Ich erlebte in Ungarn; Hintergründe und Ziele des konterrevolutionären Aufstandes*. East Berlin: Kongress Verlag, 1957: pp. 63.

STIL, ANDRE. *Je reviens de Budapest*. Paris: Maison des Métallurgistes, 1957.

STILLMAN, EDMUND, ed. *Bitter Harvest*. New York: F. A. Praeger, 1959: pp. 313.

——*The ideology of revolution: the people's demands in Hungary, October–November 1956*. New York: Free Europe Press, 1957: pp. 37 (Illustrated).

STRASSER, PETER, ed. *Ein Atemzug Freiheit. Volksaufstand und konterrevolution in Ungarn*. Bericht der Sonderkommission der Vereinten Nationen. Wien: Verlag der Wiener Volksbuchhandlung, 1957: pp. 96.

Szabadságharc (A) követelései, 1956 (The Demands of the Revolution, 1956). New York: Free Europe Press,: pp. 60.

SZABO, MIKLOS. *Foglalkozásuk emigráns* (Professional Emigrés). Budapest: Pannonia, 1959: pp. 331.

——*Hontalanok* (The Stateless). Budapest: Kossuth, 1960: pp. 191 (Illustrated).

——*Je rentre dans mon pays. Mémoires d'un émigré désabusé*. Budapest: Kossuth, 1957: pp. 40.

——*A strassburgi Magyar Forradalmi Tanács tagje voltam. Onvallomás* (I was a member of the Strassbourg Hungarian Revolutionary Council. A confession). Budapest: Kossuth, 1957: pp. 31.

SZABO, TAMAS. *Boy on the Rooftop*. Boston-Toronto: Little, Brown & Co., 1958: pp. 180.

SZAKSZERVEZETEK ORSZAGOS TANÁCSA. *Az igazság a magyar szakszervezetekről* (National Council of the Trade Unions: The truth about the Hungarian Unions). Budapest: SZOT, 1957: pp. 30.

——*A Tanács IX, X, XI. teljes ülése* (The 9th, 10th, 11th plenary sessions of the council). Budapest: SZOT, 1957: pp. 118.

SZALAY, LAJOS. *El drama de Hungría*. Buenos Aires: Délamerikai Magyarság, 1956: pp. 44 (Illustrated).

SZAMOS, RUDOLF. *Kommentár nélkül; disszidensek levelei* (Without any comments; letters from dissidents). Budapest: Kossuth, 1958: pp. 128 (Illustrated).

SZECHENYI, GYORGY, Dr Conde: *Doce anos entre cadenas 1944–1956* (Without place of publication and name of publisher.) 1957: pp. 223.

SZENES, IMRE. *Az utolsó napjuk . . .* (Their Last Day). Budapest: 1957: pp. 167.

SZILAGYI, EDIT, ed. *'Haza akarok menni', vallomás és vádirat* ('I want to go home', confession and indictment). Budapest: Magyar Kommunista Ifjusági Szövetség, 1957: pp. 47 (Illustrated).

Tájékoztató az amnesztia rendeletről (Information about the decree of amnesty). Budapest: Magyar Hirek, Athenaeum, 1963: pp. 47.

TASS REPRESENTATIVE IN INDIA. *True Facts on Events in Hungary*. New Delhi: 1956: pp. 94.

Testvérpártok a magyarországi eseményekről (Fraternal parties about the events in Hungary). Budapest: Kossuth, 1957: pp. 115.

THIERRY-TIRY, LADISLAO. *Hungria en la tornamenta*. Lima: Libraria Internacional del Peru, 1957: pp. 159.

THIERY, ARPAD. *Vádirat. Az ellenforradalom Veszprém megyében* (Indictment. The counter-revolution in Co. Veszprém). Budapest: 1957: pp. 111.

THURY, ZOLTAN. *Menekültek kalauza* (A guide for refugees). München: Grief, 1957: pp. 128.

TOLLAS, ISTVAN (pseud.). *Wir Kämpften für unsere Freiheit*. Liestal: Lüdin, 1957: pp. 93.

Too mondai shiryo. Series I of the Documents on the East European Problems. Tokyo: Shakai-Undo-Tushinsha, 1956: pp. 189.

Tross alt. Et folks kamp for friheten i dikt og prosa. En ungarsk antologi. Tresmitt av Maria Kiss. Oslo: Dreyer, 1959: pp. 198 (Illustrated).

TYRENCZY, L. *Magyars à l'assaut*. Paris: Editions Actualités mondiales, 1957: pp. 186.

Ungarische Jungen wollen nach Hause: helft ihnen. Budapest: 1957: pp. 31.

Ungarische (Die) Revolution 1956. Ost-westliche Presseschau. München: Herausgegeben im Selbstverlag von J. G. Farkas, 1957: pp. 125.

Ungarn. Ein Kampf um die Freiheit. Wien: Sozialistischer Verlag, 1958: pp. 88.

Ungarn unter Sowietherrschaft. München: Free Europe Committee, 1957: pp. 103.

Ungarns Freiheitskampf. Dokumente. Bern: Peter Sager Bund, 1958: pp. 120.

Ungheria. Il Ponte-Aprile-Maggio 1960. Firenze: 'La Nuova Italia' Editrice S.P.A., 1960: pp. 791.

UNION OF FREE HUNGARIAN STUDENTS. *Message from the Hungarian Youth to the Youth of Asia. The Hungarian Nation Fights Soviet Colonization*. (Without place and date of publication). pp. 15.

UNITED NATIONS. General Assembly. *Special Committee on the Problem of Hungary*. Report. New York: United Nations, 1957: pp. 148 (Maps, illustrated).

——*Indispensable role of the UN. A difficult year in review*. Introduction to the Secretary General's 12th annual report, August, 1957: New York, 1957: pp. 25.

URBAN, GEORGE. *The Nineteen Days; a broadcaster's account of the Hungarian revolution*. London: Heinemann, 1957: pp. 361 (Illustrated).

URQUHART, MACGREGOR. *Hungary Fights*. London: Digit Books, Brown Watson Ltd., 1957: pp. 159.

US CONGRESS HOUSE. COMMITTEE ON UN-AMERICAN ACTIVITIES: *International Communism: Revolt in the Satellites*. Staff Consultations with János Horváth, Sándor Kiss. Washington: DCUS, Government Printing Office, 1957: pp. 35.

US INFORMATION AGENCY. *Far Eastern Reaction to Hungarian and Polish Upheavals*. Washington, DC: 1956: pp. 10.

——*Hungary; American statements and actions.* The texts of key statements by United States leaders on the tragedy of Hungary, October and November 1956. London: pp. 48.

US PRESIDENT'S COMMITTEE for Hungarian Refugee Relief: Report to the President. Washington: US Govt. Printing Office, 1957: pp. 7.

US TREATIES (series 3825). *Emergency relief for Hungarians in Austria.* Agreement between the USA and Austria effected by exchange of notes signed in Vienna, 10 May 1957. Washington: Govt. Printing Office, 1957: pp. 6.

USSR LEGATION, CANADA. *The Truth about Hungary: Facts and Eyewitness Accounts.* Ottawa: Press Office of the USSR Embassy, 1957: pp. 205 (Illustrated).

VALI, FERENC A. *Idem.* (In Arabic) Beirut: Hungarian Freedom Fighters Federation, 1958.

——*The Hungarian Revolution and International Law.* New York: Hungarian Freedom Fighters Federation, 1959.

——*Rift and Revolt in Hungary, Nationalism versus Communism.* Harvard University Press, Cambridge, Mass., University Press, London: 1961: pp. 590.

VANHOPPLINUS, ROGER. *De lijdensweg van Hongarije.* Poperinge: Drukkerij Sansen, 1956: pp. 48 (Illustrated).

VASS, H. *A magyarországi 1956 októberi ellenforradalom történetének néhány kérdése* (Some questions of the history of the Hungarian counter-revolution in October 1956). Budapest; 1958: pp. 223.

VEER, IMRE. *Ma Magyarország, holnap a szabad világ* (Today Hungary, tomorrow the free world). Minneapolis: Pannonia, 1957: pp. 840 (Illustrated).

VENN, MARY ELEANOR. *Refugee Hero; a Hungarian Boy in America.* New York: Hastings House, 1957: pp. 128 (Illustrated).

Vérité (La) sur l'affaire Nagy: les faits, les documents, les témoignages internationaux. Préface de A. Camus. Paris: Plon, 1958: pp. 256 (Illustrated).

Vi kämpade för Ungern. Frihetskämparnas egen berättelse. Mullsjö: Inst. för samhällsforkning, 1957: pp. 89 (Illustrated).

Voilà comme nous sommes. Poémes de la Révolution. Bruxelles. Institut Imre Nagy de Sciences Politiques, 1959.

WASSERMANN, CHARLES. *Tagebuch der Freiheit. Als Reporter in Ungarn und Polen.* Gütersloh: Bertelsmann Verlag, 1958: pp. 202.

WEIDLEIN, J. *Der Aufstand in Ungarn und das ungarländische Judentum.*

Wiederaufflammen des madjarischen Rassen-nationalismus. Schorndorf; 1957: pp. 24.

WIEDERKEHR, EMIL and CATTANI, ALFRED. *Ungarns Freiheitskampf und seine Hintergründe.* Luzern: Schweizer Hilfe für Ungarns Flüchtlinge, 1957: pp. 112 (Maps, illustrated).

YEH, T'IEN-SHENG. *Hsiung-ya-li jen min k'ang pao chi.* 1957: pp. 240 (Illustrated).

Yougoslavie (La) et les événements de Hongrie. Paris: Articles et Documents, No. 0443, 11 décembre 1956.

ZAKHARCHENKO, V., POPOV, YU., STARODUB, A. *Budapest, oktjabr'–nojabr' 1956 g.* I tom cto my videli svoimi glazami. Moskva: Izdatelstvo CK VLKSM 'Molodaja Gvardija', 1956: pp. 104 (Illustrated).

ZATHURECZKY, GYULA. *Der Volksaufstand in Ungarn; Berichte und Zeittafel.* Köln: B. Pick, 1957: pp. 68.

ZAVOLZHSKIJ, S. G. *51 let svobodnii Vengrii.* Moskva: Izdvo Znanie, 1960: pp. 31.

ZINNER, PAUL E., ed. *National Communism and Popular Revolt in Eastern Europe.* New York: Columbia University Press, 1957: pp. 563.

——*Revolution in Hungary: Reflections on the Vicissitudes of a Totalitarian System.* Reprint from The Journal of Politics. Vol. 21, New York: 1959: pp. 36.

——*Revolution in Hungary.* London, New York: Columbia University Press, 1962: pp. 380.

Hungary: Chronology of Events 1953–65

COMPILED BY STEPHEN BARLAY

1953

January	20	Soviet Union cancels Hungarian war reparation debt.
March	8	National Assembly introduces law for 'preservation of Stalin's memory'. Rákosi leads delegation standing guard at Stalin's Catafalque. New electoral law.
May	17	General elections: 98 per cent of electors vote; 98·2 per cent of votes for the candidates of People's Independence Front'
June	27–28	Following Beria's fall, session of MDP (Hungarian Workers' Party) CC: Position of Secretary General (Rákosi) abolished and replaced by three-strong Secretariat. Past policies criticised.
July	2	Rákosi cabinet resigns.
	4	Imre Nagy becomes Premier and forms cabinet. (Several Stalinists like cultural overlord J. Révai and Defence Minister M. Farkas are out.) The 'new course', Nagy's programme introduced: criticism of past policy and practice of terror and forced industrialization; new agricultural policy with concessions to peasants, end of forced collectivization; amnesty; some strict labour regulations abolished; bread rationing abandoned.
	11	Party functionaries' meeting: Rákosi suggests that 'new course' need not be taken very seriously—implies survival of old policy.
	26	General Amnesty. Abolition of internment camps. (About 10,000 prisoners to be released.) Tax reductions for peasants. Co-operatives dissolve one after another.
August	16	General M. Farkas becomes member of Party Secretariat.

31   Diplomatic relations with Yugoslavia resumed.

November 2 Rákosi becomes 'first secretary' of MDP.

December 13 Endre Zakár, Cardinal Mindszenty's former secretary, sentenced to fourteen years imprisonment for 'organizing and heading' anti-state movement.

1954

March   13 Supreme Military Court tries General Gábor Péter, former head of State Security Police (AVO), Gyula Décsi, former Minister of Justice, and others for 'anti-state and anti-people crimes'. The accused admit guilt, G. Péter: life sentence; Gy. Décsi: nine years prison.

May   18 International Labour Organization (ILO) announces: Hungary is willing to assume obligations of membership and will send delegation to Geneva conference.

24–30 3rd Congress of MDP.

June   2 Hungary re-joins UNESCO (withdrew in 1952).

July   2 Heavy industrial output to be reviewed and decreased.

August   Football World Championship in Switzerland; Hungarian defeat followed by mass demonstrations in Budapest.

17 American aid for flood relief accepted.

October 1–3 Session of Party CC: Nagy scores important victory by successful defence of 'new course' against Stalinist revival.

9 János Kádár released from prison: becomes party secretary of 13th district, Budapest. Continuous release of political prisoners.

10 István Kovács, 1st party secretary of Budapest, admits former use of 'criminally improper methods' by AVO and 'invented and forged charges and evidence' in courts.

27 Gy. Kállai released from concentration camp.

November 7 Soviet interest in Joint Companies sold to Hungary.

21 Anna Kéthly, leader of the former Social Democrat Party, released from prison.

December 21 Grand ceremony in Debrecen to commemorate the 10th anniversary of the proclamation of democratic

Hungary. Rákosi, back from long 'sick leave' in Soviet Union, delivers speech reflecting his renewed power.

1955

March	2	Party CC sets new tasks for party and condemns I. Nagy for rightist deviation, nationalism, neglect of heavy industry and dissolution of co-operatives. (No announcement for ten days.) Disciplinary action against writers and journalists.
April	13	Five 'conspirators' sentenced to death in Budapest.
	14	I. Nagy removed from all party functions. (Later expelled from party.)
	18	National Assembly dismisses I. Nagy 'unanimously'; he is succeeded as Prime Minister by A. Hegedüs, acting Premier since February.
	19	A. Hegedüs outlines new policy—return to fast industrialization with heavy industry having all the priorities.
May	14	Hungary becomes founder-member of Warsaw Pact.
July	17	Cardinal Mindszenty released from prison; placed under house arrest.
September	7	Reduction of Armed Forces by 20,000 men. *Irodalmi Ujság* (Literary Gazette, later prominent revisionist forum) confiscated.
October	14	Archbishop J. Grösz and priests released from prison.
	18	The 'Memorandum'—prominent communist writers, scientists, artists, etc., openly object to the return of the rule of force. (Released at the November meeting of the Writers' Union party branch.) The open argument with the party leadership begins.
November	15	I. Nagy is deprived of his seat in the National Assembly. F. Erdei becomes Deputy Prime Minister.
December	5	Party CC: rebels among writers must be punished. Meeting of functionaries condemns writers.
	14	Hungary is admitted to the United Nations.
	23	Party takes disciplinary action against some leading communist writers.

1956

January	15	Trial: 'spying and anti-state activities' in Budapest. Sentences range from three years to life imprisonment. (B. Kapotsy, F. Arpás, K. Balázs, E. Márton and Mrs. E. Márton.)
February	25	Nine church dignitaries released. (Among them, Jusztin Baranyi, the only defendant in the Mindszenty trial who didn't plead guilty.)
March	29	Rákosi declares rehabilitation of victims of Rajk trial. Release of survivors of Rajk trial and of imprisoned leaders of former Social Democratic Party.
May	10	Government decree: Social Court to be set up; role of experts and managers in industry to be strengthened; minefields and barbed wires to be removed from western frontier.
	11	Amnesty to Archbishop J. Grösz—becomes Chairman of Bench of Bishops.
	30	Important public meeting of Petőfi Circle. The revolt of economists.
June	1	Petőfi Circle meeting of historians followed by literary historians (2 June) and scientists (4 June—E. Andics, Stalinist historian and prominent party functionary heckled and abused.)
	14	Petőfi Circle meeting of philosophers (led by Gy. Lukács), followed by meetings of teachers (15), former college staff members (17), former partisans (19—Mrs L. Rajk's dramatic speech), judges and lawyers (21), musicians (headed by Z. Kodály), natural resources experts (22) and the revolutionary 'press debate' of writers and journalists (27).
	30	CC condemns Petőfi Circle and its debates. Writers Tibor Déry and Tibor Tardos expelled from the party.
July	3	First public statement by B. Kovács (former Small-holders' leader) in provincial paper.
	18–21	Session of CC with A. I. Mikoyan present (then First Soviet Vice-Premier). M. Rákosi is replaced by E. Gerő as First Secretary of MDP. Kádár becomes member of Politburo. M. Farkas expelled from Party.

September 16 –21	Writers' Congress reflects spirit of Petőfi Circle debates and also of literary rebellion throughout past summer. Stalinists removed from leadership. Presidium elected by secret ballot.
22	Irodalmi Ujság publishes full report on writers' congress despite ban. Party counter-attack.
30	Tito meets Gerő 'accidentally' in Crimea.
October 5	100 m. roubles Soviet emergency loan to Hungary.
6	Silent revolution: 200,000 attend reburial of L. Rajk, Gy. Pálffy, T. Szőnyi and A. Szalai in Budapest. State funerals to be granted to other innocent victims.
11	Several AVO officers, including V. Farkas (Son of General Farkas) arrested and charged with 'serious violations of socialist legality'.
12	M. Farkas arrested.
14	Szabad Nép publishes I. Nagy's letter asking for readmittance to party (4 October) and Politburo grants it.
15	Delegation (E. Gerő, A. Apró, A. Hegedüs. J. Kádár, I. Kovács) to Yugoslavia. Rákosi emigrates to Moscow for second time.
18	Stormy meeting of 1,000 university students in Szeged.
19–22	Meetings in several towns—in spirit similar to Petőfi Circle.
22	Budapest University students decide to hold silent demonstration next day.
23	Student demonstrations banned, later permitted. March to General Bem statue and Polish Embassy. Demands: international equality, return of I. Nagy, democratic reforms. Nagy speaks to crowd at Parliament. Gerő on radio. Fighting at radio building. Stalin statue pulled down. Demonstrations turn into revolt in capital. Soviet troops and tanks used against revolution. CC session accepts I. Nagy as next Premier.
24	Fighting against Soviet and AVO units; revolt spreads outside Budapest. I. Nagy succeeds Hegedüs as Premier and appeals to fighters to stop. State of emergency declared.
25	Fighting continues. J. Kádár succeeds E. Gerő as first party secretary. Nagy and Kádár offer reforms and

negotiations for Soviet withdrawal if order restored.

26   Heavy fighting all over the country. Party offers to satisfy most revolutionary demands.

27   I. Nagy forms new government which includes non-communists like ex-President Tildy and B. Kovács, former leader of Smallholders Party. Revolution is spreading successfully.

28   Government orders cease-fire, promises Soviet withdrawal without delay, amnesty to all fighters, and also abolition of secret police. Party Emergency Committee set up: I. Nagy, J. Kádár, A. Apró, K. Kiss, F. Münnich and Z. Szántó. Revolutionary workers' councils and local committees formed. The demands now include neutrality; free elections, press, speech and worship. Units of armed Hungarian National Guards organized.

29   Some Soviet units withdraw from Budapest, replaced by revolutionary units, but fighting continues centred mainly round Killián Barracks. Szabad Nép defends revolt against *Pravda*.

30   Fighting continues. Battle at Budapest Party HQ. Nagy forms coalition government and offers return to multi-party system. Kádár supports policy. Smallholders' and Peasant Party to be revived. P. Kós, UN representative recalled; Cardinal Mindszenty freed. Hungarian Air Force threatens to bomb Soviet tank units. Revolutionary Home Defence Committee organized under General B. Király and General P. Maléter. Free Radio Kossuth goes on the air.

31   Social Democratic and above parties reconstituted; their official publications revived. In all, some forty parties are formed including Right-wing extremists and, in two counties, fascist parties.
Gen. Maléter becomes First Deputy Defence Minister. Gen. B. Király: military commander of the capital. Soviet declaration on changes in relations with sattellites. Compulsory agricultural deliveries abolished. Gradually, the release of some seventeen thousand prisoners—most of them common criminals—begins.

Order restored step by step, but several people, suspected secret-policemen, lynched. Siege of the Budapest Party HQ: atrocities; I. Mező, Budapest party secretary and others who defended the building killed. Some 3,000 suspected AVO-men and others arrested and imprisoned to await trial.

November 1 Nagy declares Hungary's withdrawal from Warsaw Pact and proclaims neutrality. Free trade unions publish 'Népakarat'.

Kádár denounces MDP and forms MSzMP, the new communist party. First Mindszenty speech.

National Guard to include all the revolutionary under Gen. Király. Soviet units surround capital and airfields.

2 Government protest against arrival of Soviet reinforcements in Hungary. UN notified. Appeal to major powers to recognize Hungarian neutrality.

3 Considerable Soviet troop movements. Shops open; production slowly begins.

New coalition government: I. Nagy, Premier and Foreign Affairs (Communist); Ministers of State— Z. Tildy, B. Kovács, I. B. Szabó (Smallholders), G. Losonczy, J. Kádár (Communists), A. Kéthly, Gy. Kelemen, J. Fischer (Social Democrats), I. Bibó, F. Farkas, (Petőfi Peasant Party); Minister of Defence— P. Maléter (Independent).

Negotiations for Soviet withdrawal. Further efforts to re-start production. Cardinal Mindszenty's programme on radio.

4 At dawn, heavy Soviet attack on capital. New all-communist government formed at Szolnok: J. Kádár— Premier, F. Münnich—Vice-Premier and Armed Forces. The last appeals of the Nagy government on radio.

UN Security Council and UN General Assembly put Hungarian issue on the Agenda. Acceptance of Hungarian UN delegates' credentials delayed. (On 10 November, after emergency session, 11th Session's agenda contains Hungarian issue. Voting result: 53 for it, 9 against, 8 abstentions.)

I. Nagy and others ask for asylum at Yugoslav embassy.

Soviet success throughout the country. P. Maléter and delegation arrested while negotiating Soviet withdrawal. I. Bibó and Writers' Union appeal to the world. SOS calls by dwindling number of free radios. New government calls for restoration of order with help of Soviet troops.

5   Fighting continues in waning pockets of resistance. Government and Soviet troops call for cease-fire and appeal to workers to start production.

6   Ultimatum to revolutionary forces. Government appeal to bloc for food and medicine. Free radios ask for Western help.

14   Népszabadság calls for end of strike. Workers' delegations receive promises from Kádár: free elections, amnesty, abolition of AVO, multi-party government, etc. Free movement of labour granted. Some Stalinists removed from office. Kádár: rejects Hungarian neutrality; 'up to Nagy to take part in politics'.

17   Workers offered Yugoslav system in return for restoring order and finishing strike.

18   Attacks on strikers. Wages to be paid only for effective work. Deportation of youths denied.

21   Law strips workers' councils of political power.

22   General strike.

23   I. Nagy and party abducted on leaving Yugoslav embassy and taken to Rumania.

24   Mass-arrests of refugees. Decree on withdrawal from and dissolution of collectives.

25   Kádár: 'Nagy camouflaged the . . . counter-revolution which began on 30 October.'

26   Kádár: firmer and harsher against counter-revolution. Denounces workers' councils and UN debate on Hungary. Speaks of Nagy's crimes.

27   Efforts to stop emigration. Amnesty to emigrées who return before 31 March 1957. Guarantee for religious freedom. Sporadic start of industrial production.

December 3   AVO officers to be investigated.

4   Soviet troops fire at 15,000 women demonstrating for their dead in Budapest. Protesting crowds dispersed, arrests. F. Münnich announces abolition

of revolutionary committees. Army officers made to sign loyalty to government (80 per cent success claimed).

5 New wave of rebellion. Writers denounce Soviet intervention.

6 Arrests. (Among them: M. Gimes, Nagy's associate, former editor of *Szabad Nép;* Gy. Obersovszky and J. Gáli, young writers.)

7 New strikes and street fights.

8 Provisional CC resolution: condemns counter-revolution; breaks with Stalinist past; calls for adherence to Leninist principles; promises socialism under 'conditions peculiar to Hungary'. Budapest Workers' Council dissolved by order. Local revolutionary councils outlawed.

11 Martial law introduced.

12 General strike. Public meetings banned. Resistance in the provinces. Mass arrests. S. Bali and S. Rácz, leaders of Budapest Workers' Council, arrested.

24 Coal and power shortage announced: the jobs of 200,000 threatened.

27 Report on use of martial law: in sixteen days 'only six were sentenced to death and only three were actually executed'. Mass arrests continue.

1957

January 1 Estimated aid from bloc about 700 million forints.

1–4 Soviet and satellite leaders meet in Budapest and pledge support to Kádár.

3 MSzMP, the reorganized Communist Party, has 100,000 members.

4 Abolition of compulsory Russian at schools.

6 Kádár's programme: dictatorship of the proletariat, democratization, new and more rational plan promised, no return to forced collectivization but defence of existing collectives.

8 General union elections postponed.

10 Kádár in Moscow.

11 Demonstration by Budapest children and Csepel workers. University unrest.

12 Eight student leaders arrested.

13 Strikes and all effective forms of resistance become punishable by death.

15 Prosecutions begin.

16 Kádár condemns revisionist views and insists on 'class content' of democracy.

16–18 Chinese Premier Chou En-lai in Budapest.

17 Writer's Union banned by government.

19 Journalists' Union suspended. Two revolutionary leaders, J. Dudás and J. Szabó, executed.

25 Prominent 'revisionist' writers and journalists—including Gy. Háy, B. Lengyel, P. Lőcsei, S. Novobáczky, T. Tardos, D. Varga and Z. Zelk—arrested for 'counter-revolutionary plotting'.

February 1 Raid on students' hostels—arrests for hiding firearms.

2 Kádár in Salógtarján condemns national communism, and blames Nagy for counter-revolution.

16 Népszabadság: only 156 were sent to jail by summary courts. F. Münnich calls for more severity by judges.

20 Kádár visits Moscow.

23 Forty sentenced to death by summary courts. (Report on radio only on 13 March.)

March 2 Russian to be compulsory in all elementary schools and preferred in secondary schools and universities.

14 Police and army alert for next day but all quiet.

17 Communist Youth League (KISz) formed to replace DISz (launched four days later).

19 Police has right to deport 'troublemakers' from Budapest.

20 Kádár and delegation in Moscow; reinforcement of Warsaw Pact; proletarian dictatorship will punish revisionism more severely; negotiations for Soviet troop-withdrawal only after order restored. Joint declaration blames imperialists for counter-revolution and declares Nagy a traitor.

23 'Anti-party propaganda gang' arrested in Budapest. Party control over Church emphasized with threats.

	25–30	New series of arrests for organizing strikes and anti-state propaganda.
April	3	12th Liberation Day (4 April) celebration. Marosán attacks writers who fight even if only with silence, claims success in restoring collectives.
	8	Ilona Tóth (death) and seven accomplices (one to eight years jail) sentenced for 'counter-revolutionary crimes'.
	11	Permission for Gy. Lukács to return from Rumania where he went with I. Nagy. Catholic Bench of Bishops declaration supports the government.
	13	Curfew ends.
	21	Writers' Union dissolved—T. Déry arrested for 'crime against state'.
	25	M. Farkas (ex Minister of Defence) sentenced to sixteen years imprisonment for serious violation of law while in office. Further sentences (J. Kiss hanged) for concealing firearms and ammunition.
May	1	Mass meetings permitted for the first time.
	5	Only one-third of former party members have rejoined party (about 300,000).
	7	Three followers of Dudás sentenced to death.
	9	First session of National Assembly since revolt. Kádár postpones promised general elections, rejects demands for multi-party system which would disrupt national unity.
	12	Some price increases—food and clothes prices remain.
	17	CC session satisfied with consolidation; method of persuasion is declared better than force in collectivization.
	27	Soviet–Hungarian agreement on temporary stationing of Soviet troops in Hungary.
June	3	1957 budget and plan—country will not be economically self-supporting this year.
	9	Trial and conviction of eighteen Transdanubian counter-revolutionaries.
	11	Announcement: eighty-nine death sentences have been passed and carried out in Budapest since revolution.

	15	Drive against judges and lawyers. Return to People's Court system (one professional, two lay judges).
	20	Hostile party branch at Faculty of Law of L. Eötvös University dissolved.
	22	Appeal to peasants for grain. Attacks on UN Report on Hungary. Zs. Sipos and two accomplices sentenced to death for assassination of major of 'security forces'.
	28	I. Tóth and three others executed.
July	1–5	Miners' strike at Sajószentpéteri.
	12	Trial of fourteen members of Christian Youth Association formed on 23 October.
	21	Thirteen Budapest counter-revolutionaries sentenced —two to death. 'Norms' wage system replaced nominally by "incentives".
August	2	Leaders of Transdanubian National Council sentenced.
	3	New wave of arrests.
	19	Attack on UN in terms used under Rákosi. (UN General Assembly voted 60 to 10 to condemn Soviet acts of aggression against Hungary; appointed Special Commission to investigate Hungarian issue.)
September	4	Writers' meeting condemns UN Report.
	27	Kádár in Peking.
October	5	Sixteen members of 'armed gang' sentenced—one to death.
	30	Mass rally at Republic Square (Budapest) to commemorate party officials and AVO men killed 'in defence of the Budapest Party HQ' during revolt on that day.
November	3	Summary Courts abolished.
	13	Writers sentenced: T. Déry nine, Gy. Háy six, Z. Zelk three years, T. Tardos eighteen months.
	22	Hungary signs Moscow policy declaration of bloc.
	24	Killián Barracks fighter executed.
December	7	State decoration to Archbishop Grösz.
	10	Execution of commander of unit which freed Cardinal Mindszenty during revolt.
	15	Prominent intellectuals, D. Keresztúry and Prof. D. Kosáry arrested.
	22	Chief Prosecutor G. Szénási admits existence of a concentration camp and claims that 3,012 persons

have been convicted for political crimes since December 1956.

29 State decorations to Church dignitaries.

31 Result of forced collectivization: 60 per cent increase in number of co-operatives (164,000 members).
Total value of loans from bloc countries in 1957: 1,138 million roubles.

1958

January	1	Decree: certificate of 'good behaviour' needed to keep or obtain any of the more important jobs.
	2	Commander of the Corvin Block fighters executed.
	11	Seventeen Catholic priests sentenced for activities during the revolution.
	27	Kádár: economic liberalization; forgiveness to those who 'genuinely erred' during revolt; new industrial plans must suit national conditions.
	28	J. Kádár remains First Secretary of party, but resigns as Premier; replaced by F. Münnich.
February	21 –22	Conference of judges—leniency towards those who were 'just misled' during revolution.
March	6	A. Sándor, writer, sentenced to eight years imprisonment for part in revolution.
	9	Two former members of Csepel National Guard executed.
	15	17,000 Soviet troops to be withdrawn from Hungary. First small detachments leave.
	16	Vice-President of Szeged Workers' Council executed.
	27	Kádár meets Tito.
April	2–11	Krushchev tours Hungary, backs Kádár in several speeches, condemns Rákosi and counter-revolution, and defends Soviet position in Eastern Europe.
	23	Several lawyers imprisoned in drive against profession.
May	18	Four 'counter-revolutionaries' executed, two sentenced for life, ten imprisoned.
June	6	T. Tardos released.
	17	Announcement of execution of revolution leaders: I. Nagy, P. Maléter, and two journalists, M. Gimes and

J. Szilágyi. Col. S. Kopácsi, life sentence; F. Donáth, twelve; F. Jánosi, eight; Z. Tildy, six; M. Vásárhelyi, five years imprisonment. Charges against G. Losonczy dropped due to his death from 'natural causes' in prison.

	19	Announcement of three-year plan for 1958–1960.
August	28	Trial of revolutionaries. I. Bibó, thought to be arrested in spring, 1957, now sentenced for life.
September	14	Four sentenced for spying for US.
October	11	Return of leading Stalinists from Moscow to Budapest: A. Hegedüs, Gen. I. Bata, J. Szalai, B. Vég, A. Berei, Gy. Alapi, V. Olti and L. Piros.
	15	Release of Z. Zelk, D. Varga and B. Németh—all sentenced after revolt.
November	16	First post-revolt general election: 98·4 per cent of those eligible vote—99·6 per cent of them vote for People's Patriotic Front single list.
December	1	Exit permit for elderly relatives of refugees.
	5–7	CC decision to speed up collectivization.

1959

January	22	Government announces end of trials for participation in revolution.
	30	About 10 per cent of the Soviet troops to be withdrawn from Hungary.
March	6	Industrial labour competition to be revived.
	20	B. Kun, leader of 1919 revolution and executed by Stalin in 1938, rehabilitated on fortieth anniversary of dictatorship of proletariat.
	30	F. Mérey, S. Fekete, J. Széll, Gy. Litván and A. Hegedüs sentenced for two to ten years imprisonment for setting up 'anti-state organization' after revolution.
April	4	Land area of collectives nearly doubled in three months. Partial amnesty—not applicable to those convicted for participation in revolt.
	6	Church leaders made swear allegiance to state.
May	28–	Khrushchev visits Hungary.
June	5	

July	Secret trial of the 'Ujpest counter-revolutionaries'. Several death sentences. Kádár denies this and news of other revolution trials.
September 25	Ban on Hungarian Writers' Union lifted but 'all literary activities must support the state in building socialism'.
November	Drastic collectivization drive begins.
30	December 5: 7th Congress of MSzMP (including those of MDP). Soviet party delegation is headed by Khrushchev. Kádár announces collectivization campaign; Soviet troops will remain in the country while the international situation necessitates their presence; condemns the '1956 events' for which he blames the Rákosi era; denounces Rákosi but claims 'he did good service, too'. J. Fock presents draft for five-year plan. Marosán becomes Permanent Deputy to the 1st Party Secretary.
31	Catholic Bench of Bishops supports collectivization drive.

1960

January	1	Census result: population is 9,976,530. (Ten million will be reached around 23 July). Census shows continued strong drift to towns.
	8	Fifteen-year plan to ease housing shortage.
	16	Gy. Kállai becomes first Deputy Premier.
February	12	Collectivization drive halted to consolidate results. (About 60 per cent of all arable land—75 if including state farms—belong to the collectives; 70 per cent of agricultural population in collectives.)
April	4	Amnesty to 'revisionists', Stalinists and common criminals: prison sentences of up to one year passed before 1 March 1960, cancelled; those who served half their terms given before 31 December 1952, now released by remittance (includes charges of war crimes and crimes against the people); sentences of more than six years passed before 1 May 1957 for same crimes, now suspended. Sentences of Tibor Déry, Ferenc Donáth, Mihály and Vladimir Farkas, Gy. Háy, F. Jánossy and G. Váradi suspended.

July   Industrial norms tightened.

December 16 1st Congress of KISz. Kádár criticises dogmatism and
   -17 peasant youths for staying away from KISz.

1961

January 7 Housing decree limits urban dwelling space per head—
       special high rent for extra space.

     18 The 1958-1960 plan is reported to have been 'over-
       fulfilled in its main targets'.

February 7 Priests, monks and lay men arrested and charged with
       plotting.

     22 Collectivization drive completed—less than 10 per
       cent of cultivable area is owned privately.

April   9 Production norms tightened. Labour discipline cam-
       paign begins.

     26 Following Soviet move, Public Prosecutor asks for
       death penalty for 'crimes against socialist property' and
       other economic offences.

May   24 Catholic Bench of Bishops (not recognized by Vatican)
       finds February arrest of priests justified.

June   19 Trial of twelve priests and monks. All but one (Mgr.
       Lenárd) plead guilty in conspiracy against state.
       Archbishop Grösz' unsuccessful attempt to save them.

July   12 Meat, fruit and vegetable shortage—price control
       introduced.

September 13 Cabinet reshuffle: J. Kádár, while retaining post of
       First Party Secretary, takes over as Premier from F.
       Münnich who retires to Minister of State without Port-
       folio. Four Vice-Premiers appointed: A. Apró, B.
       Biszku, J. Fock and Gy. Kállai.

October 3 Archbishop Jozsef Grösz dies. New Head of the Bench
       of Catholic Bishops: Endre Hamvas.

      7 Sztálinváros re-named as Dunaujváros.

     11 National Assembly adopts new five-year plan for 1961–
       65. (Raised targets to be achieved mainly through
       productivity drive; investments cut because 1956 loans
       must start to be repaid.)

December 26   Kádár attacks Albanians in *Pravda* in stronger terms than other satellite leaders.

1962

January   1   Kádár's New Year message—'He who is not against us is with us'—starts greater political leniency. Several former Stalinist leaders return to Budapest.

February   1   Draft of new Penal Code (1961) becomes law. (Penalties for political offences tightened; execution of juveniles forbidden except in 'special cases'.)
Non-party experts given important posts up to Deputy Minister level.

March   18   State funeral and full rehabilitation for M. Károlyi, first President of 1918 Republic.

23   Several populists arrested as followers of Bibó and charged with inciting against state. Secret trial follows, only sentences reported: prison terms up to $4\frac{1}{2}$ years.

April   Statistical monthly reports: food prices rose by an average 32 per cent in 1961.

May   18-19   Congress of Writers' Association 'supports party line on all the major political issues'.

August   19   M. Rákosi, E. Gerő and twenty-three others formally expelled from the party. (Six accused of having formed a 'factional group with Rákosi and Gerő' and rest as accomplices in Rákosi's 'violation of socialist legality'.)

September 15   190 'National Communists' and ex-Social Democrats— sentenced under Rákosi—now rehabilitated.

17   Hungarian section of 'Friendship' oil pipeline opened. T. Déry reappears in print.

27   UN General Assembly puts Hungarian issue back on agenda. (Votes: 43 for, 34 against, 19 abstentions.) Special Rapporteur Sir Leslie Munro reports that communist pressure in Hungary is decreasing but UN resolutions—withdrawal of Soviet troops, free elections under UN auspices, basic human rights for the people—are still ignored. Special Commission discharged. General Secretary U Thant instructed to take necessary steps.

October	12	Gy. Marosán expelled from the CC after his attack on new policy and resignation on 1 September.
November	2	G. M. Wynne, British businessman, disappears in Budapest. (Later convicted in Moscow for spying.)
	20–24	8th Congress of MSzMP: 'One-nation' policy endorsed, decision to tolerate all who do not oppose the regime actively. Final liquidation of 'personality cult'— Rákosi condemned summarily. The foundation of socialism is regarded to be completed by the results of the collectivization. Kádár: 95 per cent of those sentenced for participation in the revolt have now been released.

1963

January	1	Limited price reductions.
	20	Full-scale attack on Albanian and Chinese communists in Népszabadság. 1962 plan fulfilled.
	29	Further mergers in industry urged together with decentralization and stronger expert influence.
February	24	Elections to National Assembly and local councils 'under the auspices of the Patriotic People's Front'. 97·2 per cent of the electorate cast their votes, 98·9 of them for the single list. Among the 340, there are 125 new members of Parliament, most of them experts, intellectuals and specialist party leaders.
March	21	Kádár in National Assembly: 'Counter-revolution caused about 22 billion forints damage.' Announces amnesty without specific terms for 4 April. Release of István Bibó, E. Turcsányi, L. Kardos, S. Kopácsi, Prof. F. Mérey, Gy. Adám, P. Lőcsei, S. Fekete, priests and others. Gy. Lukács re-appears in print after seven years of silence.
May	4	New regulations for university enrolment—class origin to be deleted from application forms. Another five Catholic priests freed from house arrest.
	21	After visit to Hungary, U Thant reports (11 July): further UN action is not conceivable.

August	4	Visa requirements eased for exiles.
October	9	No visa needed for travel between Hungary and Czechoslovakia.
November	13–	Delegation, led by Bishop Hamvas, in Rome to attend
December	7	session of Ecumenical Council. (Meanwhile, Hungarians' pilgrimage to Lourdes and Rome permitted for the first time.)

1964

January	19	Report of Central Statistical Bureau: national income rose by 5 per cent in 1963; increase of industrial and agricultural production below the targets; higher productivity plan unfulfilled.
March	8	Népszabadság pays homage to 'heroic struggle' of L. Rajk on fifty-fifth anniversary of his birthday.
	18	Albanian commercial attaché expelled for interference in internal affairs of Hungary.
		Arrest of Sándor Nagy, Stalin-prize winner writer, for incitement against Kádár and the government. Text of report implies Stalinist plot.
March	31–	Krushchev in Budapest. Kádár becomes 'Hero of the
April	10	Soviet Union' and receives the 'Order of Lenin' and 'Medal of the Golden Star' which carry automatic Soviet citizenship. Final communique of visit reflects perfect Soviet-Hungarian unity in face of Chinese views.
June	27	Sándor Nagy sentenced to three years imprisonment for distributing Chinese propaganda leaflets.
September	14	Partial agreement between Vatican and Hungary.
October	11	Report that Lenin statue will be erected in place of Stalin's which was destroyed on 23 October 1956.
	14–18	International PEN Executive meets in Budapest. (First session in an East European capital since before the war.)
December	4	Talks begin on US property claims.
	8-10	CC accepts plan for 1965: lower production targets; emphasis on quality.
	12	Nine arrested (including monks) for conspiracy and political incitement among the young—a warning to

youth and to Catholics not to expect too much liberty even though the recent agreement with Vatican.

14   Five sentenced for anti-state conspiracy and for trying to revive Catholic Democratic People's Party.

15   Party elections completed (began on 1 November): about 30 per cent of the party functionaries replaced.

31   Tibor Sőznyi, leading party functionary, executed in 1949 as Titoist, fully rehabilitated in Népszabadság article.

1965

January   17   Central Statistical Office reports on 1964 Plan results: 9 per cent increase of industrial production (2 per cent overfulfilment); national income 4 per cent up (off the target by 2 to 3 per cent); agricultural production rose by 2 per cent (plan was twice as much).

29–31   Brezhnev and Podgorny visit Budapest and confer with Kádár.

February   6   András Szalai, former leading party official, executed as Titoist in 1949, rehabilitated in Népszabadság.

April   2   Lenin's statue, in place of Stalin's, unveiled in Budapest.

3   Celebration of the twentieth anniversary of the liberation of Hungary. Ceremonial session of National Assembly.

4   Military parade in Budapest—speeches by Kádár and Mikoyan.

9   Austro-Hungarian power-exchange agreement and steps towards further co-operation.

20   Several in catering industry sentenced for economic crimes. (Case starts scandal concerning public morals.)

May   22   Budapest International Trade Fair opens: US and six other countries exhibiting for the first time.

31   Long-term (1966–70) trade agreement with Soviet Union signed in Budapest.

June   30   J. Kádár replaced as Premier by Gyula Kállai (1910, filled various high government and party posts, was imprisoned when Kádár under Rákosi, Deputy Premier since 1961.) Kádár remains First Party Secretary (he relinquished Premiership once before, in 1958, when replaced, until 1961, by F. Münnich.)

July   1   Increased payments to lower categories of pensioners (mainly peasants) and higher assistance to orphans.

       7   Seven priests arrested for influencing youth in 'a way hostile to the regime'. (Among them: Rev. László Emődy, previously arrested in 1961 and released by amnesty in 1963.)

September 8   Ferenc Halász, Catholic priest, re-imprisoned on political charges.

     16   From 1 January 1966, new industrial incentive system mainly for management.

     24   Hungarian troops begin removal of mines from 'Iron Curtain'. Foreign Ministry announces: a 'new technique' will be used to protect the Austrian border.

November 18   CC session: far-reaching economic reforms out-lined
    −20   for 1966-1968; further steps planned towards market economy.

December 18   Preliminary plan targets for 1966 announced. (Third five-year-plan not yet ready.) Industrial production to rise between 4 and 6 per cent with highest target for chemical industry: 10 per cent.

Government announces changes in price system: some advantage to peasants to boost agricultural production; serious burden by higher prices (mainly food) on consumers; textiles become cheaper; some wages raised.

     29   Seven arrested and jailed in December for anti-state incitement. (Others, like M. Vásárhelyi, former associate of Imre Nagy, released from prison by amnesty, now warned against airing anti-regime views.)

     31   New investment policy devised for collective farms.